PRAISE FOR *RAISING DOUGH*

"Elizabeth Ü has created a formidable one-stop guide to the brass tacks of building a successful sustainable food business. For everyone who's ever wanted to turn their passion for sustainable food into a thriving business, this book is for you."

—ANNA LAPPÉ, founder, Real Food Media Project and
author, *Diet for a Hot Planet*

"Elizabeth has written an absolutely critical book for social entrepreneurs. She provides a unique perspective on how different kinds of capital can be blended and sequenced. If you are not familiar with how to attract grants, low-interest loans, equity, loan guarantees, etc., to grow your business, you'll find this to be a hugely valuable investment in yourself. Read it, use it!"

—DON SHAFFER, president and CEO,
RSF Social Finance

"The foundation of a new economy is an equitable society that values everyone. Localists know this requires working on multiple fronts, and community capital is one of the most important. Elizabeth's book covers the many ways to connect any local businesses—not only those related to food—with local lenders, investors, and donors."

—MICHELLE LONG, executive director,
Business Alliance for Local Living Economies (BALLE)

"Successfully financing food enterprises is paramount to building a just, fair, and healthy food system. Elizabeth's book shows us how to get it done. *Raising Dough* is an excellent addition to the literature of the sustainable food movement."

—LADONNA REDMOND, executive director,
The Campaign for Food Justice Now

"As a food entrepreneur, I learned how challenging it is not only to find money but to find the right money. Elizabeth's book is an important tool to help food entrepreneurs start and grow their businesses in a way that supports their vision—so that their food start-ups can thrive and change the world."

—SHERYL O'LOUGHLIN, executive director, Center for Entrepreneurial Studies at the Stanford University Graduate School of Business, cofounder and former CEO, Nest Collective (now Plum, Inc.), and former CEO, Clif Bar & Company

"Great business ideas need money behind them, and Elizabeth Ü shows us how to attract and steward investors who are looking beyond profit and toward the benefits that a mission-driven business brings to the community it serves. I wish this book had been around when we were looking for equity investors in Cowgirl Creamery."

—SUE CONLEY, cofounder, Cowgirl Creamery

"*Raising Dough* is an invaluable resource for socially minded farmers and food entrepreneurs. Elizabeth Ü's clear-eyed, nuts-and-bolts advice demonstrates that, like food, finance can be sustainable, too."

—AMY CORTESE, author, *Locavesting: The Revolution in Local Investing and How to Profit from It*

"Where has this book been all my life? This step-by-step guidebook to financing food businesses is vitally needed today. In this rapidly evolving field, *Raising Dough* is a key contribution."

—MARJORIE KELLY, Tellus Institute fellow and author, *Owning Our Future: The Emerging Ownership Revolution*

"Starting a food business? *Raising Dough* provides an extremely useful roadmap through the financial landscape. This is a wonderful overview of the tools and techniques for capitalizing your small food enterprise."

—WOODY TASCH, chairman, Slow Money, and author, *Inquiries into the Nature of Slow Money*

RAISING DOUGH

RAISING DOUGH

The Complete Guide to Financing a
Socially Responsible Food Business

ELIZABETH Ü

FOREWORD BY MICHAEL SHUMAN

CHELSEA GREEN PUBLISHING
WHITE RIVER JUNCTION, VERMONT

Project Manager: Hillary Gregory
Developmental Editor: Brianne Goodspeed
Copy Editor: Alice Colwell
Proofreader: Eileen M. Clawson
Indexer: Lee Lawton
Designer: Melissa Jacobson

Printed in the United States of America.
First printing June, 2013.
10 9 8 7 6 5 4 3 2 1   13 14 15 16

Cover photographs clockwise from top right:
Valley Flora produce; Justin Libby, Port Clyde Fresh Catch; Valley Flora produce; Eji Atlaw, Eji's Ethiopian; White Dog Café; Azalina Eusope, Azalina's; Christina Doerr, Neo Cocoa

Our Commitment to Green Publishing
Chelsea Green sees publishing as a tool for cultural change and ecological stewardship. We strive to align our book manufacturing practices with our editorial mission and to reduce the impact of our business enterprise in the environment. We print our books and catalogs on chlorine-free recycled paper, using vegetable-based inks whenever possible. This book may cost slightly more because we use recycled paper, and we hope you'll agree that it's worth it. Chelsea Green is a member of the Green Press Initiative (www.greenpressinitiative.org), a nonprofit coalition of publishers, manufacturers, and authors working to protect the world's endangered forests and conserve natural resources. *Raising Dough* was printed on FSC-certified paper supplied by Thomson-Shore that contains at least 30% postconsumer recycled fiber.

Library of Congress Cataloging-in-Publication Data
Ü, Elizabeth.
  Raising dough : the complete guide to financing a socially responsible food business / Elizabeth Ü ; foreword by Michael Shuman.
    pages cm
Includes bibliographical references and index.
  ISBN 978-1-60358-428-9 (pbk.) — ISBN 978-1-60358-429-6 (ebook)
1. Small business—Finance. 2. Social responsibility of business. I. Title.

HG4027.7.U23 2013
664.0068'1—dc23

                    2013009483

Chelsea Green Publishing
85 North Main Street, Suite 120
White River Junction, VT 05001
(802) 295-6300
www.chelseagreen.com

CONTENTS

FOREWORD

IN 2004, AT THE SECOND annual conference of the Business Alliance for Local Living Economies (BALLE) in Philadelphia, about twenty-five people were sitting on a University of Pennsylvania patio discussing some of the biggest challenges facing local business. I recall being grilled about possibilities for localizing investment by an exceptionally sharp CEO of a skateboard company named Don Shaffer. I explained, with dejection and frustration, that American law had made local investment by the 99 percent of Americans who were not wealthy, or "unaccredited," exceedingly difficult, expensive, and impractical. Saying pretty much the same thing at his own workshops at the conference was Woody Tasch, a pioneering investment adviser who had formed a fast-growing network of innovative investment professionals called Investors' Circle.

About half the nation's economy, by jobs and output, resides in small- and mid-scale business, and research suggests that young local businesses are our most important jobs producers. This is the part of the economy most people are referring to when they are talking about "local" business, since 99.9 percent of these firms are locally owned. We also know that sole proprietorships, which most small businesses are or start out as, are three times more profitable than C corporations, the structure embraced by bigger businesses. And we also have good reason to believe that small businesses are becoming more competitive as entrepreneurs master the Internet and take advantage of emerging small-scale technologies like 3D printers.

If US capital markets were operating efficiently, at least half of our long-term capital would be invested in the local half of the economy. All the long-term savings American households have today— in stocks, bonds, mutual funds, pension funds, and insurance funds—total about $30 trillion. So, in principle, about half those savings should be going to small- and mid-scale business. In fact, almost none is.

Americans are systematically overinvesting in Fortune 500 companies, and underinvesting—that is, investing virtually nothing—in the local businesses that are essential for regional vitality. Put another way, our capital markets are like a Mob-run casino, with the dice loaded to provide a huge edge to global business and undercut community-based businesses.

Flash forward a decade from the BALLE conference in Philadelphia, Shaffer would become director of BALLE and then president of RSF Social Finance, the first major national revolving-loan fund to welcome investments from unaccredited investors. Tasch would go on to write *Inquiries into the Nature of Slow Money*, a bestseller that spawned the Slow Money Alliance, which has since helped thousands of investors place tens of millions of dollars in local food businesses. And the movement for local investing would proceed so fast that in 2012 just about the only piece of legislation that Occupy Wall Street Democrats and Tea Party Republicans could agree on was to create, through the JOBS Act, a new crowdfunding exception to securities laws that soon will allow every American to invest at least $2,000 per local business per year.

Quietly working under both Shaffer and Tasch at different times and learning from them was a young powerhouse named Elizabeth Ü. As a recent graduate of one of nation's most innovative business schools, the Presidio Graduate School, she carefully observed, analyzed, and advised, and she gradually developed one of the richest brains of local investment experience and wisdom in the field. Surveying the universe of books on local-investment, including my own (*Local Dollars, Local Sense*) and Amy Cortese's *Locavesting*, Elizabeth saw the need for a guidebook primarily for the entrepreneur, especially one involved in farming or local food.

From her perspective, while a core group of investors have been assiduously organizing themselves to refocus their dollars on small business, entrepreneurs have been left to fend for themselves. This, to her, seemed manifestly unfair, and left small businesses vulnerable to the mercurial whims of people with money. Entrepreneurs need to be aware of the many options for finance they have—whether conventional ones like federal grants and loans or unconventional ones like crowdfunding—if the appropriate balance in investor-entrepreneur negotiations is to be restored. So the mission of this book is to help entrepreneurs to think about, weigh, and choose among the hundreds of options for investment, including the virtues of proceeding with no outside finance whatsoever.

It's truly remarkable how far this revolutionary movement for local investing has come. From "no, it's not really possible" to "here's how to do it"—all in ten short years. To continue with a food metaphor, apropos for this book: Now that the table has been set, it's time for the dinner to be served and eaten. Enter Elizabeth, who proves herself to be a chef extraordinaire.

Chances are good that you're reading this book because you're a farmer or local food entrepreneur looking for money. Or you might be an investor looking to place your money in a local food business. Or perhaps you're just interested in learning about how to start a food business. Or maybe you've just heard that this is a tremendous resource for anyone interested in local investing. Whatever your mission, prepare for a feast ahead.

Elizabeth explains, in meticulous detail, the myriad investment options that are available for small-business entrepreneurs, the pro's and con's of each approach, and the relevance of each to different business needs, goals, and stages of growth. You could think of this as a textbook, but it's too well written and has too many interesting stories to fall into that stodgy category. But if you're short on time, you also don't need to read it cover to cover to gain quick, practical advice for your own business or investment decisions.

As someone who is often looking at this subject from a 30,000-foot level, I found it extremely helpful and informative to get down into the trenches. For example, I've been looking to refinance some of my own credit lines. I read several of the chapters in the back of the book, learned how to use websites like Prosper and Lending Club, and am now taking the specific, easy-to-understand steps Elizabeth recommends to make "Shuman, Inc." attractive to outside investors. Along the way, I learned about a bunch of other sites like ZimpleMoney that I might use to invite family to invest in me and get a much higher rate of return than they would on Wall Street.

What Elizabeth doesn't say—but clearly is the underlying motivation for this book and the entire local food movement—is that we're all living on borrowed time. For farmers, business as usual means depleted topsoil, drained aquifers, climate disruptions, and more bankruptcies. For eaters, it means more global food giants selling more high-fat, high-salt, processed food through Walmarts and Safeways. For food investors, it means placing casino-like bets on distant companies whose practices are beyond your influence and whose securities are traded on incomprehensible and dangerous global financial markets. The alternative is a local food system where we increasingly buy fresh, healthy foodstuffs from farmers and local processors we know, and local financial systems that allow us to invest our precious savings in the businesses we love.

Fixing our food system requires fixing our capital markets, which in turn requires both legal and behavioral changes. The legal changes, as noted, have already begun. With the JOBS Act, we've made it easier and cheaper for small businesses to issue securities. Next, we need to make it easier and cheaper to trade these securities on local stock exchanges, to bundle them in diversified pools in local investment funds, and to allow pension-fund fiduciaries to move their money into these funds.

But the behavior changes are even more important. We need many more local businesses to accept finance from local investors, and many more investors to focus their portfolios on local business. Elizabeth shines a bright spotlight on how these changes can be made. She also invites readers like us to share our own experiences, whether as an investor or a business, through her website: www.financeforfood.com. She understands that our challenge now, as a community, is to learn quickly from one anothers' mistakes.

The next time someone asks you, "How can I save the world?," tell them the secret is that we all must go to business school—and commit ourselves to being smarter, more locally minded entrepreneurs, investors, consumers, and voters. And recommend this book as his or her first assignment.

INTRODUCTION

THIS BOOK IS WRITTEN for the entrepreneurs across the United States who are using food ventures to build healthier economies, ecosystems, people, and communities. If you're a passionate and experienced food person who has yet to take the business plunge but are headed in that direction, this book is for you, too. The new enterprise models you are pioneering— plus the traditional models you have reenvisioned to better serve people and the planet—offer a dizzying range of solutions to the well-documented cycles of environmental damage, food deserts, depressed urban and rural communities, and diet-related disease.

As a group you offer social, environmental, and economic solutions at all levels of the food chain: from seed companies that aim to preserve heritage varieties well suited to specific regions; to farms and ranches that employ ecologically benign or restorative production methods and land stewardship practices; to food hubs that make it more efficient for these producers to bring their products to market; from on-farm, value-added processing to larger-scale food manufacturing facilities that create jobs and return higher value to producers while providing healthier food to people and a reduced impact on the environment. Your food distribution businesses boast more efficient routes and delivery vehicles. Many of you in food retail, including grocery stores and restaurants, offer healthier choices and forge more direct relationships with local farmers in addition to using less energy in your buildings. Completing the cycle from farm to fork and back to the farm again are those of you whose businesses collect food waste and turn it into valuable compost, and still others who take used cooking oil and turn it back into fuel for cars or commercial vehicles. Then there are the businesses that offer people- and planet-friendly fertilizers, pest management systems, or production management software. The solutions are endless.

This book is also for people who want to better support socially responsible entrepreneurs in their efforts to raise capital, as a nonprofit service provider, a civil servant, or an engaged citizen. And finally, it is for people who already do, or want to, invest in sustainable food businesses, whether you have a little of your own money, a lot of your institution's money, or any amount in between to give, lend, or otherwise bring to the table. I hope the following pages will help you understand the experience of the people whose businesses you may encounter in your journeys.

Are you a social entrepreneur, a green businessperson, or an ecological problem solver in a field that has nothing to do with food whatsoever? Most of this book's content is relevant to people raising money for socially responsible businesses in any field—or any business at all, for that matter. The case studies all have to do with food companies that are addressing social or environmental issues in some way, but I have tried to choose a variety of business models that will mirror the experiences of a wide range of entrepreneurs.

—— Why I Wrote This Book ——

I have spent the last decade closely examining the challenges that people face when trying to raise money for socially responsible food ventures. Almost all of the food entrepreneurs I meet report that lack of access to capital presents a major barrier to planning, launching, maintaining, or growing their businesses, limiting their ability to foster positive social change. How can this be, at a time of increasing demand for food that is produced, delivered, prepared, and sold in ways that are better for the environment and for the people involved at all points in the process? And at a time when more and more financial institutions, not to mention everyday people, are interested in investing their money closer to home, and in ways that support the very outcomes that sustainable food businesses bring about?

Over the past ten years I have also done my best to create new ways to connect food entrepreneurs with the people and institutions that want to invest in them. As an employee of Slow Money (see chapter 1), I examined survey results and interviewed dozens of people in an attempt to tease out the needs of food entrepreneurs and mission-minded investors. Could we design an investment fund that would work better than existing venture capital funds to foster a more sustainable food system? The unique equity fund I designed was never actually launched, but it helped further the discussion of what might be possible. While on staff at RSF Social Finance, a pioneering nonprofit financial services organization dedicated to transforming the way the world works with money (see chapter 14), I helped design and launch a new loan fund for the highest-impact food companies. As a member of the advisory committee of the Community Capital Initiative of the Business Alliance for Local Living Economies (BALLE), I help craft a series of workshops and webinars that show both investors and entrepreneurs how to take advantage of the most promising new models to connect local businesses with local lenders; we envision that literally trillions of dollars could move from Wall Street to Main Street, creating millions of new jobs and helping to build vibrant local economies.

Even as I worked to create and share new food-financing solutions, one major conundrum continued to trouble me. I was spending the majority of my working hours trying to find and make sense of all the different capital options available for food businesses, and I could barely keep track of them all. How could anyone possibly expect a social entrepreneur—someone who was already spending 120 percent of her time building a venture that would make the world a better place *and* make a profit—to understand all the financing options? Even if someone miraculously managed to identify every single potential source of funds, how would entrepreneurs be able to quickly determine which would be the best fit for their unique business, with their particular values and priorities? There came a time when I could ignore these nagging questions no longer. I needed to write this book!

My friend Brahm Ahmadi is CEO of People's Community Market, envisioned as a small-format, full-service neighborhood food store, health resource center, and community hub that supports West Oakland families to attain healthier and more socially connected lives. I have watched Brahm struggle for years to raise money to finance construction of this project in this inner-city California community of twenty-six thousand residents who are predominantly African-American and Latino. Although residents collectively spend over $58 million a year on groceries, there are no full-service grocery stores in West Oakland. Many people who live there don't own a vehicle and rely on public transportation. Yet they must travel great distances to get to far-off supermarkets. The inconvenience, time, and cost of these shopping trips leads many residents to regularly shop at nearby corner stores that carry mostly processed, poor-quality foods sold at high prices. Meanwhile, 70 percent of the grocery spending occurs outside of West Oakland, meaning there is an unrealized potential for local jobs and local profits. One might think that banks, foundations, and wealthy individual investors would jump at the chance to financially support People's Community Market, as it would resolve so many issues that West Oakland residents face.

Brahm has an MBA. He's an excellent public speaker with a decade of experience working as a community leader within the local food system, making him a media darling. People's Community Market has a top-notch team, with industry expertise in spades. They have conducted ample research to show that People's Community Market should succeed according to plan. Despite all of this, Brahm failed to raise the necessary capital from the usual suspects (i.e., the traditional sources of capital), and I believe his experience is a textbook illustration of the barriers that stand between socially responsible food entrepreneurs and the capital they need.

The experience of lack of access to capital can stem from any number of challenges, each of which can hinder the flow of money from those who would like to invest it to those who are trying to raise it. Many of these are, unfortunately, beyond an entrepreneur's immediate control.

—— How to Use This Book ——

The good news is that the variety of capital sources available to sustainable food entrepreneurs is increasing, and there are many things that you can do to increase the likelihood of raising capital for your business. This book focuses on actions you can take and financing options that are available right now. It is not meant to be an exhaustive directory of grant makers, lenders, institutional investors, and the like. Nor is it meant to define exactly what a "sustainable food business" should be, though you may find inspiration in the entrepreneur profiles that I use throughout this book to illustrate the concepts covered.

I have organized the book into four parts. Part 1 pertains to things that you can—and in my opinion, should—do before you ask a single person for money, whether it's a gift, a loan, or an equity investment. It includes chapters on meeting the right people, making sure you know what values are most important to you, and setting up your business so that it's ready to attract new capital. The next three parts cover the many different forms of capital that are available to support socially responsible food businesses, including information about when a particular source of financing might be appropriate, how each tends to work, what financiers will likely expect from you as they assess whether or not to invest in your business, things to watch out for, what the relationship might look like over time, and where to look for more information, including places to find the actual financiers themselves. Part 2 focuses on financing methods that you would use primarily with people you know quite well, including friends, family, and existing or future customers. (I refuse to use the expression "friends, family, and fools" because I have a lot more respect for people who choose to take a risk by investing in an early-stage company with a mission they believe in.) This second part also covers online crowdfunding. Don't miss chapter 10, which covers important laws that all fundraising entrepreneurs need to know lest they end up inadvertently breaking one. Part 3 covers all manner of debt (also known as credit), wherein you borrow money and pay it back over time, usually plus interest. This part covers all the different sources of debt that might work for your company, from personal debt options to direct loans from individuals to lines of credit from a commercial lender, and more. Part 4 covers equity financing (in which you raise money by selling shares of your company), from individual and angel investors to venture capital and other institutional equity options. I put the chapter on working with foundations in this section, not to imply that foundations only do equity financing (this is hardly the case), but because foundations can do so many types of investments that it didn't make sense to include them earlier in the book. Part 4 ends with a chapter on strategies for entrepreneurs who are ready to transition out of the business but want the values to remain after they are gone.

Each of the chapters in parts 2, 3, and 4 is organized roughly in order of which sources of capital I would recommend first to new businesses, with later chapters covering financing options that are more appropriate for later-stage companies. Don't take this as a prescription, however; you'll have to use your best judgment and the information provided to determine which options to pursue and when, if they are appropriate for you at all. While you could start with the chapters that interest you the most, I highly recommend at least skimming through the whole book before jumping to conclusions about which financing methods might be the right fit for your needs. There are also aspects of earlier chapters that I refer back to in later chapters; as an example, chapter 7 describes the process of building a list of people who might be willing to give you a gift to launch or grow your business, but this is the same list that will help you identify people who might be able to make a loan or equity investment.

It is my sincere hope that this book will

- increase your awareness of the full range of capital options available to support sustainable food businesses;
- help you identify which of these are most appropriate given your unique values and goals;
- give you a sense of what it will take to successfully access the appropriate types of capital;
- increase your confidence in speaking about money and finance with different types of investors; and
- reveal additional resources that will help you in your quest to raise money for your venture.

Raising capital is rarely easy or straightforward, and the field of finance is changing so rapidly that even seasoned entrepreneurs can find it difficult to know just where to focus their efforts. For Brahm, the People's Community Market, and the residents they serve, the answer came in the form of a direct public offering that allows anyone in California to invest as little as $1,000. West Oakland residents can now become founders and shareholders of the company that exists solely to make their lives better. (See chapter 10 for more information about this financing option.)

May the insights in this book help demystify the fundraising process so that you can get back to the work you set out to do, as soon as possible, with the resources you need to do it. Thank you for your contribution to building a more sustainable food system that nourishes us all.

PART ONE

Preparing for Outside Capital

THE CHAPTERS IN THIS PART COVER STEPS THAT YOU CAN TAKE EARLY on that will make your future fundraising efforts far easier. Chapter 1 stresses the importance of cultivating relationships with potential funders long before you need to raise money. It also describes a few networks where you might find helpful partners in the fields of sustainable food and social enterprise. Chapter 2 is the shortest but most important chapter in the entire book. You need to know what values are important to you and your company, and you need to be able to effectively communicate them in order to make important business decisions—including choosing appropriate financial partners. This chapter will help you get there. Chapter 3 explains the fundraising implications of the entity type that you choose for your venture and covers some newer options available for socially responsible businesses. Chapter 4 covers personal finance basics, such as improving your credit score, separating your business from your personal finances, and building your personal savings so that you can invest both time and money into your business. Yes, these details matter to investors and other financiers! Chapter 5 will help you set up—or modify—your bookkeeping system so that it will both help you manage your business more effectively and easily generate the types of reports that lenders and other investors will ask for. It also explains how the way in which you approach your tax returns can help—or harm—your chances of raising capital. Chapter 6 will help you identify how much financing you need, then write a business plan that can help you raise it.

Even if you've been in business for years, there will be information that you can use in these chapters. For instance, you can never develop too much financial discipline when it comes to keeping tabs on your business activity, and it might be time for you to reconsider the entity structure that you started out with. If your business plan has been sitting on the shelf unopened for years, it's probably time for a new one. So what are you waiting for? Let's get started!

1
......

It's Never Too Early to Start Building Relationships

ONE DAY I RECEIVED A CALL from a friend whose company manufactures organic cotton drawstring bags that are an excellent alternative to single-use plastic bags when one shops for vegetables or bulk goods. He had a meeting that week with the regional buyer for a national natural foods retailer, at which he expected to receive a verbal commitment for about seventy thousand bags that the retailer would sell alongside their bulk bins. However, my friend would need to buy a full container of two hundred thousand bags from his supplier in order to deliver the expected order, an expense he could not afford at the time. If the deal went through as expected, he could easily pay for the full container, but he'd still be in a cash flow crunch. Did I know of any investors who might help him finance this chicken-and-egg situation?

I begin this book with the advice to start building relationships now, because you can never begin this process early enough. It's certainly too late to look for prospective investors the week before you need the money, as my friend discovered (and ultimately, the deal did not go through). Better to start building relationships gradually. By the time you are ready to start raising capital for your business, you will be able to make informed decisions about whom to approach, how, and when. "Investors and capital providers like to get to know a business before they invest," observes Bonny Moellenbrock, executive director of SJF Institute, a nonprofit that works with sustainable entrepreneurs to facilitate their access to capital, promote employee engagement, and help build sustainable economies. She is also the executive director of Investors' Circle (see chapter 16 for more information about how Investors' Circle might help you find equity investors).

"Go to the networking events, the local business leaders' cocktail hour, any conferences where people in your field are gathering," suggests Bonny. "It's all about relationships. Develop those relationships, and people will be more likely to take a look when the time comes for you to raise capital." Building relationships is not just about raising capital, of course. You never know when you might meet someone who will later turn into a colleague, customer, supplier, or other type of partner.

Even if formal networking events aren't your thing, building relationships can be as easy as being present as you go about your daily activities, being a genuinely nice person with everyone you meet, and eventually, asking for what you need when you need it. It's important to dispel the myth that you need to meet "the right people" in "the right places." That person you always chat with in the yoga studio waiting room could be the manager of the local credit union. Your softball buddy could be looking for a way to invest a recent inheritance closer to home.

Think of building relationships more as a philosophy and way of being rather than a quest to find investors. It's a matter of acknowledging our interdependence. None of us would be where we are without each other; we have all had help getting to where we are now, whether from our parents, our neighbors, our teachers, our spiritual community; whether that help came in the form of land, money, connections, or mentorship. Once we realize this, it's easier to ask for help, and it's also easier to offer what we can to help others.

Here are a few ways to maximize your chances of building relationships with people who can help you further your business goals, by connecting you to partners to help you manage the business, introducing you to suppliers or customers, offering strategic advice, or helping you raise capital.

—— Tap into Networks ——

One straightforward way to build relationships is to tap into the professional networks, associations, or other membership organizations in your region that convene the people who are part of your business ecosystem. You may be able to find a group built around the specific sector in which your business operates. Even if there is no immediate connection to your business other than shared geography, it's worth getting involved to better get to know your local leaders, influencers, and connectors. Examples of groups to consider engaging with include organic farming associations, regional sustainable agriculture working groups (SAWGs), your local grange, sustainable business networks, organizations that support local purchasing efforts, chambers of commerce, and groups concerned with issues of economic development.

As part of their missions, some of these groups may offer connections to financial resources through referrals, direct advisory services, or workshops. Some may even offer lending programs designed to support businesses like yours. For instance, the Northeast Organic Farming Association of Vermont, the Maine Organic Farmers and Gardeners Association, Financing Ozarks Rural Growth and Economy, and California FarmLink all administer loan funds for farmers. (See chapter 14 for more examples.)

The following profiles describe a few of the most important and influential networks that serve socially responsible food entrepreneurs. It is beyond the scope of this book to list hundreds of relevant local groups around the country, but I do want to stress that it is much easier to build relationships at the local level. Since people and institutions usually prefer to invest closer to home, engaging in local network activities may generate the most fruitful fundraising leads, so do not forget to explore your local network opportunities.

Slow Money

Although the term "slow money" has come to represent an entire genre of investment practices, the name also refers to a particular nonprofit organization, Slow Money, which has spearheaded the movement based on a set of published principles (see sidebar on page 13). Slow Money is a national network and a family of local networks organized around new ways of thinking about the relationship between food, money, and soil. As of this writing, there were sixteen local Slow Money chapters in the United States.

The organization also holds both regional events and annual national gatherings that bring together investors, donors, entrepreneurs, activists, and farmers from around the country and the world. These events often feature entrepreneur showcases, during which a select group of entrepreneurs representing both for-profit and nonprofit food system ventures (depending on the selection committee's criteria for that event) has the opportunity to present their business ideas to the crowd. As the result of conversations sparked during these national events, more than $21 million has been invested into 175 different small food enterprises. In addition, Slow Money chapters around the country host local discussion groups and entrepreneur showcases, which catalyze their own local investment conversations and activities. Slow Money also works to incubate new financial tools that will make it easier for individuals of all economic backgrounds to participate in making slow-money-style investments. One of these, Credibles, is covered in more detail in chapter 8.

"Our members include a wide range of individuals—angel investors, foundation staff, entrepreneurs, farmers, and just plain regular folks who want to know where their food comes from and where their money goes," explains Woody Tasch, founder and chairman of Slow Money and author of the book *Inquiries into the Nature of Slow Money: Investing as if Food, Farms, and Fertility Mattered* (Chelsea Green, 2010). "We all believe that putting some of our money to work in local food enterprises makes tremendous sense—in terms of financial diversification, in terms of biological diversity, in terms of security, and in terms of local resilience."

If your goals go beyond raising capital to include becoming actively engaged in a conversation about the nature of investing in socially responsible food companies as part of a larger movement to build sustainable communities, then do yourself a favor and tap into this community. While companies seeking financing for extensive growth have made good investor connections through Slow Money, there is no other organization that has spent as much time and energy focusing directly on the financing needs of food entrepreneurs, whether they intend to grow their businesses beyond the local or community scale or not. "The food entrepreneurs who have successfully raised capital through Slow Money see themselves as part of something bigger. They become members and actively participate in the network, at the national or local level, in order to foster that purpose," says Michael Bartner, Slow Money's vice president. "Be part of the community-building first. Be enthusiastic about what you're doing to impact your local food system, but don't appear pushy," he suggests.

The Social Venture Network

If you are committed to issues of social responsibility, there are two national networks to be aware of. Even if you can't directly engage in their conferences or local chapter activities, they all offer services to help you stay connected and informed about issues relevant to social entrepreneurs. The first, founded in 1987, is the Social Venture Network (SVN), a peer-to-peer membership network of close to five hundred social entrepreneurs and impact investors. Its mission is to connect, support, and inspire business leaders and

THE SLOW MONEY PRINCIPLES[1]

I. We must bring money back down to earth.

II. There is such a thing as money that is too fast, companies that are too big, finance that is too complex. Therefore, we must slow our money down—not all of it, of course, but enough to matter.

III. The 20th Century was the era of Buy Low/Sell High and Wealth Now/Philanthropy Later—what one venture capitalist called "the largest legal accumulation of wealth in history." The 21st Century will be the era of nurture capital, built around principles of carrying capacity, care of the commons, sense of place and non-violence.

IV. We must learn to invest as if food, farms and fertility mattered. We must connect investors to the places where they live, creating vital relationships and new sources of capital for small food enterprises.

V. Let us celebrate the new generation of entrepreneurs, consumers and investors who are showing the way from Making a Killing to Making a Living.

VI. Paul Newman said, "I just happen to think that in life we need to be a little like the farmer who puts back into the soil what he takes out." Recognizing the wisdom of these words, let us begin rebuilding our economy from the ground up, asking:

VII. What would the world be like if we invested 50 percent of our assets within 50 miles of where we live?

VIII. What if there were a new generation of companies that gave away 50 percent of their profits?

IX. What if there were 50 percent more organic matter in our soil 50 years from now?

social entrepreneurs in expanding practices that build a just and sustainable economy. "There are in fact many impact investors amongst the SVN membership," says executive director Deb Nelson. "It's not specifically designed to foster investments, but active SVN members often raise capital from fellow members." SVN hosts two national gatherings, one in the spring exclusively for members and another in the fall that is open to members and others by invitation only. The events are where much of the SVN magic occurs, though you should not attend solely with the intention of raising capital.

In addition to the national gatherings, SVN also hosts regular local gatherings in several cities around the United States. The network offers a variety of additional benefits to members, including personalized connections to other network members, meetings of peer groups for mutual support and mentoring, promotion and media opportunities, discounts, and other resources. Approximately 75 percent of SVN members are leaders of and investors in some of the nation's most innovative socially and environmentally responsible businesses. The remainder are founders and directors of nonprofit and philanthropic institutions. Most SVN members are CEOs, presidents, or owners of companies with $2 million (the standard revenue threshold to qualify for membership) to $100 million in annual revenues. Members representing socially responsible food businesses include Myra Goodman of Earthbound Farm, Gary Erickson of Clif Bar, and George Siemon of Organic Valley.

If you don't meet the standard criteria, don't fret: you can still get involved. Emerging entrepreneurs who do not meet the financial criteria for membership and have been in business fewer than five years are eligible for membership at reduced rates. SVN further offers affiliate membership that covers most but not all membership benefits. SVN also publishes a series of books that walk readers through the practical steps of starting and growing a socially responsible business, written by authors that are leaders in this field and, of course, members of the network.

Jim Slama is founder and president of FamilyFarmed.org, which encourages the production, marketing, and distribution of locally grown and responsibly produced food through its events, publications, technical assistance, and other programs. He met Jim Epstein, a real estate developer, at a national SVN conference in Chicago in 2009. "We connected at 2 a.m. one morning while watching the SVN band. I was talking about the need for infrastructure for local food, and he was talking about his interest in sustainable real estate development," Jim Slama recalls. A major component of the discussion centered around FamilyFarmed.org's publication *Wholesale Success: A Farmer's Guide to Food Safety, Selling, Postharvest Handling, and Packing Produce*, which covers all the things that small farmers need to do to sell in larger-scale wholesale markets. "After talking for hours, we agreed, 'Let's do something together,'" Jim Slama says.

FamilyFarmed.org then did a feasibility study that validated the demand for local produce for wholesale markets. "In this process, we realized that there was a strong need for an aggregator to work with growers to sell and transport the product," Jim Slama says. As a result, Blue Ridge Produce was born, as Jim Epstein decided to launch a food hub in Virginia to aggregate produce from nearby farms and supply it to buyers throughout the region. While doing the feasibility study, they looked at several sites and facilities, including one that seemed perfect, with fifty thousand square feet of warehouse, two acres of greenhouses, and office space. They just had to come up with the money to buy it.

Not only did the SVN conference catalyze the genesis of this food hub, but connections made through the network helped with raising the capital needed to purchase the property and launch Blue Ridge Produce. "After completing a very extensive business plan, the company raised $1.4 million in four months," Jim Slama says, still somewhat amazed at the quick turnaround for such a fundraising effort. "Jim Epstein put in some of his own money, plus he was able to bring some family money to the table," he reports. "In addition, one longtime SVN member that Jim Epstein knew from having been active with the network put in $700,000, and there were a few other SVN investors as well."

BALLE

SVN also has a successful history of catalyzing new networks that serve the needs of the socially responsible business movement. One of these is the Business Alliance for Local Living Economies, or BALLE. Started by longtime SVN members Laury Hammel and Judy Wicks (see chapter 20 for more of Judy's story as the pioneering entrepreneur of the White Dog Café in Philadelphia), BALLE's mission is to catalyze, strengthen, and connect networks of locally owned, independent businesses dedicated to building strong local living economies—economies that function in harmony with local ecosystems, meet the basic needs of all people, support just and democratic societies, and foster joyful community life. As North America's fastest-growing network of socially responsible businesses, BALLE consists of over eighty community networks in thirty U.S. states and Canadian provinces, representing over twenty-two thousand independent business members.

BALLE offers a wide range of services to its constituents and local networks, including support for Buy Local campaigns and the development of community energy programs, zero-waste manufacturing loops, and local food systems. Their annual national business conference convenes hundreds of innovative community leaders, entrepreneurs, independent business owners, policymakers, economic development professionals, funders, and investors to share ideas, resources, and models for unleashing local prosperity. Of particular interest to entrepreneurs raising capital is BALLE's Accelerating Community Capital initiative, which consists of monthly webinars showcasing successes in connecting investors with local investment opportunities, intensive workshops, and a full track of programming at the national conference. (Full disclosure: I'm part of the advisory committee.) You can engage with BALLE by joining one of the local networks, attending the national workshops and conferences, or participating in the webinars.

—— Seek Out Advice ——

"If you ask for money, you'll get advice. If you ask for advice, you'll get money." Though I do not actually suggest that you avoid asking for money, I love this tongue-in-cheek rule. Why does it ring so true? Is it because the people who are wise enough to ask others for advice are more likely to run well-considered businesses? Is it because advisers who have seen you learn and grow over time are more likely to give good references when investors start kicking your tires and asking around for character references? Is it because prospective investors themselves appreciate being considered as sources of wisdom rather than giant wallets?

It's likely a combination of the above, plus other factors. But the underlying message is always the same: ask for the help you need. Reading books and poring over Internet sites may help, but also seek out advice from actual people who can point out what you didn't even know you needed to study up on. Talk to people to check your assumptions and confirm that your ideas make sense. Conduct lots of informal market research by asking questions of anyone who is remotely related to your business: Do you think people will buy these frozen apple pies at this price? What about wholesale customers? Where can I find the best organic ingredients, recycled packaging, manufacturing equipment, or e-newsletter software? How were you able to develop a relationship with the nearest farmers' market or Whole Foods regional buyer? Stay humble and always keep learning. In your quest for advice, you may very well discover you have found some investors.

U.S. Small Business Administration

If you want access to more formal programs offering business assistance and mentorship, you have several options available through the U.S. Small Business Administration (SBA). The SBA's Small Business Development

Centers (or SBDCs, which are often partnerships between the government and colleges or universities), Women's Business Centers, and Minority Business Development Centers all provide free and confidential in-person counseling and training services for small-business owners. They cover many aspects of starting and running a business, from getting loans and financing, to developing business plans and marketing strategies. The SBA also has special programs to provide assistance to Native Americans, veterans, youth, and entrepreneurs over the age of fifty. The SBA's Service Corps of Retired Executives Association (SCORE) offers free mentoring, business counseling, and low-cost workshops, thanks to its network of over thirteen thousand volunteer counselors. In addition to delivering services in person at over 364 chapters nationwide, SCORE makes counseling, workshops, and other resources available online via their website. (The SBA also has several financing programs; see chapter 15.)

Food Business Incubators

You might also find advice on starting or growing your venture from a food business incubator. Full-service food business incubators go a good step beyond the shared kitchen space, commercial equipment, and storage space offered by kitchen incubators (though the terms used to describe kitchen incubators are fuzzy, so double-check the list of services provided rather than make any assumptions based on the name alone). Food business incubators usually offer classes and even one-on-one technical support on topics such as recipe development, food packaging, business planning and strategy, marketing, sales, bookkeeping and accounting, finance, food safety, permitting, international trade, and operations. They may present specialized workshops on topics such as developing food cart businesses. Some also facilitate joint purchasing of ingredients and supplies on behalf of their clients, allowing for economies of scale that small businesses might not otherwise be able to access on their own.

Food business incubators may also be able to connect you to lending institutions and other types of investors; a few even offer their own lending programs. "We recommend that anyone who graduates to a certain stage of our incubation process take out a loan from our guaranteed loan program," says Caleb Zigas, executive director of La Cocina, a nonprofit that cultivates low-income food entrepreneurs, primarily women of color and immigrants, as they formalize and grow their businesses. La Cocina provides affordable commercial kitchen space, industry-specific technical assistance, and access to market and capital opportunities. "Even if our clients don't think they need a loan, and they pay it back within a week, it builds their credit records," he explains. "But more importantly, it allows them to feel the power of capital when they see how much easier it was to start their businesses with a thousand or two extra dollars!"

Also consider reaching out to general business incubators near you, even if they do not have a food-specific focus. "Kitchen incubators, like arts incubators, are one small niche of the total incubation industry," explains Mary Ann Gulino of the National Business Incubation Association. A non-food business incubator may still be able to provide you with office space, mentorship, and other resources and referrals that can help your socially responsible food business grow, even if they can't help you with shared commercial food processing equipment.

Keep in mind that general business incubators are likely to be better versed in more traditional business models and may not lead you to mentors and advisers who have experience with socially responsible food businesses and more cutting-edge financing methods. Although you shouldn't let this deter you from engaging their services, keep in mind (as you would any time you receive feedback related to your business) that the person giving the advice may not actually have the best insights into the specific niche that your business addresses. If something you hear doesn't seem right to you, trust your instincts and seek out a second (if not third and fourth) opinion.

2

......

Clarifying Your Values

IN 2007 KATIE MCCASKEY and her boyfriend, Brian Wiedemann, moved from New York City to the small town of Staunton, Virginia, where Katie had grown up. One night they realized they needed feta cheese for the recipe they were preparing for dinner. Whereas they would have had no problem finding feta in New York City, there were no grocery stores left within walking distance of their home in Staunton. When Katie happened to mention her feta-free dinner experience to the owner of her local coffee shop, she learned that a man named George Bowers had operated a grocery store in the very same building around the turn of the twentieth century. "Wouldn't it be great to have a grocery store in the neighborhood again?" Katie mused.

A few weeks later the coffee shop owner told Katie that he and his wife had decided to reopen the grocery store in the location next to their shop. They had already invested a significant amount of money into the business; would Katie and Brian like to join them as minority partners? "These people were fun, enthusiastic, and nice! It sounded like they had great experience, connections in the community, and connections to local farmers," Katie recalls. "Personality-wise, it seemed like a really good fit. They were talking about all the things that we cared about: community, neighborhood, local food." She and Brian liked the idea of being able to invest in the community while also helping create the kind of neighborhood store that they themselves would like to spend time in—one that would carry both local products and gourmet "essentials," including feta cheese.

Katie and Brian invested $20,000 of their own funds, which gave them a minority ownership stake in the business. In 2008 the George Bowers Grocery Store received the first microloan from the newly established Staunton Creative Community Fund, a grand total of $5,000. "This was a small percent of the overall cost of renovating the 130-year-old building and buying inventory for the store," Katie says, "but we weren't going to say no! Fortunately, we were also able to get a $17,000 line of credit from a community bank." The two couples opened the new grocery store at the end of 2008, much to the delight of the community.

Within a few months, however, the business partnership began to sour. Katie and Brian found themselves shouldering the bulk of the daily work of operating the store, and their partners—who were going through a divorce—were less and less available to share the workload. In addition to differences over appropriate work ethics, the couples found themselves at odds over the procurement standards for the store's inventory, despite the fact that they had seemed to agree that purchasing local food was a major priority. "One day, one of our partners came back with a load of cheese from Costco. I was shocked. I asked, 'Why did you do that? This isn't local at all,' and the response was, 'Well, it's from our local Costco.' It was agonizing! We clearly didn't share the same values around what 'local' means."

Then came the real zinger. In January 2009 the other couple, who had already shuttered their coffee shop because of personal financial troubles, threatened to close down the grocery store, too. Katie and Brian, determined to see their own dream through, had no choice but to buy out their partners. "They were asking an outrageous price," says Katie, "considering we were also renting the space from them. But we couldn't negotiate it down." They came up with the money by draining the last of their savings, all of which added quite a bit of stress to their lives.

Katie says that the next couple of years were challenging, but she and Brian made a series of smart decisions, including moving the George Bowers Grocery Store to a larger location closer to the main street in town and adding an outdoor beer garden that hosts popular community events. (They were also able to secure an additional loan of $10,000 from the Staunton Creative Community Fund in April 2010, a loan made possible by U.S. Department of Agriculture (USDA) programs and a Community Development Block Grant; see chapter 15 for more information about these options.) Their business is thriving, and they are proud of what they have accomplished, despite having learned the hard way about the importance of choosing partners with aligned values. "Looking back, we realized we had failed to do sufficient background checks," Katie says of the couple they had gone into business with. "We took them at their word as far as their professional backgrounds were concerned, which was a mistake." She wishes they had asked for resumes and followed up with their references. "Had we done that," she says, "we would have quickly uncovered some of their exaggerations in terms of their management experience, qualifications for running a business, and connections within the community."

"It is so important to find people with values that match your own. I can't emphasize that enough," Katie stresses. This is true whether you're setting out to find business partners or investors—and often, as in the case of the George Bowers Grocery, your business partners and investors are the same people. But it's very difficult, if not impossible, to gauge a good values fit if you haven't first determined your own values and priorities. This chapter helps lay out several concepts and principles that many socially responsible food entrepreneurs incorporate into their own businesses. Once you're clear about what is most important to you, it will be much easier to find the types of people you want to work with and the types of financing that will make the most sense for your venture.

—— What's Most Important to You? ——

As you read through the following list of values, note which of them resonate most strongly with you. Where on the spectrum of options do your own values lie? If you had to sacrifice some to stay true to others, which would rank as the highest in priority? Which values are most closely connected to your vision of success? (If your business has more than one founder, or if you have already built a managing team, make sure that you each go through this section so that you can compare notes. Like Katie, you might be surprised at what you discover!) I might have called this section "How Do You Measure Success?" because your vision of success will reveal your true values. How would you measure the ones that are most important to you? Where would you draw hard lines? Values are complex and inter-related. Some may be mutually exclusive, meaning that if you focus on one it could be harder to achieve the others. But many of them can happen simultaneously and may in fact reinforce one another.

Here are some values to consider for any type of business:

- **Place.** How important is the place where you do business, such as the farm, the neighborhood, the city, the state, or the region? It might not matter at all. But in many cases a venture is inextricably connected to its place, such as in the case of a family farm that operates on one's family land or a retail business designed to serve a particular community. The wildly popular Zingerman's Deli in Ann Arbor, Michigan, for instance, chose to leverage its success by spinning off several complementary businesses in the same town (including a creamery, a bakery, a coffee company, a candy "manufactory," and a consulting company) rather than expand through franchising the deli in different locations. Another situation in which commitment to place might be important to you is if you intend to stay involved in the business and you are not willing to move, whether or not it might make more sense for other reasons to take the business elsewhere.

- **Control.** Do you intend to stay at the helm of your venture until your dying day? Does the thought of having to answer to someone other than yourself make you cringe? Or perhaps it is important to you to be able to pass your business on to your children or to your employees. These are a few cases in which staying in control would be an important value. On the other side of the spectrum, you might be a serial entrepreneur who frequently has great ideas, and you don't mind at all if other people take over what you have started, so long as your idea or product gets out there. If you have one or more business partners, you need to discuss various scenarios for what will happen if one of you decides to move on to other things, both in terms of control and in terms of buying out the departing partner.

- **Scale.** How big is big enough? Whether you measure by annual revenue, number of jobs created, customers reached, market share, pounds of food waste diverted from landfill, acres of farmland converted to organic, retail locations opened, or some other metric, you probably have an idea of what success looks like. Bigger is not necessarily better! If you would prefer that your home-based business stay small enough that you and your partner can handle all its operations yourselves from your garage, don't be shy about saying so. Likewise, if you want your breakthrough product to be available in every major grocery store across the country, you value scale in a different way.

- **Pace of growth.** Once you have a clear goal in terms of scale of your business, how quickly do you intend to get there? Rapid growth requires a different mind-set and a different set of tools than slower growth. You may be perfectly satisfied with a slow-growing business or one that doesn't need to grow at all once it's breaking even. Think carefully about your personality, work ethic, and lifestyle expectations. Are you willing to pour all of your life energy into your business? Or do you intend to make time for other priorities as well, such as spending time with your family or volunteering? If you yourself are not willing to put in the hours that rapid growth may require, would you consider hiring someone else to take the helm and giving them the autonomy to do so?

- **Financial success (and for whom).** How much money do you want the business to generate for yourself and for your partners, employees, vendors, and other stakeholders, which may include shareholders? Maybe your business is a labor of love and not your primary source of income, and the social mission is more important than your own earnings. But maybe you want to be able to generate enough income through this venture to support your entire family, including sending your kids to college. It might be challenging to juggle these conflicting values. For instance, if your mission is to support local farmers, a policy of paying them a premium price for their goods might be at odds with the goal of paying yourself a higher salary, unless you can achieve efficiencies in other parts of your business.
- **Time horizon.** Do you want the business to last a few years, a few decades, or long after you are gone? Or perhaps it's a onetime project with a short duration, such as a pop-up restaurant. Make sure your time line is clear to any potential partners.

Socially responsible food businesses often incorporate one or more of the following additional values:

- **Buying locally.** If local food is at the core of your venture's mission, then this value is obviously very important to you. But depending upon where you live and what grows there in which season, you might discover that it's hard to commit to exclusively purchasing local food. How much money or energy are you willing to spend working with local growers or manufacturers so that they can meet your procurement standards? What about your other vendors? Will you purchase other inputs, such as packaging, printed materials, and office supplies, as locally as possible? Do you prioritize independent service providers for taxes, accounting, legal counsel, and so on over national-brand services?

- **Supporting organics.** Whether you produce or purchase grains, fruits, vegetables, or animal products, the question of production methods is an important one. For you, is "organic" more about keeping toxic chemicals out of the environment, keeping farmworkers safe from chemical exposure, healthier food, or something else entirely? Will you insist upon third-party certification and the federal definition of "organic"? (Many farmers who meet or exceed organic standards choose not to get certified because of the costs and record keeping involved.) If your business focuses on ensuring access to low-cost fresh fruits and vegetables, organics may not be your highest priority if they are more expensive.

- **Humane treatment of animals.** Again, it's a question of how far you want to go with these issues and considering the trade-offs. Perhaps you would prefer to avoid any animal products from concentrated animal feeding operations (CAFOs). Or will you insist upon products that are certified humane by one of several third-party organizations?

- **Sustainably sourced seafood.** If you want to protect the ocean's re-sources and procure seafood only from the most sustainable fisheries, can you commit to only the "best choices" as specified by the Monterey Bay Aquarium's Seafood Watch program, or perhaps only products that are certified by the Marine Stewardship Council, for instance? Or would you prefer to support small, independent fisherpeople and pur-chase whatever they can provide? Would committing to all of the above be too challenging—or expensive—to make it work for your business?

- **Food justice, food sovereignty, and food security.** Ensuring that all people, regardless of economic class or location, have access to healthy, fresh, just, sustainable, and affordable food is just one aspect of this value. How does your venture relate to helping communities grow, process, and retail their own food? Does your business factor into a larger community democracy?

- **Healthy and safe conditions for employees.** How far down the sup-ply chain does your commitment go? For instance, if you want to support improved conditions for farmworkers, how will you confirm that your vendors meet your standards?

- **Healthy food.** How do you define "healthy"? Will you manufacture or provide healthy foods only, even if you could sell a lot more, at higher margins, of the unhealthy options?
- **Energy use and carbon footprint.** Every business uses energy and emits carbon at multiple points in its operations and in the lifecycle of its products. Is your equipment and physical infrastructure energy efficient? Will you source your energy from more ecologically friendly utilities? Will you purchase carbon offsets? You might run your vehicles on biodiesel or even used vegetable oil, or contract with distributors or delivery companies that address their own carbon footprint. Your product design also has an impact; for instance, you might design your heat-and-eat products so that they remain stable at room temperature rather than requiring refrigeration.
- **Minimizing waste.** What can you do to reduce the amount of waste that your company produces? Will you use recycled and/or recyclable packaging? What about compostables and bioplastics? If avoiding genetically modified (GM) products is important to you, you might need to think twice about some of your options.
- **Investing in your community.** This could take a number of different forms in addition to purchasing local goods and services. Will you host community events at your place of business or sponsor other local events? Will your company donate money to local charities or match employee donations? Does your company policy cover paid volunteer days for employees? Maybe you will commit to hiring local people, even if this means providing extra training.
- **Employee compensation, benefits, and decision-making processes.** Which of the following would you like to provide for your employees: paid time off for holidays, vacation, illness, bereavement, care of family members, maternity, paternity? Flexible work schedules? Subsidized health, disability, and life insurance premiums? Matched contributions to retirement plans? A generous definition of what constitutes "full-time employment" for the purposes of providing benefits in the first place? Meal plans? Affordable housing? This is just the start, as there are many other benefits you could choose to provide. How do you engage your employees in making decisions about your business? For some, democratic and/or consensus decision making is an important value.

- **Transparency.** You may be committed to transparency of your venture's activities, but of which specific details and to whom? What will you share with your board, your customers, your suppliers, the public? How will you make this information available?

—— Putting It in Writing ——

Once you've determined what is most important to you and your business, make an effort to clearly articulate your commitment to these values. Will Rosenzweig is cofounder and partner at Physic Ventures, a venture capital firm that invests in breakthrough technologies, products, and services in health and sustainability. He's also a successful food entrepreneur (he was founding CEO and minister of progress at the Republic of Tea) who served on the faculty of the Haas School of Business at the University of California, Berkeley. "A company's values need to be explicit, not just in terms of 'what are we doing' but also 'how are we going to do it' so that there is a constitution to follow," he says. If possible, use specifics to describe your commitment to the value, such as, "We commit to spending at least 50 percent of our store's produce budget on farms located within seventy-five miles." Keep in mind that these commitments might change after you have been in business awhile, as you learn through experience what is realistic and sustainable for your operations. (You'd be wise to avoid printing your commitments on every sign, doormat, and T-shirt associated with your business until you're sure that you can keep them.)

These value commitments might become part of your venture's mission statement, operating principles, or other guiding document. You'll want to refer back to them as you read through the chapters to come, as they will help you evaluate which options are the best fit. Your statement of values will also serve as a guiding star when you come up against challenging management decisions. Not sure which vendor to commit to, which distributor is the best choice, or even which customers to focus on? Checking for a match in values will help you determine the correct path of action. Clearly articulating your values and priorities will also give you and your prospective investors a sense of whether or not you're on the same page.

Finally, consider how you would explain your position on these values to somebody else. As a social entrepreneur, this is a skill you will need to cultivate. You might already know exactly why your values feel right, but others might not be so understanding. The overriding assumption in the world of business is that a company exists to make as much money as possible through whatever means necessary. Entrepreneurs with a wider value set bear the burden of justifying their actions not only in terms of the financial but also in terms of their other stated areas of impact.

3

······

Choosing an Entity Type

BEFORE YOU BEGIN THE PROCESS of raising capital from outside investors, you will need to make some decisions about how to legally structure your business. The entity type you choose affects your capacity to fundraise, and not always in the ways that you might expect. "Choosing an entity is about finding the possible in a sea of perceived constraints," says Joy Anderson of Criterion Ventures, a business that offers what it calls Structure Lab training sessions to help social entrepreneurs consider the benefits and implications of various structures. "Legal structures are often a deafening thud in the moment when people are thinking about what is possible. 'Really? We can't do that?' people say, thinking their venture can't take grants if it's structured as a for-profit entity, or that it can't make a profit as a nonprofit. Often, these statements are radically erroneous."

The entity type you choose can also impact your ability to keep your values embedded in the venture as it evolves over time. Marjorie Kelly is director of ownership strategy at the consulting firm Cutting Edge Capital, where she works with companies to design ownership and capital strategies that maximize social mission. She is also a fellow at Tellus Institute, where she directs a number of large research consulting projects in rural development and impact investing. "Choosing an entity structure is not primarily a legal exercise," she emphasizes. "You end up with a legal structure, but it's really about how you manage human relationships and identifying the purpose of the business. You start there. What are you trying to do?"

There are many for-profit entity options to choose from, each of which might offer benefits in some areas and disadvantages in others. As if choosing an entity structure weren't confusing enough to begin with, a social entrepreneur can consider additional options above and beyond the usual for-profit models. This chapter covers the basic entity types in three categories: nonprofit, for-profit, and newer social enterprise structures that are available in a growing number of states. You'll go through a series of questions to help you determine which entity might be the best fit for your venture, given your values and intentions. While the majority of this book is designed to help entrepreneurs who choose for-profit or social enterprise structures, it is entirely possible that a nonprofit might best serve your goals.

—— Nonprofit Entities ——

Nonprofit organizations can—and often do—engage in social enterprise activities that generate revenue with the purpose of furthering their charitable missions. Nonprofits can even generate "profits" from their operations, but this net income must be reinvested into the organization to further its mission. There are some major benefits to choosing a nonprofit entity structure, assuming your venture meets the legal qualifications to become one. Eligible nonprofits are exempt from federal and state income-tax requirements, and gifts to nonprofits are tax deductible to individual donors, giving them added incentive to support you. Foundations are far more likely to make grants to nonprofits rather than for-profit entities. The social "brand" of a nonprofit is also immediately clear to prospective supporters: your organization is committed to its mission.

However, you severely limit the number of financing tools at your disposal if you choose a nonprofit structure. Many of the financing tools covered in this book (including the entire equity section) work only with for-profit entities. Even if it is technically possible to make debt investments in nonprofits, many people are simply more comfortable making gifts to nonprofits and investing in for-profit businesses. Meanwhile, more and more for-profit businesses have deeply social missions at their core. As Marjorie points out, "You can operate a social mission company within any entity type, for-profit or nonprofit." As the line between nonprofit activities and for-profit activities gets blurry, it can be confusing to understand which model might be the best fit.

Red Tomato is a nonprofit with a mission of connecting farmers and consumers through marketing, trade, and education and through a passionate belief that a family-farm, locally based, ecological, fair trade food system is "the way to a better tomato." Many of the marketing activities that Red

Tomato engages in on behalf of the farmer network it serves resemble work that a for-profit farmers' cooperative might have done. "I have been a co-op groupie my whole life," says Michael Rozyne, the organization's founder and executive director, who seriously considered a for-profit cooperative model for Red Tomato. Having cofounded and worked for nine years growing Equal Exchange, a worker-owned cooperative that imports and markets Fair Trade coffee, chocolate, and snack foods, he has intimate knowledge of how to run a food business that way. "But I decided in the mid-1990s that Red Tomato would be better as nonprofit rather than as a farmers' co-op. We work in the public interest, not only for the interests of our farmers, although worker democracy and influence is still a critical part of our culture," he explains. In his experience many of the farmers' cooperatives were conservative marketing entities, sometimes becoming dominated by the interests of one or two farmers with particularly strong voices. "We wanted to be able to focus on the best quality and the best programs, including educating the public, buyers, and growers, no matter what it takes."

"Being a nonprofit has given us a lot of flexibility to be both entrepreneurial and mission driven, not purely member driven," says Sue Futrell, Red Tomato's director of marketing. Like Michael she had worked with a cooperative wholesale company in the natural and organic industry prior to joining Red Tomato in 2006. "A co-op is really powerful if it's directed by a set of goals built around its members. In the case of Red Tomato, our goals have more to do with building a larger movement, and that would have been harder to get done in an ownership structure where the owners needed to see direct benefits. I love working for a small, entrepreneurial nonprofit."

In deciding to choose a nonprofit structure, Michael had also considered how the numbers would pencil out. From the very beginning he expected that operating Red Tomato's multiple programs—which include significant research and educational components in addition to developing a new approach to marketing, buying, and selling local produce—would require grants in addition to the revenues their work would generate. "We strive to cover the costs of actually buying, selling, and marketing produce through the fees we charge to do that, which are about 10 percent of the price that the grocery stores pay us for the products," Sue explains, adding:

> But we don't expect that part of our program to cover the cost
> of our research into new apple production methods that reduce

pesticide use, or the work to leverage what we have learned to help build the larger sustainable food movement and bring it more into alignment with our vision. We're one of the longest-running programs in the country that pools produce to sell into wholesale channels. There's more and more conversation now about the need to build distribution and marketing and wholesaling capacity, and we get several calls a week from people who want to know how we've succeeded. We're able to answer those calls, do workshops, and even take on consulting projects because it's part of our mission to share that knowledge however we can. Because we have donors and supporters who value that part of what we do, it fits into a nonprofit funding model. There's no way we could do all of this on produce industry margins.

In the case of Red Tomato, it was a clear vision of, and deep commitment to, serving the general public that made a nonprofit entity the right fit for the enterprise. If you can answer yes to the following questions, a nonprofit structure might make the most sense for your social venture:

- **Is the purpose of your organization primarily charitable?** In other words, do nearly all of your activities fall under the IRS definition of exempt activities (see sidebar on page 33)?
- **Do you intend to raise the majority of your funding for your venture from foundations and tax-exempt gifts from individuals?** If so, exempt nonprofit structures are all you should consider, as they are the only entities that can raise funds from foundations and through individual gifts that are tax-deductible to donors. (Gifts to for-profit entities are not tax-deductible, but see chapter 7 for more information on individual gifts to for-profits.)
- **Do you expect that your business model may need to be subsidized by outside funds indefinitely?** In other words, is it unlikely to ever become fully self-supported through the revenue it can generate, even in the best-case scenario? (Note the important difference between a well-executed nonprofit venture that meets all its revenue targets and still needs to raise grants to operate and an organization that is unprofitable because it fails to meet its goals. Be realistic about your

intentions. Fear that your venture may not break even is not, on its own, a good reason to choose a nonprofit structure.)

Even if you can answer yes to all of the questions above, there are some contraindications to a nonprofit structure. If any of the following are true, you (with the help of an attorney) may decide it makes more sense to choose a for-profit structure:

- **A private entity (such as a person or for-profit organization) benefits from the activities of the organization.** The IRS has specific regulations that prevent nonprofit organizations from providing "inurement," or private benefit, to the creators of the organization, their families, or any shareholders. This can be tricky to determine, and you'll need to refer back to your values. If you're in business solely to benefit a few farmers, for instance, as opposed to having a goal to improve conditions for farming in general, a cooperative or other for-profit structure may be a better fit.
- **You expect to be able to pay yourself and/or other managers a lot of money if your venture is successful.** There is no shame in wanting to be able to reap financial rewards for all the hard work you have put into launching and growing a successful enterprise. And since you cannot give yourself equity shares, it might seem that paying yourself really well once the venture is thriving would be a good option. But you do need to be aware of the possibility that the IRS has the power to deem nonprofit executive compensation "excessive" (and therefore a form of inurement), in which case you and your board may be fined, and you run the risk of losing your nonprofit status. That said, the line can be a bit confusing, as nonprofits are allowed to pay their executives "market-rate" salaries, and the "market" in question can include comparable for-profit salaries.
- **You want to be able to sell equity to raise money for your venture or give yourself shares so that you can benefit from the upside of your venture.** This isn't an option if you choose to organize as a nonprofit. Because the state technically owns nonprofits, you cannot sell equity shares to raise capital for them. (Note: you may encounter the terms "nonprofit equity" and "philanthropic equity," but these refer to the money that nonprofits need to build internal capacity

THE IRS DEFINES EXEMPT ACTIVITIES

The exempt purposes set forth in section 501(c)(3) are charitable, religious, educational, scientific, literary, testing for public safety, fostering national or international amateur sports competition, and preventing cruelty to children or animals. The term "charitable" is used in its generally accepted legal sense and includes relief of the poor, the distressed, or the under-privileged; advancement of religion; advancement of education or science; erecting or maintaining public buildings, monuments, or works; lessening the burdens of government; lessening neighborhood tensions; eliminating prejudice and discrimination; defending human and civil rights secured by law; and combating community deterioration and juvenile delinquency.[2]

infrastructure, as distinct from the money that they need to operate their programs. It does not actually refer to transferable equity shares in nonprofit entities.)

A word of caution: do not expect that just by organizing it as a nonprofit entity, charitable gifts will flow to your organization. You will still need to fundraise to bring those funds in, and you may find it more difficult to raise gift money than investments from people or institutions that are willing to put money into your venture in exchange for the possibility of financial returns.

Even if you have convinced yourself that a nonprofit structure is the best fit for your goals, you will still need to convince the IRS that you are eligible for one of the nonprofit entity options. The following entities differ based on qualification requirements, level of complication to set up, and sources of funds.

A **public charity** is a tax-exempt 501(c)(3) nonprofit corporation. This is the structure that most people think of when they envision a nonprofit organization. To set one up you must first establish your organization as a nonprofit corporation with your state, a process that involves filling out a form and paying a filing fee. The next step, applying to the IRS for exempt status, is much more involved. As defined by the IRS, public charities must receive at least one-third of their funding from the general public (i.e., through gifts from individuals) or from government sources rather than grants from foundations or investment income. And you must regularly prove that this is the case to maintain exempt status as a public charity.

If you cannot prove to the IRS that you are eligible for exempt status, by default your organization will be considered a **private foundation**, another kind of 501(c)(3). This entity type is usually controlled by a smaller number of people, which might be the family that provides much of the financial support to the organization or that donated the endowment that provides investment income to support the foundation's activities. Private foundations must follow stricter regulations than a public charity, which include increased reporting requirements and lower dollar limits on gifts from individuals and corporations. They enjoy fewer tax benefits than public charities as well, and it can be harder to raise money from other foundations or individuals into a private foundation.

The most common entity structure for a nonprofit social enterprise that cannot be considered a public charity is the **private operating foundation**, a form of private foundation that devotes the majority of its resources to the delivery of its charitable, exempt activities rather than to making grants. The steps for starting a private foundation are essentially the same as starting a public charity, with the exception of applying for exempt status if you are certain that your organization will not qualify.

An eligible organization can reap the benefits of nonprofit public charity status without organizing a new entity, filing for 501(c)(3) status on its behalf, or filing appropriate reports to the IRS annually—all expensive and time-consuming—by choosing **fiscal sponsorship**. In this model (sometimes referred to as using a "fiscal agent"), an existing 501(c)(3) organization sponsors your project; all funds are raised and distributed through the sponsoring organization. Many start-up nonprofit organizations choose this model. Some 501(c)(3) organizations exist solely to provide fiscal sponsorship to other projects; others may offer fiscal sponsorship only in rare cases involving very close mission alignment. Many fiscal sponsors offer a range of services, including money management and tax reporting, financial reporting, bill paying, payroll and benefits administration, technical support such as workshops or one-on-one consulting, and the publication of annual reports. Fundraising is almost always the responsibility of the sponsored project, not the sponsor.

If you decide to look for a fiscal sponsor, you'll have to find an organization that is a good match for your mission and your activity. Many organizations require a minimum budget, if not also a minimum amount raised toward the project, in order to consider fiscal sponsorship. The costs of fiscal sponsorship vary depending on the services rendered by the sponsoring organization and are usually charged as a percentage of the funds distributed to the sponsored project. Fees between 5 and 10 percent are typical, depending on the services offered, and you may be able to find lower rates if you have a close relationship with the sponsoring organization.

Finally, you may want to consider one of several **nonprofit–for-profit hybrid models**, such as launching a for-profit entity that is fully owned by a nonprofit or creating contractual agreements between a for-profit and a nonprofit. Though they can be quite complicated both legally and operationally, they can also offer flexibility not found in a pure nonprofit entity. Consult your attorney and accountant to identify all of the implications of choosing a hybrid model.

For-Profit Entities

There are many reasons a for-profit structure might make the most sense for your venture. You might prefer to have a wider variety of financing options at your disposal. You may want to reap the financial benefits of growing the business, or you may want to share those benefits with a wide range of stakeholders, including investors. Your reasons may be more philosophical; perhaps you want to be part of the movement that is showing the world that businesses can do well *and* do good. Or your venture may simply not qualify for charitable status based on the nature of its primary activities.

Whatever the reasons, it's likely that most readers of this book will end up choosing (or have already chosen) a for-profit entity for their enterprise. This section gives an overview of each of the for-profit entity types, including cautions and fundraising considerations for each. Note that there are many additional steps involved in starting a for-profit business that are not covered here, such as registering a business name, getting a tax identification number, and securing all appropriate licenses and permits. Since each state and local government has different rules and requirements for the above, it is important to confirm the local formation process (and associated fees) for the entity type that seems to be the best fit for your business.

Sole proprietorships are the simplest for-profit business form for a single owner: you and the business are the same legal entity. There are few if any forms, licenses, payments, or taxes required to set up and operate a sole proprietorship (this varies from state to state). Sole proprietors pay taxes on all business income on their personal tax forms rather than separately for the business. This simplicity, however, comes at the expense of considerable risk: a sole proprietor is also personally liable for all business debts with this type of structure. This means that if you cannot pay any bills associated with the business or if someone sues you based on something that happens during the course of operations (let's say your helper accidentally drops a case of your cookies at the farmers' market, injuring a customer's foot), your personal assets are at risk, including your home. A sole proprietor also cannot sell equity shares (stock) as a way to attract investors, though it is possible to raise money through debt from individuals or lending institutions.

Partnerships, also known as general partnerships, are for-profit structures that are similar to sole proprietorships in terms of taxation and registration, except that more than one person actively manages the business. As with sole proprietorships, the catch with this structure (and the reason they are not very popular) is that all partners are personally liable for business debts and in the event of lawsuits, even if the liabilities are due to actions of the other partner. Although states recognize a partnership as soon as two or more people begin doing business together, the people involved in the partnership should draft a formal partnership agreement dictating exactly how to handle governance, return on investments (particularly important if the partners do not bring equal contributions of cash or other assets to the partnership), dissolution (what happens if one or more partners want to leave), and other factors, such as milestones at which the partners will adopt a different entity structure. All partners are responsible for reporting their share of the partnership's profits or losses on their personal tax returns. While partners technically can sell their interest in the partnership, this is not a very practical way to raise capital from sources outside the partners themselves, and debt is the most common fundraising option.

Limited partnerships are similar to but more complicated to set up than general partnerships. The trade-off is that it is much easier to raise capital from outside investors with this structure, as it allows for certain partners (known as limited partners) to have limited personal liability and/or management responsibility. In other words, limited partners can be passive investors, and their financial liability in the partnership is limited to the amount that they have invested in the business. In limited partnerships, there are still one or more general partners who run the business and who are personally liable for business debts and liabilities. States are more likely to require formal filings and partnership agreements for limited partnerships than for general partnerships, and again, it's in all partners' best interests to have a partnership agreement that clearly spells out how all parties will be treated under different scenarios, whether related to governance, return on investment, dissolution, or other factors.

Corporations are independent, for-profit legal entities that are entirely separate from their shareholders or managers. They are much more complicated to set up and maintain than the entity structures described above: you must appoint formal directors, file articles of incorporation, draft bylaws, and document all important corporate decisions made at formal meetings of the directors and shareholders. You must file a separate tax return for the corporation, in addition to filing annual reports with the state.

Corporations are relatively expensive to form and to maintain compared to the previously described structures, with most states requiring annual fees. At the formation of a corporation, the manager formally issues stock to all owners. The main fundraising benefit of choosing this entity type is that people who own stock can sell their shares of the corporation to other people. A corporation's shareholders and managers all have limited personal liability, so long as the directors adhere to the state's laws regarding corporate formalities.

There are two main types of corporations: **C corporations** pay taxes on profits, and shareholders pay taxes on any dividends they receive from the corporation on their personal tax returns. **S corporations** do not pay taxes on profits, but shareholders pay taxes on their share of profits whether or not they are distributed as dividends. Another important distinction when it comes to raising capital is that C corporations may issue a number of different classes of stock (such as common stock and preferred stock; see chapter 17), to an unlimited number of shareholders, anywhere. S corporations can issue only one class of stock and can have no more than one hundred shareholders,[3] all of whom must be U.S. citizens or residents.

Cooperatives (co-ops) are for-profit corporations that are owned and operated by the people who mutually benefit from the operations of the business. Common examples in the food world include worker- or consumer-owned retail food co-ops and farmer- or rancher-owned marketing co-ops. Co-op members themselves generally invest the start-up funds required to launch the business, though they can sell preferred stock (see chapter 17) to raise money from outside investors. Farmer cooperatives that meet certain requirements can apply to the IRS for special tax status found under section 521 of the Internal Revenue Code. This gives eligible co-ops special treatment under both federal and state securities laws, allowing them to raise money from outside investors without the burden of federal or state registration requirements. Your state may also offer securities exemptions for certain types of agricultural co-ops (see chapter 10 for more information on securities laws and how exemptions can work in your favor). In short, it can be much easier for eligible cooperatives to raise capital from the public than it is for other kinds of businesses, though you'll definitely need to consult an attorney who is well versed in such cases to be sure what is possible in your situation.

A **limited liability company**, or LLC, is similar to a corporation in that it is its own entity, separate from its owners, and offers owners limited liability. Like a sole proprietorship or partnership, however, the owners report their portion of the LLC's profits or losses on their personal tax returns, provided they opt to pay taxes that way (you do have options and can choose to have your LLC taxed like a corporation). LLCs do not have to abide by the same administrative formalities (such as holding and filing minutes of regular director and shareholder meetings) as corporations do. It is much easier to make changes to an LLC's operating agreement than it is to make changes to a corporation's bylaws—and for socially responsible businesses, you can include social purposes in that operating agreement, which is one way to build your mission into your entity structure without using one of the new entity structures described below. "If you put a social mission into a regular LLC, you may become subject to L3C rules [see below] unintentionally," warns attorney Susan Mac Cormac. Depending on your state, LLCs may pay higher tax rates and fees than corporations with similar revenues. Some more traditional investors shy away from investing in LLCs for a number of reasons, including the fact that LLC operating agreements can vary widely (as opposed to the standard format of corporation articles and bylaws), making them harder to assess; that the LLC is a newer (and therefore less familiar) entity type; and that taxes from LLC investments are not always calculated in their favor.

—— New Entity ——
Options for Social Enterprises

In addition to the traditional entity options described in the previous section, social entrepreneurs have three additional options to choose from. Each of the following entity types allows directors some protection from the usual expectation that they need to manage their businesses to maximize profits, even if financial gain comes at the expense of other social or environmental factors. When it comes to raising capital, choosing one of these entity structures may be good branding, with a "halo effect" potentially giving impact-oriented investors—not to mention customers—more confidence about your commitment to social mission. Ask your network of advisers, peer entrepreneurs, and investors about their experiences with these options to get a sense of how they perceive them, recognizing that this is a rapidly evolving field. These entity structures are available only in certain states, though there are efforts in more states to introduce additional entity structure options for social businesses, and you can incorporate your business in one of the states where the newer entity structures are already available.

The **low-profit limited liability company, or L3C,** is a special type of LLC that attempts to bridge the gap between for-profit and nonprofit entities. It was developed to make it easier for for-profit social enterprises (that is, companies with the potential to generate high social returns) to qualify for program-related investment (PRI) from charitable foundations (see chapter 19 for more information about PRI). That said, there is little evidence that this entity type has actually encouraged additional PRI activity. "The IRS did propose regulations in April 2012 that added new examples of PRI," says Ken Merritt, an attorney in Vermont who works with venture capital and growth-stage companies, but these regulations had not yet been adopted as of this writing. This may be because the IRS requires a private ruling letter to ensure eligibility of PRI investments or because LLC structures in general are so flexible that a foundation has no reasonable guarantee that the L3C's activities will remain as charitable as they were at the time the investment was approved. As of this writing, the IRS has yet to formally issue any guidance to foundations related to L3Cs. "The only thing you have to do is state in the articles of incorporation that you want to be an L3C," explains Ken, who has worked with several pioneering social enterprises. "An L3C can say they're low-profit," he says, "but there are no transparency requirements and no standards for measuring that."

Benefit corporations have resolved the lack of transparency and accountability issues inherent in the L3C structure. States that allow benefit corporations hold them to most of the same administrative and taxation standards as other corporations. The notable differences are as follows:

- Benefit corporations must create a material positive impact on society and the environment, and they must note this in their articles of incorporation.
- Benefit corporations allow directors to take into account the nonfinancial interests of stakeholders beyond shareholders (including the workforce of both the business itself and its suppliers; community and societal factors where the business and its suppliers are located; the customers of the business; and the local and global environment), and the corporation's bylaws must reflect these interests.
- Benefit corporations must provide annual reporting on social and environmental performance as measured by recognized, third-party standards.

While the annual reporting requirement increases the amount of work for managers of benefit corporations, it may provide the added reassurance that an impact investor will need in order to feel confident investing in such a venture. Note that the benefit corporation legislation is not exactly the same in all states, so you will need to check the specific statutes in the state where you intend to incorporate. As of this writing, twelve states have passed legislation recognizing benefit corporation status, with additional states expected to follow suit.[4]

The **flexible purpose corporation**, or FPC, is another type of corporation that allows its directors to consider a wider range of stakeholders in their decision making, which makes it an interesting option for social entrepreneurs who fear that shareholders may file claims that a business was not managed in a way to maximize their financial returns. As the name implies, FPCs are more flexible than benefit corporations in that board members and shareholders can choose which "special purposes" the company will pursue; these can, but do not need to, include as many stakeholders as the benefit corporation, and they can certainly include fewer. The reporting requirements for your chosen purposes are robust. Because the "flexible purpose" of this type of corporation, which must be specified in its articles of incorporation, need not include any social benefits, it is unclear whether FPC status will confer the same socially responsible brand benefits or halo

DISTINGUISHING BETWEEN BENEFIT CORPORATIONS AND CERTIFIED B CORPORATIONS

People often use the terms interchangeably, but there's a major distinction between a benefit corporation and a Certified B Corporation, or B Corps: in short, the differences are availability, verified performance, and access to services and support. A benefit corporation is a legal entity option available only to businesses incorporated in certain states. B Corp is a third-party certification conferred by the nonprofit organization B Lab, and it's available to businesses in all fifty states and around the world. B Lab did help develop model benefit corporation legislation, and it works with the community of Certified B Corporations and others to marshal support for passage of such legislation in states where it does not already exist.

Both benefit corporation and Certified B Corp status may have benefits in terms of how customers and prospective investors view your company, but even here it's worth noting the distinctions. Directors of both benefit corporations and Certified B Corps are required to consider the effect of decisions not only on shareholders but also on other stakeholders, such as workers, community, and the environment. Both are required to publicly publish a report assessing their overall social and environmental performance against a third-party standard. Benefit corporations can choose from a list of standards, and the reports need not be verified, certified, or audited by a third party; the B Impact Assessment survey is the standard for all B Corps, and the results of this survey are certified by B Lab. As of this writing, twelve states have passed legislation recognizing benefit corporation status, with additional states expected to follow suit.[5]

Benefit corporations need not be certified as B Corps. Furthermore, any for-profit entity type can apply for B Corp certification, a distinction that is reserved for businesses that both meet the certification eligibility requirements and pay the annual certification fee. Certification confers access to a portfolio of services and support from B Lab to help them with marketing, attracting talent, raising money, saving money, and learning from and doing business within the community of Certified B Corps.

effect as benefit corporation status. That said, some believe that it may be more attractive to mainstream investors, because the structure appears more similar to the corporations they are used to. FPCs may be the better choice for companies that want to focus on a very specific social benefit rather than the entire gamut of sustainability. "You could have a company primarily devoted to twenty or more factors, or you could have a company devoted to just one specific social or environmental goal," explains Susan, who helped usher in the flexible purpose corporation legislation in California. "It can be just as socially responsible, or even more socially responsible, than a benefit corporation, depending on which goals shareholders agree to focus on," she says. As of this writing, California is the only state that offers the flexible purpose corporation option, though Washington State passed legislation for a **social purpose corporation**, which is a similar structure.

——— Guiding Questions ——— for Choosing an Entity Type

Now that you have a sense of what is possible, which is the best entity type for your venture? As you read through the following questions, see what resonates most closely with the intentions and values you identified in chapter 2.

- **How many owners does (or will) the business have?** If you are the only owner of your business, you can choose to operate as a sole proprietorship or incorporate as a corporation or LLC. If there is more than one owner—and even if you are the only owner now, there will be others if you intend to raise capital by selling equity shares—your options include a partnership, a corporation, or an LLC. If you anticipate raising money from a significant number of equity investors, a corporation is a good fit.
- **Is the cost of setup and maintenance of your business entity an issue?** Corporations and LLCs are more costly to set up than sole proprietorships and partnerships because of state filing fees, and most states require payment of annual franchise taxes as well.
- **Are you willing to commit to complicated formalities required by certain structures, at start-up and beyond?** Sole proprietors and partnerships are relatively easy to set up and maintain, requiring very little ongoing documentation. Corporations, on the other hand, are much more complicated to set up and maintain. LLCs are more complicated than sole proprietorships or partnerships to set up and maintain but have much simpler reporting requirements than corporations.

- **How much flexibility do you want in your business structure?** Corporations are also more complicated to update if the business evolves significantly over time and you need to make adjustments to the incorporation documentation. LLCs are more flexible to update than corporations, requiring only a change to the operating agreement. Sole proprietors have the most flexibility.
- **If there are risks inherent in your business, will you or your partners need to protect personal assets?** In the event of major losses related to a business, neither sole proprietorships nor partnerships protect the owners' assets, potentially putting owners' personal property at risk. Owners of LLCs and corporations that are properly maintained are not personally liable for business debts that they have not personally guaranteed.
- **How do you want taxes to be handled for yourself, your business, and your investors?** If you want to be able to pass through taxable income—or write off eligible losses—to the owners, consider a sole proprietorship, general partnership, S corporation, or LLC. C corporations are subject to double taxation in that they owe taxes on profits and owners must pay income taxes on dividends they receive.
- **How much flexibility and/or control do you want to maintain over your business?** You'll have the most control if you operate as a sole proprietorship. The management structure of LLCs offers far more flexibility within its operating agreement than is possible with corporations, which are required to have a board of directors, who appoint officers and make major decisions. Corporation directors can decide to fire the founders, so keep that in mind if maintaining control is important to you. If you want to maximize your ability to consider factors beyond maximizing profits, consider one of the new social enterprise models.
- **From whom do you intend to raise capital for the business?** While lending institutions and individual investors may not care if your business is a sole proprietorship or partnership, angel investors, venture capital funds, and other institutional investors may only invest in corporations or LLCs. If you intend to raise the majority of your funds from foundations, then a nonprofit corporation makes the most sense (see previous section). Be careful about choosing an entity type based solely upon what one interested funder wants. "This is the worst possible way to decide what type of entity to build," warns Joy

Anderson of Criterion Ventures. "You'll do all this work to set it up and find that you will have the wrong type of structure for the next potential investor, and there's still no guarantee that the first funder will actually invest!"

- **Are you willing to choose a relatively new structure that may be unfamiliar to potential investors?** You might be most interested in the new entity options designed specifically for social ventures. While these structures could potentially make your business a more appealing investment opportunity to certain types of investors, you may find yourself spending time and energy educating prospective investors about the new entity type you have chosen.
- **What is actually possible in your state?** Not all states treat all entities in the same way. Some states limit the types of businesses that can form as LLCs, for instance. Others tax LLCs as corporations. The newer entity types are not yet available in all states, although you can incorporate your business in another state that does offer the options you are looking for.

Regardless of the for-profit entity structure you pick, and whichever stakeholders you choose to consider in your business operations, financial profitability is crucial to all for-profit enterprises—social enterprises included. "You still need to make intelligent business decisions," warns Ken Merritt, adding, "you still have to be profitable! Financial profitability gives you so much more in terms of resources to change the world, in terms of your employees, your community—profitability is a good thing." Jay Coen Gilbert is cofounder of B Lab, and he agrees. "No margin, no mission," is his mantra, referring to the margin a company earns on the difference between its expenses and revenues. "If you're not running a profitable business, you'll never get the opportunity to scale your impact, whether your strategy to scale is growing in your own good organic time or accelerating your growth through outside capital," he says. "If you want to attract outside capital, you need to have a sound business model and operations that are exceptional, with an incredibly talented and deep management team that is able to execute and make the trains run on time."

4

......

Putting Your Personal Money House in Order

NO DOUBT YOU HAVE ALREADY NOTICED that your business is inextricably connected with the rest of your life, particularly when it comes to money. Your personal credit history, your ability to separate your personal finances from those of your business, your capacity to save, and your personal investment in your business all can affect your ability to raise money for your business. This chapter covers these aspects of your personal relationship with money, with tips for cultivating the conditions that will prime you for fundraising success.

—— Personal Credit ——

Your credit report is the first thing that many financiers will look at to determine whether or not they want to work with you. Particularly with commercial lenders, your personal credit will also affect the total amount of money they will lend you, and at what interest rate. The better your credit, the better your chances of getting a larger loan at a lower interest rate. If you have bad credit, you might not qualify for a loan at all. While this might frustrate those of you with lower credit scores, it's not that surprising if you think about it from the financier's point of view. "The general rule that lenders follow is that if someone has a credit score, or FICO score, of 700 or above, they are low risk, because there's only a 5 percent chance that they will default on their loan," says Irma Ranzuglia, a certified financial counselor with Santa Cruz Community Ventures, a nonprofit affiliate of the Santa Cruz Community Credit Union in California. "When someone's FICO score is 600, the default risk jumps to 50 percent." So it makes sense that lenders would be wary of prospective borrowers with lower scores or would at least charge them more in an attempt to recoup their potential losses.

It's important to monitor your credit reports for inaccuracies that might be working against you. You can order them free of charge once a year from each of the three credit reporting agencies, TransUnion, Equifax, and Experian, or you can get all three at once at www.annualcreditreport.com. Clear up any issues as soon as you can. If you have a history of bad credit, check for tips at the website of the National Foundation for Credit Counseling: http:// www.nfcc.org. You can also use their site to identify free or low-cost credit counseling services near you. Remember that the best thing you can do to build or repair your credit score is to pay all of your bills on time, period.

Peer-to-peer (P2P) lending sites such as Prosper and Lending Club (described in more detail in chapter 12) offer another option for repairing credit scores. Many people have been able to take out P2P loans at significantly lower interest rates than the rates on their credit cards, which allowed them to pay off those higher balances and get a better handle on their debt situations. Unlike using other credit cards to consolidate debt, P2P loans have fixed rates, which makes it easier to plan ahead to make the payments. And because these loans are for a fixed amount, it is less likely that you would find yourself in another credit pickle if the temptation to use the credit available on your card proved to be irresistible.

If your credit history shows some scars, you will definitely experience some challenges accessing credit, but you're not necessarily out of luck. Keep excellent records of the ability of your business to earn revenues, and you may still be able to find a lender to work with you. Gary Matteson of Farm Credit (see chapter 14) suggests, "Be honest with the person who is evaluating your financial situation. Say, 'I did something really stupid—I started this business on credit cards.' They'll want to know why you did it and how you've spent the money. And they'll want to see evidence that you can earn money."

Separating Business from Personal Finances

As soon as you can, separate your personal finances from those of your new business. This is important even if you launch your business as a sole proprietorship, S corporation, or another entity that involves pass-through taxes (see chapter 3). Not only will this make it easier for you come tax time, but it can help prevent an IRS audit: tax laws regarding hobbies are much different from those pertaining to businesses, and intermingled finances are more likely to indicate a hobby than a business to the IRS. Finally, when you begin seeking outside investors or talking to lending institutions, you will have a much easier time conveying your professionalism, verifying revenues, and compiling the necessary financial statements if your business finances are clearly separated from your personal finances.

The easiest way to keep personal and business finances apart is to maintain a separate bank account for your business, even if the account is in your name rather than that of the business. Then pay for all business expenses (and only business expenses) using funds from that account. Likewise, deposit all income related to the business into that account rather than your personal account. If you have a personal need for the money coming into your business, make the deposit into the business account first, then write yourself a check, accounting for the expense in your business records. The sooner you can incorporate your business (see chapter 3) and open a separate bank account in its name, the better. "The longer you've been in business, the easier it is to borrow money," explains Ted Levinson, director of lending at RSF Social Finance (see chapter 14). "A filing with the secretary of state or a bank reference will both confirm your time in business."

Your business itself will not at first qualify for a credit card in its name, much the same way that a person with no credit record will find it more difficult to get one. If you must use a credit card (as opposed to a debit card, which withdraws money from an existing bank account) to pay for business expenses, see if you can qualify for a new personal card in order to keep business expenses off any personal cards you might already have." Just keep in mind that this option does not protect you from being personally responsible for paying off the credit card debt, and any mishaps in paying off the credit card will reflect poorly on your own credit record. Another alternative is to use your personal card for business as well as personal expenses and to carefully account for all business expenses every month, then reimburse yourself for the business total with a check from your business account. You'll have to figure out what percentage of your credit card's annual fee you'll charge to your business or just accept the fee as a personal expense. (See chapter 12 for additional examples of personal debt that you might use to finance your business, so long as you keep the personal and business accounting separate.)

Common problem areas with regard to the risk of an IRS audit include home office expenses and using personal assets (such as your car or cell phone) for business purposes. The clearest way to deal with separating a home office, for instance, would be to physically measure the percentage of your home that you use for business purposes and have the business write you a monthly check for rent and the associated proportion of your home's utilities (a formal rental agreement would also help). But do you really want to keep track of the percentage of cell phone minutes you've used for business calls? As with many of the decisions in this book, you'll have to think how carefully you want to proceed, taking into account the balance between your appetite for risk, your willingness to track every last detail, and how these decisions will affect your ability to raise capital for your business.

—— Boosting Your Personal Savings ——

There are several reasons to build your personal savings prior to launching a business. Many entrepreneurs find themselves in the position of needing to live off their savings at some point or another. Particularly as your business is just getting off the ground, you may have to weather long stretches of time before you can pay yourself a living wage. If you do not have another source of income, your savings will be there to cover your living expenses during these stretches, so that your own cash-flow crises will not put undue financial stress on your business.

How much should you save? Many personal finance experts recommend that people living within their means set aside an emergency fund of three to six months' worth of living expenses—and this is for anyone who has paid off her debts, whether or not she has plans to start an expensive endeavor such as a new business. You would put these funds in a savings or money market account that you can access easily in the event of an emergency so that you can cover rent or mortgage payments, utility bills, food, gas, and other nondiscretionary expenses. As an entrepreneur with a new or growing business on your hands, consider this emergency fund rule of thumb as a bare minimum, since your savings may have to cover not only personal emergencies but business emergencies as well.

Calculating how long it will be before your new venture will start paying you a living wage—and by extension how much you will need to save to cover living expenses in the meantime—is a tricky affair. (A statement of cash flow is a good place to start; see the section "Preparing Financial Statements" in chapter 5.) If you are working another job while launching your venture, you may also be wondering when it makes sense to leave that job. In addition to the cash-flow consequences of this decision, there is the issue of projecting your personal commitment to your new venture. Financially, you may need to continue working another job (or two) while your business is getting off the ground. When you start raising capital for your new venture, however, prospective investors may get the impression that you are not fully committed if you have other professional demands to meet. Or you may discover that in order to build the business to the point where it can support you, you need to give it your full-time attention. Clearly, there are many factors to consider, and only you will be able to determine the best path for yourself and your business. One fact remains clear: the more you have saved, the more options you will have.

While this book doesn't go into the various techniques for building your savings—you can find ample resources for doing so on the Internet or in your local library—I do want to draw your attention to individual development accounts, or IDAs. Usually available only to low-income people, IDAs are the closest thing to free money that I've encountered. Eligible savers sign up with a program's sponsor and open a savings account. Thanks to funding from federal or state government agencies, private foundations, and even individual donors, the saver's deposits into that account are matched— sometimes two or three dollars for every dollar saved—up to a certain limit.

—— Skin in the Game ——

One very important reason to save as much as you can as soon as you can is so that you will have funds to invest in your own business. Unless you are one of the very fortunate few who can attract investors before you've invested any of your own money into your business, you will be your business's very first investor, through the hard work you put in, the personal assets you commit to business use, and infusion of real, hard cash. In other words, you will be covering all of the business's expenses yourself until you are able to secure outside financing, and this is a process that often takes much longer than you expect or hope it will. "Take the amount of time you think it will take you to raise the money, and triple it," advises Don Shaffer, who had launched two businesses prior to becoming president and CEO of RSF Social Finance (see chapter 14).

Not only is investing your own money a necessity from a cash flow perspective, but it's an important prerequisite to attracting other investors to your venture. If you are not willing to invest your own money, why should your friends, relatives, or a lending institution? When you invest personal funds in your business, you show potential investors that you have skin in the game, increasing their confidence in your level of personal commitment.

When you invest in your own business, document the transaction as formally as you would with an outside investor: draft a legal agreement between yourself and your business, and stick to the terms specified. You want it to be very easy to explain to potential investors how much you have invested so that when it comes time for you to reap the financial rewards of having built a successful company, you will be compensated appropriately.

5

......

Befriending the Books:
Tracking and Reporting Your Venture's Finances

IT MIGHT BE TEMPTING to stay loose with your venture's numbers at first—"What a pain to keep track of every dollar that goes in and out, and who's ever going to know the difference anyway?"—but this is a dangerous attitude. It is impossible to effectively manage a growing business without a good bookkeeping system. "Inaccurate or incomplete records will also make it very, very hard for you to raise capital, so it's in your best interest to get your system down before you need the money," says Bonny Moellenbrock of SJF Institute and Investors' Circle. That way, when you're ready to start seeking financing, you'll be able to focus on fundraising rather than scrambling to organize that box of receipts so you can put together the necessary financial statements (see the section on this topic, below). Good records can also help you work with your existing investors in the event that you encounter a significant problem, such as a health crisis, crop failure, or catastrophic damage to facilities. With good records you can say to your lender, for instance, "Here's what happened, here were the exact consequences, and here is how I plan to move forward." If you don't have good records, it's all just an unsupported story, and it's less likely that your creditors will work with you on a creative solution.

This chapter covers the why and how of bookkeeping, financial statements, and tax returns that make it easy to manage your venture *and* communicate its value to prospective lenders and investors.

——— **Bookkeeping** ———

Julia Shanks is a chef and entrepreneur who consults with food businesses and farms, helping them maximize profits and streamline operations through business planning, feasibility studies, and operational audits. As a business consultant and serial entrepreneur, she has firsthand knowledge of the challenges that business owners face when starting up or raising funds, and she helps her clients overcome the obstacles. She reports that a large part of her job is getting people to overcome their aversion to keeping excellent records. "People see record keeping and bookkeeping as being able to pay bills on time, avoiding bounced checks, and filing taxes at the end of the year," she observes. "But that leaves out a huge amount of information that could help you reduce your expenses, better manage your cash flow, and grow your business." A good bookkeeping system allows you to quickly gauge important information, such as where you are spending your money, how profitable your business is, how much you owe, and how much your customers owe you. You'll also be able to deliver this information quickly to current or prospective investors, who will inevitably ask for it. Even if you do hire an accountant or bookkeeper to help out, good record-keeping habits mean you'll need to pay these specialists only to handle the more complicated aspects of the job, which ultimately saves you money.

If you ignore good bookkeeping, even at the very beginning stages of your business, you put yourself at a disadvantage later when you're negotiating with prospective investors. Tera Johnson of tera'swhey, a socially responsible company that produces high-quality and all-natural dietary supplements, learned this lesson the hard way. "Long before you're officially in business, there's so much that happens. When I look back I realize that I really should have kept track of all these things," she says. "I chased around the universe doing things like finding the perfect site for our manufacturing plant, which I needed to identify before I could write the business plan. I spent a lot of time and some real money driving around to different towns to look at potential sites." Tera says she was "fairly good" about tracking expenses in instances where she literally wrote a check to an attorney or an accountant. "There's so much else that you just do and you think to yourself, 'I don't need to keep track.' But it really would have been good to have documented everything." When Tera started talking to investors, they wanted to know exactly how much money she had put in so that they could convert that amount to owner's equity. Had she tracked and been able to report all of her time and expenses, the dollar amount of her contribution—and the corresponding number of shares of the company she owned—would have been higher.

As soon as you begin to contemplate going into a particular line of business—even if you start informally engaging in business activities before forming the legal business entity—start keeping records of any activity that might be related to the venture you expect to launch. Not only will this help you develop good business management habits (as the old saying goes, you can't manage what you don't measure), it will help you make accurate projections related to future costs you may incur and future revenue-generating potential. And all of this will make it much easier for you to raise money for your venture later.

What should you keep track of? Maintain a detailed financial accounting of all the money you spend for business purposes, no matter how insignificant those transactions seem. Also document all revenues, no matter how insignificant they might seem. Let's say you sell only a couple of hundred dollars' worth of goods at a roadside stand in your first season. If you don't record the prices you charged for each item (particularly if you tried a few different prices to see which worked best with your customers), will you remember a couple of months from now? You'll certainly have a much easier time convincing a bank or other investor that your projected prices are reasonable if you can show records that this is what you successfully charged customers in the past.

If you do any production test runs, such as field tests to see how many pounds of vegetables you can produce in a season or a test to see how many brownies you can produce in the commissary kitchen in your four-hour time slot, keep records of those results, too. "I once worked with a farmer who hadn't sold anything at all yet, but he had been testing the fields," Julia recalls. "I asked him, 'How many tomatoes did you grow last season?' and his response was, 'Oh, lots and lots!' There was no way to project future revenues with that. If we had known that he had grown fifty cases of tomatoes, we would have had much more to work with when it came time to writing the business plan." As this story illustrates, it's much easier to log these details as you go rather than racking your brain trying to fill them in later.

Finally, you need to note any funds that you or anyone else has invested in the business.

Setting Up a Bookkeeping System

If you're starting from scratch, the first step is to compile and organize all the loose bits and pieces of paper that represent your venture's financial transactions and get them into a hard filing system that allows you to quickly find a particular item when you need it. In this day and age, it's possible that you don't have hard copies of some of the following. Determine for yourself whether or not it's worth printing them out to help you reconcile your books, or whether it's easier for you to work with the electronic versions.

- **Purchase receipts and invoices.**
- **Bank statements and your checkbook register.** Yes, it's important to balance your checkbook, keeping track of which checks and deposits have cleared versus which have yet to clear.
- **Credit card statements.**
- **All other bills.**
- **Sales invoices.** If you are not already doing so, start numbering your sales invoices sequentially so that it's immediately obvious which invoices came before others. This will help you identify and collect overdue payments if you don't have a software system that alerts you automatically.
- **Mileage registers** for personal vehicles that you are using for business purposes. If you're not already recording this information, start now.
- **Payroll records, staff timesheets, and contractor invoices.** Don't forget to keep track of the time that you put in, whether or not you have begun to pay yourself.

Separate invoices (for purchases you have made), bills, and credit card statements that you have already paid from those that you still need to pay so that it's clear which require further action. Likewise, keep sales invoices (for your customers' orders or purchases) that you have already collected separate from those that you have yet to collect.

Once you've got all of these documents organized, you will need to enter all of the transactions they represent into your bookkeeping system. How exactly will you keep track of everything? I highly recommend you use some type of accounting software to manage your financial information. Not only will it be easier to add and maintain information, but you can easily assign different categories to transactions so you can see exactly what you're spending money on and where your revenues are coming from. It will also instantly generate the kinds of reports that allow you—and your investors—to understand what is actually happening under the hood of your business; these are covered in the following section. Still, be sure to keep your paper records organized so that you have all your sources ready if you need to verify your numbers or if the IRS decides to audit your business.

There are several software systems that are designed to make the process relatively painless, while also offering the capacity easily to generate a variety of reports that give you excellent visibility into your business activities. Julia, along with many other advisers, recommends QuickBooks. "It automatically puts things in the appropriate categories for you. It also has a great system for tracking your time." Most computerized bookkeeping systems have default settings or wizards to help you get started, but be careful about blindly accepting these settings. "It's a good idea to sit with a professional bookkeeper or accountant that understands managerial accounting *and* QuickBooks to help you get set up the first time," Julia recommends. "A system that is set up properly in the first place makes it really easy to get the information you want out of it later, such as accurate financial statements and reports." At the very least, go through every one of the system's settings to make sure that you're choosing the options that make the most sense for your unique business. If you do hire professional help, make sure you communicate well during the process, as both you and your accountant or bookkeeper bring important expertise to the table: you have an intimate knowledge of your venture's operations, and she should understand the ins and outs of the bookkeeping system itself, plus all relevant tax laws.

No matter how sophisticated a bookkeeping system you have, it won't do you any good if you do not continue to use it. Develop a practice of entering your transactions regularly so that you don't fall too far behind, creating a monster of a catch-up project. Julia recommends setting aside ten minutes every day for this task. "If you do it once a week, the task gets onerous, and if you only do it once a month, it can take you hours," she says. By alerting you to when bills are due, a well-designed and well-maintained bookkeeping system can help you avoid late fees, hits to your credit score, or even being dumped by your vendors. It can help you collect payments from your customers in a timely manner. And it can generate valuable reports that reveal hidden patterns and opportunities for improving your business, insights that you would never discover while staring at a box of receipts, bills, and customer invoices.

—— **Preparing Financial Statements** ——

Yes, prospective investors will look at your venture's financial statements when considering whether or not to work with you, but first and foremost these statements are tools to help you manage your business. This section covers the basic elements of the core financial statements, why each is important, and things to keep an eye on. Refer to your bookkeeping software for instructions on preparing these financial statements, which is usually as simple as clicking a button, assuming you have entered everything into your bookkeeping system properly. You can also generate these reports using the many templates that you can find online, although this option requires that you manually compile the information that each report requires, introducing the possibility of error and difficulty in making quick updates to projections if you make any changes to your assumptions. If you don't have historical data in your bookkeeping system, you will need to make estimates about your future revenues and expenses. It is a good idea to run these reports for yourself on a monthly basis, checking for areas where you might be able to increase margins or take advantage of other efficiencies. Ask your accountant or bookkeeper to help you review them the first few times, but you'll quickly get the hang of it. You might prepare these statements for your investors once a quarter, and you will also want to use them to help explain significant changes to your business plan or operations.

Income Statement

Also called a profit and loss statement, or P&L, an income statement shows revenues, expenses, and profit (or losses) for a specific period. If your bookkeeping system breaks down your revenues into different categories, you'll be able to see right on the income statement where your revenues come from. This report should separate out the expenses that are directly related to the cost of sales (i.e., variable costs) and subtract those from your revenues to show gross profit. Keep a close eye on your cost of goods sold and gross profit margins, both in terms of how they are changing over time and how they compare to industry standards. To make it easier to see where you are spending money, you will also want to break down your business's other expenses into different categories, such as salary and payroll expenses, overhead and operating expenses, interest, and taxes.

Balance Sheet

A balance sheet lists the assets of a business (everything it owns, including cash on hand, inventory, accounts receivable, prepaid expenses, fixed assets such as buildings and equipment minus accumulated depreciation, and any intellectual property) on one side, and its liabilities (everything it owes, including accounts payable, expenses that have been incurred and not yet paid, and long-term debt) plus equity (which includes any capital that has been invested in the company, whether by the owner or other shareholders, plus retained earnings, or the company's earnings that are not distributed to shareholders) on the other. As the name of this statement implies, both sides must balance, such that assets equal liabilities plus equity.

The balance sheet tells you—and investors—at a glance what all of the company's assets and liabilities are. It also shows how the company is doing in terms of its ability to meet short-term debts (i.e., those due within a year) and long-term debts (i.e., those due a year or more from the date of the statement). Most managers and investors also pay attention to the financial ratios that you calculate from information contained in the balance sheet. Current ratio is the ratio of current assets divided by current liabilities, and it is a measure of liquidity. You want this value to be greater than one, meaning that the company has enough assets to cover its liabilities. Cash-to-debt ratio is similar to the current ratio, except that it compares cash to liabilities, and a value greater than one would indicate that you would not need to sell any assets to cover your liabilities. There are many more financial ratios you can use to give yourself a picture of your business's profitability, operating performance or activity, and investment valuation. Ask your accountant or bookkeeper which would give you the strongest sense of how your business is doing, and pay close attention to those.

The balance sheet refers to a specific point in time (often the end of a month, quarter, or financial year), and the income statement refers to a specific period of time (such as an entire month, quarter, or financial year). You will also want to draw up reports that project how each might look at various points in the future, based on your assumptions about future business activities. If your business is brand new, all of the periods shown in your reports may be projections. Because it's harder and harder to predict what will happen the further out into the future you go, you probably don't need as much granularity in your projections for three years from now as you do for the immediate future. You might want to see your projections on a monthly basis for the next two years, for instance, and annually for three years after that.

Cash Flow Statement

A cash flow statement shows you how much cash your business has on hand and how the various activities of your business affect how cash comes into and goes out of your business over time. It is important to have this information at your fingertips so that you can avoid running into a negative cash situation, where you owe money and there's no cash in the bank to cover your immediate expenses. A good cash flow statement lets you quickly gauge how certain business decisions (or changing certain assumptions) will affect available cash balances in the months to come.

Cash flow statements usually include three main categories of information: cash flow related to operations (this is the bulk of the report), cash flow related to financing (such as money the business received in the form of loans or other investments, plus any payments toward loan principal or dividends to investors), and cash flow related to your business's investing activities (which refers both to investments made with excess cash and also to money spent on assets such as buildings or equipment). When put together, this information gives you a complete picture of your cash situation. Cash flow statements add back in noncash items that are part of the income statement, such as depreciation and amortization.

Each column of a cash flow statement refers to the end date of a specific period (such as the end of a month, quarter, or year). Each column will start with the cash balance on hand at the end of the previous period, then add all new revenues and subtract all new expenses to show the new cash balance. Pay close attention to any periods in your cash flow statement that show very low or negative cash balances. You will need to implement changes—such as negotiating more favorable payment terms with customers or vendors, increasing a line of credit, or taking out an additional loan—in time to prevent the possibility of a cash shortfall.

Break-Even Analysis

This statement tells you how many units of your product you need to sell at a certain price in order to break even, or cover all the costs of producing those products in the first place. When you exceed this sales volume, your business is making a profit. To calculate the break-even quantity (also called

FIXED VERSUS VARIABLE COSTS

//

Fixed costs are those that do not change depending on your volume of production. Expenses in this category include rent, salaries, and any other overhead expenses, such as telephone, Internet, and office-cleaning services. Variable costs, on the other hand, go up as your production increases. Examples include vegetable-packing boxes; labels and packaging; electricity to run processing equipment; hourly wages for people you hire to help harvest, process, or package product; delivery costs; and fuel for the delivery fleet.

the break-even point; BE in the formula below), you'll need to look over your records or make estimations to calculate the total fixed costs (FC) involved in operating your business, the average sale price that you charge for your products (P), and the sum of all variable costs per unit sold (VC). The break-even quantity is the sum of your fixed costs divided by the difference between the price and the variable costs, or $BE = FC / (P - VC)$. If you have yet to start the business, do some research to generate some estimated values, and list your assumptions on the statement itself.

You can calculate a break-even point for each type of product you sell, which is a good way to help you prioritize which products to focus on; if you do this, you'll need to allocate a portion of fixed costs to each product's analysis, rather than expecting that the sales of each product will have to cover all of your fixed costs. For example, if jarred tomatoes make up one-third of your business and jarred salsa the remaining two-thirds, you would calculate the break-even point for the tomatoes using only one-third of the total fixed costs across your entire business and the break-even point for the salsa using two-thirds of the total fixed costs. "You need to identify the profitability, advantages and risks of different farm enterprises and sales outlets," says Reggie Knox of California FarmLink. "Where are your profit centers? Leeks or flowers, the CSA or the farmers' markets? Break-even analysis can help you figure out when to open a new sales channel to expand your revenues or customer base, or when you need to increase sales of higher-margin products. We help farmers figure these things out so they can focus on the things that help them flourish economically."

A very high break-even quantity indicates one of several things, some of which you may have control over and some of which you may not. You may not be charging enough for your products given how much it costs to produce them. If this is the case, you could consider raising your prices; your customers might be willing to accept an increase if you share the information about your costs with them. If this isn't possible, and especially if other businesses seem to be able to charge less for similar products, your costs may be too high. Could you be paying too much in fixed costs? Do you really need that shiny administrative office in the high-rent district? Could you take a lower salary while your business grows? Maybe you need to figure out a way to reduce the variable costs associated with your product sales. If it won't be possible to either raise your prices or reduce your costs, a high break-even quantity may simply mean that a business like yours needs to operate at a very high volume to be profitable. In this case, you need to revisit your values and consider a few different scenarios. Do you want to operate at this scale? Is it feasible given your situation? Are you confident that you can come up with the money you'll need to cover your costs until you hit the break-even point? If you don't expect to be able to front this money yourself, will you be able to convince investors that you can reach this sales volume? If you cannot answer yes to all of these questions, it's possible that it just doesn't make financial sense for you to go into this line of business.

—— Filing Tax Returns ——

Yes, even the way that you fill out your tax returns can affect your ability to raise money for your business. If you plan to approach a commercial lender or other thorough investor to help finance your business, you need to fill out your tax returns such that they reflect the activity you have included (or will include) in your business plan. The most important message to take away from this section is that the tax code is complicated, and you should consult with a tax accountant who has experience with food businesses like yours. Once your business gets to a certain size, and certainly if you are a food manufacturing company, you will need professional help with your tax returns.

The first trap that you can fall into is to simply maximize all your business deductions and reduce your business income on your tax returns. This strategy can definitely work against you when it comes to lenders or prospective investors. As the former national program leader for the Office of Advocacy and Outreach, Small Farms and Beginning Farmers and Ranchers Program of the USDA, and former California CPA, Poppy Davis has worked closely with many first-time farmers. "Show too little profit and banks or other lenders might determine you are not credit-worthy," she warns. "On the other hand, if your tax returns demonstrate that you make a profit year after year, they can help you qualify for loans." If there are major differences between the numbers reported on your tax returns and those reported in your business plan, you may have a hard time proving your credibility to lenders and investors.

If you're hoping to reduce your tax liability by maximizing deductions and minimizing income, note that this strategy will actually cost you more in taxes if you qualify for the earned income tax credits. "Particularly if you have children in your home and have low income, not an unusual situation for beginning farmers," Poppy explains, "the earned income credit can be financially significant." The IRS may pay you an earned income credit as a refund even if you do not owe or pay any taxes. Deductions will lower your earned income, which in some cases will eliminate not just the taxes you owe but also an earned income tax credit due to you from the IRS.

There's also the question of which forms to use for your business taxes. This can get particularly confusing for farm businesses that are operated as sole proprietorships. Schedule F is the form to use to report farm income and expenses. Schedule C is for any other nonfarm, unincorporated business expenses. It is also important to distinguish between the business deductions to report on one of those two forms and other itemized deductions that belong on your Schedule A.

There are other confusing aspects of filing taxes for farm-based businesses. One is that the IRS does not consider value-added processing activities to be farming for tax reporting purposes, which considers farming activity to end when the farm product is in a condition that you can sell it in your local market. Here's an example: almonds are typically sold hulled, and in many places it would be difficult or impossible to sell them in their shells, so the cost of hulling almonds is typically a farming expense that you should report on your Schedule F. It is not necessary to turn almonds into nut butter in order to sell them, though, so you cannot deduct the costs of buying jars, grinding the nuts, filling the jars, and labeling them as part of the farm's expenses; instead, you must report these as a separate business activity.

For tax purposes the IRS usually considers food manufacturing to be like any other manufacturing business, so it is subject to all the manufacturing tax reporting requirements, which are incredibly complex. Don't even try to attempt a manufacturing tax return on your own without studying the regulations. When you enter into nut butter territory or go from whole tomatoes to salsa—or launch any business in which you're creating your own inventory (as opposed to buying inventory that you turn around and resell), it's time to hire a professional with experience completing manufacturing returns.

Because filing taxes for food-based businesses can be so confusing, it's always a good idea to consult a professional accountant or tax preparation specialist to help you fill out your business taxes. Make sure to check references, and find a professional who has experience with your particular type of business. If you have a small, diversified farm, an accountant who has worked only with huge farms, for instance, can do you more harm than good. "There are lots of tax preparers who have no idea how to correctly file simple farm tax returns," says Poppy. "It's sad but true. If you find a qualified small business accountant, they're always worth their fee relative to what you can do on your own. If you insist upon using quality ingredients in your products, why are you skimping when it comes time to hire qualified professionals?" Poppy asks. (See chapter 10 for more information on finding professional service providers, including accountants.) When it comes time to approach a commercial lender or professional investor, they will be able to take one look at your tax returns and see if you have made an obvious mistake, such as filing a Schedule C for a farm or failing to report inventory costs appropriately. If they see that you have not invested in a qualified accountant, and potentially owe thousands in back taxes, why would they want to invest in your company?

6
......

Getting Down to Business

CAN YOU LIST ALL of your capital needs before writing a business plan? Can you write your business plan without knowing where you will need to spend money? If you're already in business, it might be easier to identify where exactly you need to invest capital, and you might write the business plan to justify the expense. If you are still in the planning process, you might find it easier to write out the business plan first to help you identify where you will need to spend money. Either way, you need to identify your exact capital needs before you can ask anyone to invest. Most lenders and savvy investors won't even consider your request until you can show that you need their money and that once you have it you will use it effectively to fuel your business's success—and, ultimately, pay them back.

While not all investors will require a business plan, most will want to see a simplified version that shows that your business model makes sense. And it's hard to provide that without having first developed a more detailed one. This chapter covers the basics of identifying your capital needs and the whys and hows of writing an effective business plan that will both attract investors and help you manage your venture. It also covers business plan competitions as a potential source of capital.

—— Identifying Your Capital Needs: —— How Much Is Enough, When?

Exactly how much you will need to raise depends on several factors, including the type of venture, where you are in the business cycle, and your goals for the immediate (or distant) future. Ventures that are in the earlier stages of development and have yet to make any sales will need to raise sufficient capital to get through what Michael Burgmaier, investment banker with Silverwood Partners, calls "the Valley of Death." A former venture capital investor and management consultant, Michael has worked with many natural consumer products companies and organizes regular workshops on financing for entrepreneurs. "You're spending money ahead of revenues," he explains. "Your goal is to escape the valley." The so-called Valley of Death will look quite different for a small farming business that already has land than it will for a large-scale food manufacturing company that needs to build out its warehouse and processing infrastructure or a technology company that is developing CSA management software. To estimate how much money you will need to raise, consider start-up costs (if appropriate), fixed costs, and variable costs. Start-up expenses may include building renovations, website development, and onetime equipment purchases, such as a tractor for a farm or the silverware, plates, glasses, and enough salt and pepper shakers for every table in a restaurant. Include any research or consulting costs associated with completing the various sections of your business plan. You may also need to account for initial marketing fees, such as the cost of printing up fliers or the cost of giveaways or other promotions to introduce your business to new customers. Mentally walk through every aspect of your business to identify what you will need to get up and running. Also consider both the fixed and variable costs that you will incur during your first several months of operations, if not even further into the future.

How big is the valley? It depends upon how quickly you expect to generate revenues. Refer back to the estimates you provided in order to generate your financial statements; your cash flow analysis in particular will help you determine how much you need to raise, given the fixed and variable costs you have identified, so that you can stay cash flow positive until your monthly revenues exceed your monthly expenses. Make sure that your cash flow statement accounts for the monthly payments for any amount of debt you expect to incur.

If your business is already up and running and you're raising money to purchase a building or specific equipment (these are known as capital expenses), your financial goal might be more straightforward to predict. For instance, you might know exactly how much the equipment costs, and you can get an estimate for the costs of installation; likewise for the cost of the building and any necessary improvements. Raising money ahead of a growth spurt can be trickier. Will you need to invest significant cash into a new product division long before you will see any revenues? Are you ramping up your marketing, hiring new staff, and moving into a new building all at once? The more detailed your business plan, the better chance you stand of anticipating how much money you will need to raise and when. Even if you have no growth intentions, you may be in a position where you need to raise working capital to cover cash flow gaps that occur regularly over the course of your business cycle. These might occur monthly, seasonally, or according to some other cycle that affects when your revenues come in compared to when you incur expenses.

There are two schools of thought regarding how much money to raise. One encourages you to raise only what you really need to get to the point where you can bootstrap your way up on the money you earn through revenues. Certainly, the less money you raise from investors, the less you will have to repay them, either on a monthly basis (in the case of debtors) or in the form of shares of the company (in the case of equity investors). Additionally, some people argue that too much money leads to fiscal irresponsibility; the more money an entrepreneur raises, the less incentive there is to be careful with that money. There are other factors at play, as well. "Whether you choose to bootstrap or not also depends on your appetite for risk," Julia explains. "Bootstrapping means things will come along a lot more slowly, but it's probably safer if you are worried about the risks of needing to repay others."

On the other hand, sometimes it's not possible to grow slowly. "If you're developing a smart-phone app, and you need to pay your developers last month," Julia says, "then you don't have time to bootstrap." In cases such as this—and proponents from the other school argue, in all cases—you should raise more than you think you need, because you will always underestimate how much things will cost or how long it will be before the business generates sufficient revenues to cover expenses. It can be quite stressful to try to run a business without enough cash on hand, especially when unexpected challenges arise. "One of the top reasons for businesses' failing is undercapitalization," Julia warns. "But a solid business plan with contingencies for critical risks means you can plan for the appropriate amount of capital."

Whether you intend to raise debt or equity capital alters the equation as well, because investors and financiers will pay close attention to your debt-to-equity ratio. Carry too much debt and you'll have a hard time raising more, not to mention eat into your cash flow with repayments. Raise too much equity and you might find yourself challenged in the future when the investors want their money back—plus whatever return they expect to receive. These are just a few of the things to consider when estimating how much money to raise. There's no one formula that fits all businesses and no easy rule of thumb. The best advice is to spend some good time and energy writing your business plan.

—— Writing a Business Plan ——

A well-considered and dynamic business plan is a critical tool for attracting capital to your venture. It shows prospective investors that you have considered all the factors that contribute to meeting your goals and that you have a reasonable plan for getting there. (Of course, investors will be looking closely at your business plan for assurance that they will receive a return on the money they invest in your business.) You can also use your business plan to attract talent and recruit employees. Most important, however, your business plan is necessary for proving to yourself that your business makes financial sense and that it's worth the life energy and money that you and others will invest in it.

Do everything you can to show investors that you have a solid plan. While this is generally a good principle of successful fundraising, it's even more critical in the case of food entrepreneurs. Investors interested in sustainable food ventures often report a lack of business savvy among the food entrepreneurs they encounter, something that no degree of passion or mission-mindedness can make up for. "Compared with entrepreneurs working in other sectors, we've found that people in food don't have the same capacity to put together strong business plans, and that needs to change if more capital is going to flow into this space," says Bonny of SJF Institute and Investors' Circle. "Enthusiasm for sustainable food products is growing, but entrepreneurs in this space have not traditionally valued business-planning skills." Julia Shanks is a consultant who works closely with food entrepreneurs and coauthor of *The Farmer's Kitchen: The Ultimate Guide to Enjoying Your CSA and Farmers' Market Foods*. She has had a similar experience. "A lot of people pooh-pooh the business-planning process," she observes. "I hear a lot of statements like, 'I know what my business is. I don't need to write a plan.' But this is very shortsighted."

If you haven't already got a business plan, start pulling one together *now*, even if you are a long way from raising outside capital. If you feel some resistance to this process, ask yourself why. Many people experience some fears when it comes to digging into the numbers, either because they don't consider themselves to be "numbers people" or because they have a nagging suspicion that their unconfirmed hunches (such as when the business might break even) won't actually pencil out. Patrick Crouch teaches business-planning skills to urban farmers as part of his work as program manager of the Capuchin Soup Kitchen's Earthworks Urban Farm in Detroit, Michigan. "Most people don't think about planning at all until they've been in business for a while without making any money," he notices. But planning ahead can save you a lot of wasted money and energy. I wish I had done this myself. I was two years into my first business, a publishing company, when I finally sat down to write a business plan. As I worked through the financial model and mapped out what it would take to be able to pay myself a living wage, I quickly realized that I needed to shut the business down before it drained any more of my life energy or savings. There was no way I was ever going to be able to meet my goals without growing the business substantially, and that was not a path I was willing to take.

"It can be a smack in the face," Julia says of making the important details of your venture visible, which is essentially what the business-plan-writing process entails. Still, it is far better to identify and anticipate potential pitfalls early so that you can figure out ways to address them. "Be ambitious with your goals and conservative with your estimates. Do as much work on feasibility as you can before you launch your business," counsels Caleb Zigas of La Cocina, who says that some clients might spend six months working intensely with La Cocina's advisers and end up with a recommendation to not launch. "The power of your business plan is that it's like making mistakes without having to pay for them."

Alternately, you may simply be so busy doing everything it takes to get your business up and running that stopping to write a plan never feels like the most urgent priority. "So often people have all these ideas bouncing all over the place, and the actual process of writing the business plan really helps tie everything together neatly," Julia has noticed. Indeed, you may find you're a little less frantic in your running around when everything is written out and your various processes are clearly outlined.

Elements of a Business Plan

There is no single correct way to write a business plan. If you need some inspiration, search the Internet or visit your local library or bookstore; you will find a wide variety of guides to business planning, including templates, outlines, and formats. I also suggest that you check out the application guidelines for the social venture business plan competitions (see sidebar on page 71), as these will include sections that may well speak to impact-oriented investors more so than the business-as-usual templates. Business plans designed to attract investors should always include some version of the following sections, regardless of what order you include them in: products and services, market analysis and competition, management team and organization chart, operations, funding request and use of funds, financials, and exit strategy.

Here are some additional tips for putting together a business plan that will serve as a tool both to help you and to attract investors:

- **Build in a much longer ramp-up period for growth than you might hope.** "Even under most conservative assumptions, it will still take you longer to ramp up than you expect," says Julia. Greensgrow Farms, a nonprofit urban farm and education center in Philadelphia, grows and harvests specialty crops to sell at a city farm stand, as well as through a CSA and mobile market program. It also operates a licensed commissary kitchen where it processes unsold fruits and vegetables into preserves, baked items, and ready-to-eat foods. Their expansion into nearby Camden, New Jersey, took more time—and therefore was much more expensive—than had initially been planned. Cornerstone Ventures LLC consultant Carol Coren worked closely with them during this time. She explains that there were no municipal or county urban agriculture ordinances to guide officials in zoning and licensing, nor did the state's 2010 Urban Agriculture Law address these issues; it took several weeks to identify and secure the appropriate license. "Greensgrow's Camden team also had to dedicate time and effort to building collaborative relationships with a larger group of community stakeholders than had been anticipated," Carol says. "The Greensgrow team had to show that they respected the work of neighborhood residents and local leaders and that they were prepared to make a long-term commitment to promoting economic development through sustainable agriculture."
- **Make sure you clearly understand every aspect of your plan yourself,** whether or not you enlist help writing your plan. It doesn't matter how impressive your plan appears; if you can't explain the logic when someone asks, you're going to undermine the plan's—and your—credibility.

Sure, it may make sense to hire an accountant to help you build your first financial model or verify that your numbers are accurate and reflect your stated assumptions, and the accountant may suggest changes in your strategy based on something she discovers. Just make sure that you fully agree with—and can fully explain, to yourself or to prospective investors—any changes before including them in the final plan.

- **Avoid painting too rosy a picture just to attract investors.** What they really want to see is that you've thought very carefully about the risks and have contingency plans for what will happen if things do not go as planned. "Think of every possible thing that could go wrong," Julia suggests, "and explain how you will address them."

- **Keep your language practical.** "It's a good thing to be passionate about your business," Julia says, "but leave out the emotional pieces. Instead of saying, 'This is going to be the best tapas bar ever!' say, 'This is going to be a very successful and sought-after tapas bar because of its unique combination of excellent, high-quality food and ambience.'"

- **Choose your market comparisons carefully.** Every experienced investor has heard statistics such as "The organics industry has been growing 20 percent annually for the last decade." You really need to be more specific, citing research that is relevant to your particular niche. Another danger is comparing your company to one that shot the moon, an event that isn't likely to happen again, or comparing your company to a brand that is well loved by the general public but that didn't do so well for its investors. Michael suggests that if you are a beverage company, citing VitaminWater's sale to Coca-Cola as a comparison is not helpful. "Coca-Cola is not going to pay eleven times the revenue, or over $4 billion, for another brand like that again," he explains. "That is why they created an investment arm: to get into companies at an earlier stage. I doubt any company will ever show growth like that again," says Michael. "Burt's Bees isn't a good comparison either. Yes, Clorox bought Burt's Bees, and that shows interest in the space. But they eventually took a write-down on the purchase. They and everyone else knows they overpaid."

- **Be prepared to explain to investors how you're going to survive** if your plan shows that you'll be taking a reduced salary—or no salary at all—for any length of time. "We didn't pay ourselves for months," says Pam Marrone, a serial entrepreneur and founder of Marrone

Bio Innovations, a company that innovates biopesticides and other sustainable solutions for more productive farming. "Our investors did ask how we were going to live. They didn't want us to be stressed out; they wanted us to be focused on running the company." Julia adds, "They want to be sure that you have sufficient savings so that you won't quit to take a job if your plan takes longer than anticipated."

- **If you are going into business with one or more partners, describe what will happen if one of you wants to leave.** Consider drawing up a legally binding (and sane) exit agreement that covers such details as how to determine the value of the business assets and how the departing partner will be compensated for her contributions to date. Will she keep her company shares, or will you agree to buy her out with cash? If you decide to buy out departing partners, how long will the remaining partners have to come up with the cash? Not only will a clear plan help put your own minds at ease, but it will help prospective investors assess their own level of risk.

- **Identify any thresholds you must overcome to formally launch a start-up or to proceed with plans for expansion.** For instance, if you know that your plan will work only if you raise a minimum of $500,000, increase revenues by a certain percent, or complete construction of a new facility, mention this. Alternately, you can describe different scenarios: "If we can secure orders for two thousand units by February, we will proceed according to scenario one. If we do not meet our sales goals, we will pursue the more conservative scenario two."

- **Consider your audience.** You may have several versions of your business plan, depending on whom you will be presenting it to. The one for yourself will include every last detail. Your bank or other lenders may need only a very abbreviated version. Even equity investors are likely to glaze over if your plan is too long. Offer up a simple version at first, though be sure you can answer any questions that might come up or provide further information if asked.

Remember that your business plan is the foot to get you in the door with your prospective investors—but you're not likely to secure an investor with the plan alone. "It's just a conversation-starter," Julia explains. Your conversations with investors will take place over weeks, months, even years in some cases. Investors will want to sit back and watch what happens over

BUSINESS PLAN COMPETITIONS

Don't overlook these opportunities to win cash prizes, publicity, and validation of your idea. Most business plan competitions also offer winners technical assistance, connections to relevant networks, and in-kind support for projects. Even if your plan isn't a winner, there can be benefits to applying, including help preparing your business plan and presentation plus valuable feedback. Business plan competitions can also help you face some of the major roadblocks to successful capital raising, including fear of public speaking, challenges in summarizing your business and its value proposition, and difficulty in talking about or asking for money, to name a few. Just calibrate your efforts to the odds and benefits, and stay focused on your reasons for applying in the first place.

A variety of organizations sponsor business plan competitions, including colleges and universities, economic development authorities, and other nonprofit organizations. Their motivations for hosting competitions vary. A few are specifically interested in promoting sustainable food entrepreneurship; some want to promote social entrepreneurship in general; and some may be more interested in building the local economy but have no focus on social impact beyond job creation. Your business might be a good fit for any of the above. I highly recommend the William James Foundation's Sustainable Business Plan Competition, which offers cash prizes in several different categories, plus thousands of dollars of in-kind services to winners. More important, every single applicant receives several pages of detailed feedback on their plan from the judges: "This is our primary prize," says executive director Ian Fisk.

time; they want to know that you can manage the business according to the plan. Will you actually hit the benchmarks that you outlined? Don't let your business plan collect dust on the shelf; it's a living document that you need to refer back to and update regularly to make sure you're on the path you set out for yourself.

PART TWO

It Takes a Village:

RAISING MONEY FROM YOUR COMMUNITY

THE CHAPTERS IN THIS PART OF THE BOOK COVER A RANGE OF FINANCING models that involve close relationships between the entrepreneur and her community members. Often these relationships are closely connected to a specific geographic place, but this need not be the case. Chapters 7, 8, and 9 describe fundraising methods for which the return on investment takes the form of product rather than money, if there is any tangible "return" at all; in the case of gifts, your supporters may not require anything in return for their contributions.

Community-supported financing turns the usual business-financing approach on its head. Rather than raise a large amount of capital from a small number of investors, with these models you raise smaller amounts of money from a large number of supporters, including friends, family, neighbors, and existing (or anticipated) customers. These models can also be excellent community-engagement strategies, strengthening the relationship between your customers and your business. There are countless ways to engage your community to support the financing of your food-based business. All you need is a little creativity combined with the ability to both listen and respond to the needs of your community. Of course, depending on how you approach them, you might consider many of the fundraising methods described in other sections of this book to be "community-supported" as well. There is no need to limit the possibilities. Just make sure you keep any applicable laws in mind, which these chapters will help you do.

Chapter 7 covers the basics of identifying prospects, estimating how much they might give, and putting together a plan for reaching out to them. Most of these techniques are useful for fundraising campaigns of any type, whether you plan to offer your "investors" products or a financial return on their investment, so read through them even if you don't intend to raise gifts to support your venture. Chapter 8 covers everything from financing techniques based on community-supported agriculture (CSA) to selling product in advance through subscriptions, gift cards, or other forms of stored value.

Chapter 9 focuses on raising money through online crowdfunding platforms, but there are tips in this chapter that will help get the word out about any fundraising effort.

Before we go any further, it is important to mention that many of the financing models in chapters 8 and 9 exist in a gray area of the law that is confusing to begin with and made more complicated by the fact that it's a body of law currently in flux. Technically, if your business isn't up and running yet and you use a community-supported or crowdfunding financing model that promises goods that will be delivered only after the money is raised and the business has launched, then it is possible that state securities regulators will view your community-supported offering as a security and therefore subject to securities regulations. Even if your business is already up and running, it's still possible that your offering might fall under the very broad definition of a security, triggering the associated securities laws and filing requirements. Chapter 10, "Investment Offerings and the Law," covers the laws you need to be aware of when you start even thinking about seeking investors who will expect a financial return.

All of this said, very few entrepreneurs who have employed the techniques covered in chapters 8 and 9 actually file their offerings with any state or federal regulators. It is unlikely that these regulators would even know what you are up to unless someone filed a complaint against you. This scenario is rare, but it does happen, and it's definitely a risk: an investor who loses her money (or who doesn't earn as much as she had hoped on her investment) might report you, as might a disgruntled employee. Still, many entrepreneurs have used these techniques successfully, and nobody I interviewed had heard of a single case of trouble with securities regulators because of a community-supported financing effort that did not involve financial returns. Do read chapter 10, and consult an attorney to make sure you fully understand any risks inherent in your particular situation.

7

....

Raising Gifts from Individuals

·

WHO WOULDN'T WANT GIFT MONEY to help get a business off the ground? When you have little if any revenue coming in, you may have very little cash on hand to make monthly payments on loans or credit cards. Selling equity in your business during its early days isn't necessarily a great idea either, as it means selling a larger percentage of your company for the same amount of money, since your business isn't worth as much in the beginning as it will be (you hope) later on. If you can find people who are willing to make gifts to help get your food business started, and you use that money wisely, you could be in a much better position to access credit or attract equity investors down the road.

While this chapter covers the basics of seeking out gift money for your business and documenting the gifts you do receive, there are several reasons it's important to think of raising gifts as just one aspect of your overall plan for engaging your community. One is that it is highly unlikely that you will raise all the money you need for your business through gifts alone, and you'll need to spend time and energy seeking out other forms of capital as well. Another is that if you offer people only the opportunity to give gifts rather than a full menu of ways to support your venture (including the other forms of investment described in part 2), you risk losing their interest. Finally, don't miss chapter 9, which offers additional tips for managing campaigns to raise gift money and some notes about what to keep an eye on as this field evolves.

In 2010 Noam Kimelman and a couple of friends were thinking about how they might improve access to healthy food choices in the city of Detroit, Michigan. "When we founded Fresh Corner Cafe, a fresh food distribution business, experts listed Detroit as one of the most toxic food deserts in the country," he says, citing growing levels of poverty and inadequate public transportation. "People rely heavily on corner stores, with their limited and unhealthy food options, for a majority of grocery needs," he explains. "This creates obvious health problems whose ripple effects include increasing incidence of obesity, diabetes, and cardiovascular disease." Instead of working around these corner stores, Fresh Corner Cafe (formerly Get Fresh Detroit) would transform them by partnering with local restaurants and food producers to provide fresh and healthy prepackaged meal kits and meals, which they would deliver to liquor stores, gas stations, small grocers, cafés, and corporate offices throughout Detroit.

At first Noam and his partners delivered their goods to seven corner stores, a food pantry, and a café in a '96 Buick station wagon. But their expansion plans and growth trajectory meant they would quickly outgrow the station wagon, and they knew it was time to invest in a refrigerated delivery truck. "We looked into loans, but we didn't qualify," Noam explains. "So we put up half the money for the truck ourselves and encouraged supporters to meet us halfway." They launched a $10,000 fundraising campaign with the help of Kickstarter, an online crowdfunding platform (see chapter 9 for more details). In exchange for people's gift money, the Fresh Corner Cafe offered small tokens of appreciation: a basket of in-season fruit and vegetables for a gift of $25 or more; a T-shirt, apron, and tote bag for a gift of $50 or more; a food tour of Detroit in the new truck for people who gave $250 or more. One hundred and forty people contributed a total of $10,968.

Noam says the experience had its plusses and minuses. Yes, the Fresh Corner Cafe was able to purchase the new truck in July 2011, but he suspects this successful gift campaign encouraged the Fresh Corner Cafe to expand before it was ready. The business continued to lose money even as distribution picked up, and it took months longer than anticipated to reach the break-even point. "When the gift money came in, we were still in the process of figuring out the business model," he says, wondering if the rigor of having to apply for financing from commercial lenders might have forced him to tighten up his plan before taking on additional customers. As of this writing, the business plan has shifted slightly—Fresh Corner Cafe now focuses on healthy prepared foods and has added a catering service—and the business is in a much better financial position, with several paid staff members and dozens of delivery locations. Noam hasn't written off fundraising for gift money. Only a year after his Fresh Corner Cafe campaign, he raised over $12,000 using Kickstarter for the Detroit Youth Food Brigade, a collaboration of high school students, food producers, and neighborhood markets to build the local economy and promote food justice. "The campaign created tremendous buzz and local buy-in, which, in the end, is far more valuable to our long-term success than the money we raised."

Here are some tips for launching your own fundraising campaign:

- **Identify the people or businesses in your networks that might be willing to give a gift to support your business venture** and perhaps become your most committed customers. This list could include grandparents, parents, relatives, and friends. It may also include businesspeople you know in your area or those who have successfully launched similar businesses elsewhere. Consider people who will directly benefit from the products or services that your business plans to offer. Before assuming that only well-to-do people would be interested in giving to support your venture, remember to think of your gift-raising campaign as a community-building effort rather than simply an attempt to raise money as efficiently as possible. Besides, small gifts can add up quickly. Also think of the businesses that stand to gain if your venture takes off—the businesses from whom you purchase your supplies or ingredients and those that purchase your goods. If you plan to open a brick-and-mortar storefront, the neighboring businesses might be excited to support another venture that may bring more traffic to their doors.
- **For each person (or business) on your list, estimate how much they might comfortably give.** If you suspect that they might prefer to make a loan or otherwise see some financial return rather than give a gift, note that, too. (This list will come in handy when you're trying to identify potential investors, and you'll revisit it in later chapters.) You want to gain a sense of how much you might reasonably expect to receive over the course of your gift-raising campaign, which you can do by adding up the estimates for each person. Of course, this number is just an estimate, and you'll want to avoid making any plans to spend money based on the expectation of gift money you have yet to collect.
- **Decide whether to offer incentives for people to give.** Think through all the possible motivations that each person could have for giving you money to help launch your business. What might you do to satisfy these reasons? Close relatives may simply want to support you in pursuing your dreams and may need no more recognition than a warm hug and to watch you succeed. Neighbors may be excited about the possibility

of shopping at your new retail store or farm stand rather than having to shop at a big-box store or other chain store; perhaps you can offer them a discount on future purchases. Others may just want to be part of something they think will be successful, in which case you can offer to display their names and faces on your business's website or on a prominent wall in your new building. An e-newsletter with regular updates—including the names of people who have supported your campaign and how much you have raised to date—might motivate people who would like to be part of your successful campaign.

- **Set a time limit for your campaign.** A concentrated period of time for your fundraising effort helps you stay focused and keeps the energy high. If you don't put some parameters around the effort, it could drag on indefinitely, which isn't ideal. Not only will you lose steam, but your existing donors could end up feeling that they have contributed to something that never gained momentum. Of course, if you fail to meet your goal by the specified deadline, you have a choice: continue fundraising in spite of the time line or move on to other efforts with the amount you have raised.

- **Determine how you will approach your prospective donors.** You might be lucky enough that one or more of your contacts may offer you a gift without your having to ask for it. This might happen if people are already aware of what you are doing and if you've made it clear that you are embarking upon a campaign to raise gifts. More likely, though, you will need to ask, which requires coming up with a plan for reaching out to your potential donors. What method(s) of contact will you use, and how will you convey the important project details? For instance, you might decide that mailing a packet of information about your business to your prospects is the best way to get your message across. Will you write each of your prospects a personal letter to include in the packet, send a standard letter to everyone, or do some combination of the above, such as a standard letter with a personal note added at the end? Do you want to schedule formal meetings to talk about your venture and ask for donations, or do you plan to bring it up casually whenever you run into potential donors? Many people find that following up letters with phone calls works well; who will make those calls? How long will you give yourself and your team to complete the campaign?

- **When the time is right, make your requests.** No matter which contact method(s) you choose, it is important to make a direct question that includes the specific amount you are asking for. In a letter you might write, "Would you consider giving a gift of $250 to support the launch of my new business? We're going to be a key part of strengthening our local food system; supporting local, organic farmers; and giving our entire community access to fresh fruits and vegetables." Ask with a sense of confidence about your project, and a tone that reveals your faith that the venture will succeed. Explain the value that a gift at this stage of your business's development provides to you and the community it serves. Lest the person believe you are asking for a loan, make it clear that you do not intend to offer any financial incentives in return for a gift, only the sense of satisfaction of having contributed to your project. If you do offer incentives for people to give, be clear that these are merely tokens of gratitude rather than purchases or investments. Avoid using any phrases or even a tone of voice that sounds as though you are entitled to a gift or that the person needs to give; let her give freely if she is so moved. The energetic debt of having guilt-tripped someone into giving you a gift is not something you'll want to pay off later.

If your friends and family say they're interested in giving but they never seem to get around to writing the check, it's possible that a matching gift program with a time limit would be helpful. Imagine being able to say, "If you make a gift by the end of March, the local Rotary Club [or Aunt Sally or whoever] will match every dollar one to one, so that your gift will be doubled." Of course, you will need to find an organization or person who would be willing to help you offer a matching gift program, leveraging their own gift by catalyzing additional contributions from people who would be more likely to give if they knew it would mean additional money for your cause. Rather than matching dollars you receive during a certain time period, your donor may agree to match your gifts only if you raise a certain amount, a hurdle that might give you extra motivation to go out there and make requests. You and your matching donor will have to work out these details. Even if you are not able to set up a matching program, see if you can think of a way to motivate people to give within a specified time frame, such as offering a certain reward for giving by a certain date.

—— Turning a No into an Opportunity ——

When asking for gifts (or any other type of investment, for that matter), you will likely hear quite a few "no" responses. In these cases accept it graciously, and take the opportunity to ask if there is anything about the plan that makes the person uncomfortable. You may receive some valuable feedback, which, if addressed, could open up the door to a future conversation about a gift. If it seems appropriate, you could also ask whether there is any possibility that the person might reconsider if you are able to hit certain milestones. You never know; Aunt Sally may be feeling more generous once she's actually set foot inside your storefront or once you've successfully pulled off your first booth at the Saturday farmers' market. You can also ask the person if she would feel more comfortable making a loan instead of giving a gift, either immediately or at some point in the future. It can be helpful if you have prepared for this possibility in advance, bringing a few different scenarios for loans with terms that you know your business can handle (see chapter 11 for more information about loan terms).

Gifts come in many forms, so make sure to cast your net far and wide. Cash is king, but you might also be able to find gifts of equipment or in-kind services, and these possibilities expand your universe of potential donors. Ask other, more-established food entrepreneurs in your networks, locally or otherwise, if they might be willing to donate used equipment. If they're planning to upgrade anyway, they might even save money by giving you the older equipment rather than having to pay to have it hauled away. Or perhaps there is a food business in your area that would be willing to donate the use of their space or machinery during times when they are not as busy. Tatiana Garcia-Granados is executive director of Common Market, a values-driven wholesale consolidator and distributor of local food based in Philadelphia. "We have always had a close relationship with Share, a large, nonprofit food distribution organization that works with low-income residents," she explains. "Not only do they rent us storage and cooler space in their warehouse at a steep discount. They also let us use their forklift for free. We are growing at such a pace that we are planning to build an expanded cooler space in their warehouse. There is no way we could have gotten to where we are now if it weren't for Share. During the harvest season when food is most affordable, they've even become one of our largest customers."

—— Is It Really a Gift? Document It! ——

According to the IRS, a gift is money or other property that a person gives freely to someone else, without receiving equal value in return (see sidebar on page 82 for the full IRS definition). Of course, this legal definition won't stop your friends, family, or other donors from harboring some sort of expectation from you, and herein lies the shadow side of gifts: because they are usually from people you are close to, there is ample opportunity for hidden (or not-so-hidden) resentments to fester, jeopardizing your relationships.

Lack of clarity about whether money you receive for your business is a gift or a loan can cause problems for your personal relationships, your balance sheet, and your cash flow. Interviewing people for this book, I often heard some version of this story: "I got a loan from my parents, but they're not really expecting to get that money back." Or "My brother gave me some money as a loan, but we never wrote up a promissory note, and he told me he's not planning on asking me to repay him, so really it's more like a gift. And if I do ever have the money to pay him back, he'll be thrilled." Because these entrepreneurs kept using the word "loan" to describe the transactions, I could never quite tell if they were accurately representing the expectations of both sides of the financial relationship. How many of these relationships might sour in the future if the "loans" are not repaid? If expectations are very clear, and both the giver and the recipient view the transaction as a gift, your balance sheet will be stronger if you account for this money as a gift to the business rather than a loan. Clear agreement that the money is a gift rather than a loan can also prevent any lingering feelings of guilt or obligation that you will need to pay the money back someday. It can also prevent the unfortunate situation that you may at some point need to pay the money back in a hurry, at a time when you do not have sufficient cash to cover repaying the loan, leading to a cash flow crisis. If the money is truly a loan, treat it as a loan; this includes listing it as a liability in your books and making every effort to repay the loan according to its terms.

A simple gift letter is all it takes to formally document a gift, providing clarity, peace of mind, and a healthier business balance sheet. Ask your donor to write up a letter stating the amount and date of the gift, whom it is intended for, that there are no expectations about how the recipient will use the gift, and that the donor expects nothing in return for the gift. If it feels awkward to request such a letter, you can write up a gift receipt letter that contains all the same elements and ask the donor to sign it as acknowledgment that the

IRS DEFINES GIFT AND FAIR MARKET VALUE

//

Any transfer to an individual, either directly or indirectly, where full consideration (measured in money or money's worth) is not received in return, is a gift.

The fair market value is the price at which the property would change hands between a willing buyer and a willing seller, neither being under any compulsion to buy or to sell and both having reasonable knowledge of relevant facts. The fair market value of a particular item of property includible in the decedent's gross estate is not to be determined by a forced sale price. Nor is the fair market value of an item of property to be determined by the sale price of the item in a market other than that in which such item is most commonly sold to the public, taking into account the location of the item wherever appropriate.[6]

money or property is indeed a gift. If you do end up in a position where someone forgives a loan, either in part or in full, the forgiven amount becomes a gift. Again, it is important to draft a loan repayment forgiveness letter that specifies the original terms of the loan, how much has been forgiven, and on what date. Don't forget to adjust your books by both reducing your loan liability and accounting for the gift by the forgiven amount.

There are tax implications associated with gifts to individuals over a certain amount, whether they are in the form of cash or other property. Gifts to individuals are generally not tax deductible for the donor, but the IRS does offer an exemption that allows a person to give up to $13,000 a year to another person without triggering any tax liability; couples may give up to $26,000 a year, and there are no tax implications for giving a gift to your spouse.[7] (There is no gift-tax exemption for giving a gift to a business, so your donor will need to make the gift to you personally in order to qualify for the exemption.) The donor must pay gift taxes on any gifts over that amount, whether it is a single gift or the cumulative value of several gifts in the same calendar year. Gift-tax limits can vary from year to year, so it is important to check the current IRS rules. If you expect to receive a gift that is over the exemption limits and would like to pay the taxes on behalf of your donor, the IRS does offer that option. Consult an accountant or attorney with experience in gift taxes if you have questions about the laws regarding gift taxes to determine the best course of action in your situation.

8

......

Community-Supported Models

YOU ARE PROBABLY FAMILIAR with some form of community-supported agriculture, or CSA. The earliest CSAs in the United States were based on models already popular in Europe and Japan. In these traditions, farmers and a community of eaters add up the farmers' total costs of living for one year, including operating the farm itself, and divide that by the number of members who commit to being part of the community. Each member pays a share of the farm's costs, usually in advance of the growing season, and receives a share of the farm's produce every week. In true CSAs the farmers have no other source of income outside of the cost shares contributed by the association of CSA members.

These days CSAs like those just described are rare. When most people think of CSA, they think of prepaid subscriptions for weekly boxes of produce. And the benefits of this model are no longer limited to fruit and vegetables. A wide range of food ventures can reap the benefits of offering prepaid subscriptions, in which the return on investment up front takes the form of products, usually of the producer's choosing. There are also community-supported bakeries, dairies, restaurants, and other types of food businesses that raise money by selling gift certificates or other forms of stored value that customers can redeem for their choice of products later on. This chapter covers these forms of community-supported financing.

———— Cape Ann Fresh Catch: ———— A Community-Supported Fishery

The city of Gloucester, Massachusetts, is the oldest settled fishing port in the United States and home to a community-supported fishery (CSF) program.

In 2008 the Northwest Atlantic Marine Alliance (NAMA) brought local fisherpeople and other concerned citizens of this coastal town together to start thinking about a way to preserve the working waterfront and its fishing infrastructure, which was under threat from development pressure. That same year NAMA also started the Fish Locally Collaborative, bringing together a diverse set of stakeholders representing fisherpeople, local fishing families, seafood consumers/users, local community-focused marine and social scientists, and other fisheries advocates with a clear mission: the recovery and maintenance of marine biodiversity through community-based fisheries. The Fish Locally Collaborative creates tools for fishing communities to succeed at changing the marketplace and policies that put them at an economic, social, and ecological disadvantage. "Most of the stakeholder initiatives in the past only included members of the fishing industry, but this time we wanted to broaden it to the eating part of the community as well," explains Niaz Dorry, a tireless advocate of the rights and ecological benefits of the small-scale fishing communities as a means of protecting global marine biodiversity. Based in Gloucester, she is also coordinating director of NAMA.

The Fish Locally Collaborative meetings unearthed some of the unique opportunities and challenges in Gloucester. "Though it is under threat, Gloucester still has a fishery infrastructure here. Some fishing communities do not, such as Port Clyde, Maine, where the nearest markets and buyers are three hours away," Niaz explains. Fish buyers are very much part of the community in Gloucester, and most shared fisherpeople's concern about the possibility of losing the fishing infrastructure; they also welcomed the possibility of improving it. "We also realized that fisherpeople here had a reputation for being extractors. This was because most of the small-scale fishermen had lost power to the larger, extractive boats that did most of the damage to the fisheries. Unfortunately, they also did most of the lobbying," she says. "Many of the small-scale boats were edged out of the market because of that."

The Gloucester Fishermen's Wives Association joined the conversation, bringing in its deep roots and knowledge of the community. The combined group determined that a CSF could solve many of the issues they faced in Gloucester, provided it could do the following: it had to highlight the role that the remaining small boats could play in achieving marine conservation and providing local seafood while helping maintain and preserve the community's fishing infrastructure. And eventually the CSF would need to help channel that awareness into political action. The Cape Ann Fresh Catch community-supported fishery was born and made its first deliveries in June 2009. They offered two different whole-fish share options, of five and ten pounds each. The response was far greater than anyone expected. "We hoped one hundred people would sign up in the first year," Niaz says, "but the CSF started with eight hundred!" All in all, Cape Ann Fresh Catch netted nearly $1 million that first year. Twenty percent of this went to the Gloucester Fishermen's Wives Association to cover administrative costs. The fisherpeople themselves received about 30 percent more than the traditional market would pay them for the part of their catch that ended up in the CSF.

Of course, any community-supported program needs ongoing maintenance to keep shareholders in the loop and happy over time. Cape Ann Fresh Catch has had to carefully communicate issues to members, such as why they couldn't honor all of their delivery dates or extend the season in the winter of 2010, when strong winds prevented small boats from going out, or why they chose to include cod in the CSF shares. "There's such a stigma around cod. People have this idea about what sustainability means when it comes to seafood. They assume all cod is bad," Niaz reports. "The ocean is made up of microecosystems. If you're getting cod from some parts of the sea, particularly offshore, where the huge boats fish, that's bad. But in some parts of the sea, particularly near shore, where small boats fish, cod is considered a healthy fishery now."

Despite these minor setbacks, the Cape Ann Fresh Catch CSF has been a huge success and an inspiration to many other communities. Nearly thirty CSFs have started in North America with the help of the tools NAMA and the Fish Locally Collaborative created, including financial forecasting tools, best practices, principles, surveys, and public outreach materials. Niaz points out that the usual system of economic efficiency in fisheries—bring in the greatest possible volume of fish, even if that means earning less per pound—leads to environmental destruction, while also destroying communities. "In terms of sustaining the local economy, we designed a system in CSFs where the fisherpeople are paid more for the fish they catch, versus having to catch more fish." In places such as Port Clyde, Maine, the CSF was the catalyst for rebuilding the community's infrastructure and bringing a processing facility back to town. In many coastal communities with CSFs, cooperatives have started to give fisherpeople more negotiating power and control over their livelihoods and their impact on the ocean. Just as important, the CSF conversation has sparked a broader debate around sustainability of seafood. As a result, NAMA and the Fish Locally Collaborative are now working to scale up the model to reach institutions, in particular health care, that are looking to go deeper than the previous standards they used to define sustainability. This work has led to a regional look at aggregation, processing, and distribution needs of the fishing communities in New England and how community-supported models can help achieve those.

—— Prepaid Subscription Models ——

There are plenty of financial benefits to prepaid subscription models. One is that your shareholders, members, and subscribers are more likely to understand should you find yourself in the position of needing to make compromises (such as choosing to use less expensive, nonorganic feed for your chickens rather than raise the price of your eggs). Another is that they may be more likely to trust your own reports of environmentally and socially responsible practices, saving you the time and money required to secure formal certifications. You can also use your subscriptions to move products that you might have a difficult time selling in other contexts, such as cosmetically challenged items that don't meet the size or visual quality standards for your other sales channels but are otherwise fine. (This isn't to say that you should try to fleece your subscribers by giving them subpar products; you still need to set expectations and effectively communicate what you are doing and how preventing waste benefits everyone.) In the case of farm-based businesses, you'll likely do the majority of your marketing for your subscription program before the season even begins, giving you more time to spend your energy in the fields or marketing to other types of customers when the season is in full swing. Subscription programs that encourage members to pick up their shares at retail locations also encourage your loyal customers to walk through your doors more frequently. And who knows? They might be tempted to buy items not in their regular share while they're at it.

The subscriber benefits of community-supported subscription programs vary depending on how each is structured, and there are several choices that you can make during the design process. "The first thing that you need to do is really understand the purpose behind your community-supported program, and from that you can pick the right model," says Niaz. "I'm not interested in just pushing seafood. I'm interested in pushing broad social change that comes from community-supported fisheries," she explains. "In different communities there are different needs to meet and different challenges to overcome. So we have to use a variety of different models."

Here are some of the subscription program design decisions you will need to work through:

- **Which stakeholders to include in the program design process.** This will depend on many factors, including the motivation for starting a subscription program, how deep a connection you hope to foster with your community, and your willingness to engage in group process. Many organizations and individuals contributed to the design process for the Cape Ann Fresh Catch CSF program, but this need not be the case. Frequently, farmers or retailers will design an entire subscription program based on their own assessment of what would be most helpful to the business at that time. In this case it's prudent to conduct some market research to determine whether or not your community members will accept your pricing and subscription structure.

- **Whether to collaborate with other producers or retailers.** This kind of collaboration can take a variety of forms, from working with other producers to design a whole program to simply purchasing goods from another producer to include in your own subscription. On the one hand, supplementing your own offerings with produce or products from other sources might increase interest from members who seek variety. On the other hand, this might make your community-supported program less attractive to customers who want to have a close relationship with the business that provides their food. Know your audience, and weigh the logistical challenges of coordinating with other businesses to handle aggregating your products, collecting payments, and distributing shares.

- **What to include in a standard "share."** If you are a farmer, will you include only vegetables or fruit from your farm as well? You may also decide to offer different types of shares, such as half shares for smaller families or shares that include value-added products. You could also sell things like eggs, fruit, or value-added products as add-ons rather than including them in a different type of share. Community-supported fisheries might offer one share type that includes whole fish only, another type that includes boneless filets, or a combination of both. Food processors or retail stores might offer a share that includes a standard "basket" of items each week, plus a surprise selection at the entrepreneur's choice.

- **Whether to offer your members any other choices regarding what they will—or won't—receive in their share.** Will you allow substitutions? As an example, I belonged to a meat CSA that offered members the option to exclude pork or goat from our weekly boxes of frozen steaks, roasts, and ground meat. We all received the same number of pounds of each type of cut, but we didn't have any choice about which cuts or which species we would receive beyond those exclusions. You may be able to attract more members if you offer a higher number of options, but don't underestimate what it will take to manage everyone's different choices.

- **How often to deliver shares.** Depending on your business, you might encourage people to subscribe to a certain quantity of product every month. If your products are rapidly consumed staples (such as bread or milk), you could even offer weekly subscriptions. I have friends in San Francisco who subscribe to weekly deliveries of seltzer water; if you can find a market for your products at a retail location, you might be able to find people willing to prepay for a subscription.

- **How much to charge for shares.** This is a crucial calculation, particularly if you anticipate the majority of your revenues to come from the subscription program. Make sure you have a good sense of your overall costs of production so that you can charge enough not only to break even (see the section on break-even analysis in chapter 5) but also to pay yourself a reasonable wage, provide benefits, put some money aside to invest in any future business projects, and/or cover any other expenses that your values dictate are important to you.

- **What discount—if any—to offer customers for paying the entire year, quarter, or month in advance.** Entrepreneurs offering subscription programs usually offer larger discounts to customers making longer commitments in advance as a way to encourage this practice, which is the most advantageous in terms of your own cash flow. It's still important to make sure that even the most discounted share covers the full cost of producing it, unless you build a premium into the usual share price to subsidize a number of shares that do not break even on their own. Some CSA producers do this in order to be able to offer steeply discounted shares to people who might not otherwise be able to afford the regular share price.

- **Pickup or delivery location(s) and schedule.** Will members need to drive to your farm, dock, or store to collect their shares? Or will you deliver the shares directly to members' homes or to one or more locations closer to where they live? Sometimes members offer to host pickup locations, which works well if they have a secure and shaded area near their home that has enough space for the share boxes plus coolers if you need them. If you offer more than one delivery or pickup option, will there be an additional cost associated with any of them? In terms of timing, you might coordinate drop-off schedules with other regular delivery or farmers' market runs already on your calendar, or you might prefer to stagger the deliveries to ensure that you have sufficient supply. Specify the pickup or delivery hours in the agreement. Don't forget to ask members to return any boxes, cartons, or other packaging to the place of pickup if you want to reuse them. As an alternative to offering weekly half shares, which involve the hassle of packing and keeping track of boxes with different contents, you might offer your customers the option of receiving a share every other week.
- **What happens if members cannot collect their shares.** Many community-supported programs ask that members find someone else to collect their shares if they go out of town or cannot make it in person on a particular pickup day. This is entirely reasonable, particularly if you have offered a discount for paying in advance. If your business is not terribly seasonal and it isn't problematic to skip a delivery, you might consider putting the members' subscriptions on hold for the requested number of weeks and extending their subscriptions by the same amount of time.
- **How to communicate any news related to your program.** Many farmers include hard-copy newsletters in their members' boxes. Others communicate with members using e-mail or post updates on their website, making it the members' responsibility to check for news that might affect the pickup schedule, the contents of the share box, or other details related to life on the farm, in the kitchen, or wherever the action of the business takes place.

—— Gift Cards, Prepaid Sales, —— and Other Forms of Stored Value

Gift cards, gift certificates, prepaid or stored-value cards, advanced sale coupons, scrip, community-supported certificates—no matter what you call them, they basically amount to the same thing: you raise money by selling pieces of paper, cards, or some other virtual form of value that customers keep and use later to purchase goods or services. When people talk about community-supported restaurants, bakeries, or other retail outlets, this is usually the financing model they are referring to. These models work for any food-based business that sells products directly to customers, including coffee shops, farm stands, booths at farmers' markets, and food carts. Existing businesses can use this technique, as can businesses that have yet to launch, provided that the entrepreneurs have a compelling business and the charisma to make sales to people who have never tried the products.

As with subscriptions, you can choose to offer customers a discount to encourage them to purchase a gift card or other stored value. But unlike subscriptions, in which the entrepreneur usually decides what a subscriber will receive, here the customer decides what she will purchase. Still, you have quite a bit of flexibility around how you structure your prepaid, stored-value system, provided you record and track the transactions in a way that allows your customers to redeem their goods or services accordingly.

Before launching a prepaid sales program, you will have to make some decisions about the following:

- **The value of the cards or certificates.** If you are selling printed gift certificates, you might sell them at pre-specified values (for instance, each one is worth $100), or you might specify the value each time someone purchases one.
- **The physical form that the stored value will take.** If you print actual certificates, just make sure to incorporate some kind of mark or code to ensure that dishonest people cannot duplicate them easily. If you choose to issue credit-card-like cards with value that you load electronically, expect to pay something in exchange for this convenience; check with your existing merchant bank, as some do offer this service. Make sure that whatever form you choose is compatible with both the terms of your stored-value program and your point-of-sale system.

- **Whether or not to offer a promotional discount.** For instance, you may offer a 10 percent bonus for customers who prepay a certain value (e.g., they could pay $1,000 now for $1,100 in value to be redeemed later), or you might offer a certain discount off cards in excess of a certain value.
- **Setting a redemption schedule.** Though gift certificates are a great way to invite customers into your business, what would happen if everyone that bought gift certificates used them the very first week your new restaurant was open for business? Brand-new businesses in particular may want to encourage paying customers rather than gift card redemptions at a time when they really need cash coming in the door. Even established businesses may prefer to offer gift cards with staggered redemption periods to prevent a cash flow crunch right after the marketing period. When Claire's Restaurant in Hardwick, Vermont, designed their community-supported restaurant program, they sold $1,000 worth of $25 meal coupons prior to opening the restaurant. Customers could use one per month (ten months per year, at the customer's choice) over four years, preventing a rush of redemptions when the restaurant first opened. It also gives customers an incentive to keep coming back, month after month, year after year, to redeem their coupons. You might also consider structuring the coupons so that they can be used for only a percentage of the total bill, ensuring that at least some cash reaches the register with each visit. Or you could choose not to worry about this factor. "I'd rather my clients be prepared for the problem of too many gift card redemptions all at once than have to pay accumulated interest on a loan from a bank," says Caleb Zigas of La Cocina. There are both federal and state laws governing the issuance of gift cards, particularly regarding expiration, so check for appropriate laws to ensure that your redemption schedule is legal.[8]
- **How to keep track of a customer's balance.** In the most accessible (but somewhat cumbersome) system, you can simply write down your customers' balances on a sheet of paper that you keep at the cash register and train all cash handlers to manually subtract any new purchases. Electronic card systems, on the other hand, keep track of balances for you. Also consider questions such as whether you will offer cash change for purchases of less than the value of the cards and whether to offer replacements for lost or stolen cards.

- **What to do if people do not redeem their stored value.** Savvy retailers realize that people tend to lose their cards, forget about them, or just don't get around to using them, resulting in a very high percentage of unredeemed gift cards and other forms of stored value. This means that you've essentially made a sale on goods you ultimately do not end up having to deliver. Although you might be tempted to count this in your financial favor (and many retailers do), be aware of the escheat and unclaimed property laws in your state, which may require that you return the value of unused gift certificates or stored value cards to the state after a certain period of time has gone by. Whether or not you choose to abide by these laws is up to you, of course, but it certainly does not foster goodwill in your community to design a system that you expect will short change your customers.

Not long ago the Northern California chapter of Slow Money realized that many small, sustainable, food-related businesses preferred to repay lenders in kind, with their products and services, rather than cash. It appeared to be a great way for these businesses to raise funds for improvements to their operations. "People get to know and love products from certain farmers, producers, and eateries," says Arno Hesse, one of the leaders of Slow Money Northern California. "We wondered, why wouldn't these customers pay for these purchases in advance? That would really help farmers and other food producers." Arno and his fellow Slow Money Northern California members realized that there was no streamlined way for the businesses to promote this opportunity to existing or potential customers, handle the actual sales process, or keep track of each customer's balance. "If you run a restaurant and sell print gift certificates, how can you predict how much a customer is going to spend?" Arno asks. "Giving cash back if they don't spend the full amount defeats the purpose of prepaying." For their part, the customers had no convenient way to keep track of their own prepaid balances either.

Enter Credibles, an online service that resolves these challenges and more. Arno had already created a system to track individual account balances for Bernal Bucks, an alternative currency for his neighborhood in San Francisco. With encouragement from Chris Lindstrom, a board member of Slow Money, they adapted the system for use with prepayments to sustainable food entrepreneurs. In 2011 Credibles.org launched as a platform that allows entrepreneurs to promote their business, collect prepayments, track redemptions, and view customers' outstanding balances online. Customers can browse businesses that offer prepayment, use their bank accounts or credit cards to prepay businesses, and view their own credit balances. "We call these 'edible credits' Credibles," Arno explains. "The platform is open to businesses that are ready or close to deliver. It's not for start-ups or businesses that are still in the concept stage," he says of Credibles' sweet spot. "But if you're in production mode and have produced before, and you need working capital or financing to expand your business," he says, "that's the type of business that we can help presell." Arno has observed that food businesses feel empowered and proud to use their own products as a source of funding rather than asking for donations or just offering a proverbial T-shirt as a crowdfunding reward.

"Most of the businesses do offer an additional bonus for customers who prepay, either in the form of extra Credibles or through intangibles like invitations to special events," Arno explains. "Customers can later redeem such bonus Credibles at other businesses on our platform." Credibles can also be transferred to other people, meaning that customers can give them away as gifts to others. These features support the interconnectedness of local food systems, including the businesses and the eaters that compose them, and makes Credibles unique in the universe of online crowdfunding platforms (see the next chapter).

To redeem Credibles with your business, you can use a computer or a web-enabled mobile device, such as a smart phone or tablet. Instead of running a credit card transaction, you (or the person handling your cash register) will go to the customer's account in the Credibles system and deduct the dollar amount of the Credibles that this particular customer spends for that transaction. "With Credibles you can make a transaction immediately, in real time, so both parties can see the current balance on an account," Arno says. "Since the customer has a vital interest that the business stays around to make good on her store credit, chances are she'll beat the drum in her network. This is good for the business and good for the community."

9
......

Money from the Masses:
Crowdfunding Online

PEOPLE USE THE TERM "CROWDFUNDING" to refer to any of several fund-raising techniques, so it can get a bit confusing. This chapter covers the practice of using online crowdfunding platforms (such as Kickstarter, IndieGoGo, StartSomeGood, Credibles, or Three Revolutions) to raise gift money or collect prepayments for products you intend to deliver later. The type of crowdfunding in which an entrepreneur solicits small investments from a large number of nonwealthy investors with the intention of providing a financial return to those investors is covered in the next chapter, "Investment Offerings and the Law."

In 2008 Samantha Abrams and Ian Gaffney of Ithaca, New York, were excited to channel their collective passion for healthy food, community, and sustainability into a business. They tested early recipes for their raw, vegan, gluten-free, and organic desserts in Ian's mother's kitchen and named the company Emmy's Organics in her honor. Excellent-tasting products—combined with lots of elbow grease—led to sales beyond their expectations, and by the middle of 2010 Emmy's Organics hit $30,000 in monthly revenues.

That same year, one of their distributors invited Samantha and Ian to share a booth at the Natural Foods Exposition in Boston. They jumped at the chance to attend this important industry event, excited for an opportunity to meet new suppliers, get inspired by other successful small companies, and check out the competition. Observing and taste-testing their way through the booths of companies offering similar products, Samantha and Ian noticed a trend. "The other raw, vegan, and gluten-free goodies were really eye-catching in their professional packaging," Samantha recalls, "but none of them actually tasted very good." The Emmy's Organics team knew their own products had a clear competitive edge when it came to taste, "but we realized we needed to step up our branding and improve the look of our packages to compete in the marketplace."

Back home in Ithaca, a little research showed it would cost an estimated $13,000 to 14,000 to design a new logo, develop more professional packaging, and purchase the materials. But Samantha and Ian did not have that kind of cash on hand. "Plus, we were already paying back a $20,000 credit union loan that helped pay for cookie-making equipment and didn't want to go into any more debt," Samantha explains.

Around the same time, Ian's brother, Conor, had just finished raising the money his band needed to complete production of their new album using IndieGoGo, an online crowdfunding website. One hundred and fourteen people gifted a total of $5,810 toward his project. "Conor convinced us to try crowdfunding to finance our packaging redesign," Samantha says, adding that she had never heard of anyone doing something like that before. "He also helped us create a short video to promote our campaign."

Over a period of thirty days in late 2010, Samantha and Ian used Indie-GoGo to fund their package redesign, ultimately raising $15,326 from 102 people—some of whom they had never even met—in exchange for recipes and various combinations of Emmy's Organics products. The new packages reached shelves in the fall of 2011. Their broker, confident that the new packaging reflected the quality of the products inside, presented Emmy's Organics to some of the bigger distributors for the first time; indeed, within a few months, sales were up more than 100 percent. Online crowdfunding made it possible for Samantha and Ian to invest in their company's growth without going into further debt or compromising cash flow.

This story is not unique, and crowdfunding (sometimes called "micropatronage") is an increasingly popular fundraising technique among food entrepreneurs. In exchange for perks or rewards that you offer depending on the amount contributed, the supporters you attract pledge money to your project, in increments of anywhere from one dollar to thousands of dollars, with no expectation of financial return; some contributors may even choose to forgo their rewards. Most food entrepreneurs use online crowdfunding platforms in one of three ways:

1. To support their campaign to raise gift money, offering creative token gifts as rewards (this is what Noam did to raise money for Fresh Corner Cafe; see chapter 7);

2. To support a campaign to finance general expansion of an existing business, offering current products as rewards, either alone or in combination with other creative rewards (this is what Samantha and Ian did to raise money for Emmy's Organics); or

3. To support a campaign to finance a start-up or add a new product line, offering products that the business intends to produce at some point in the future as rewards, often at a discount. This is what the Windowfarms team did in their second crowdfunding campaign; see sidebar on page 97. (Note that in some cases, this type of crowdfunding might fall under the purview of securities law, particularly if your company has never delivered product before or there is some other risk that backers might not ever receive their products. See chapter 10 for more details about these laws.)

As with any financing effort, it requires some serious work to pull off a successful online crowdfunding campaign, but these campaigns can be much more than a way to bring in necessary capital. A company that has no prior sales can use an online crowdfunding campaign as a way to test the market, essentially seeing if they can attract a critical mass of customers before committing to manufacturing any products. If the campaign is successful, the customers' prepaid purchases can fund the first production run. These campaigns can jump-start a company's marketing and distribution as well. A truly effective crowdfunding campaign will also help you build a team of ambassadors for your business, loyal customers and fans that will be your bread and butter over the long term. Finally, your crowd of supporters can serve as validation of your business idea, encouraging other types of investors to come aboard later.

Online crowdfunding is a good fit for manufacturers of customer-friendly products, community-scale retail outlets (such as food trucks, co-op markets, breweries, and restaurants), projects with potential to garner broad public appeal (such as urban gardens, food education businesses, nonprofits), and any project with a charismatic leader or team that has a very deep social network. Most successful food-related businesses raise between $5,000 and $30,000, but as the field of online crowdfunding matures, the number of successful campaigns that raise tens of thousands of dollars or more is increasing. A few exceptional projects have raised six figures (including Windowfarms), but this is rare.

After you've decided how much you want to raise using an online crowdfunding platform, you design a system of rewards, varying by contribution amount, to entice people to support the project. Meanwhile, you post a

WINDOWFARMS SETS ONLINE CROWDFUNDING RECORDS

//

Windowfarms is a social enterprise based in New York that promotes healthy eating through the grow-it-yourself movement. Their unique products allow people to grow vegetables inside their homes, using natural light from a window. Through a Kickstarter project in early 2010, the enterprise raised $28,205, a record at that time, to support staff salaries and to prove that there was public support for its filing for 501(c)(3) status. To entice people to give, they offered rewards such as handwritten postcards, a book chronicling the evolution of the indoor hydroponics kits, and for donations of $500 or more, a kit that Britta Riley, one of the project's cofounders, would assemble herself. A total of 231 people supported the campaign, giving anywhere from $1 to $5,000.

A year and a half later, the Windowfarms team had completed the design of a new product: an easy-to-use, complete, hydroponics in-window growing system. But they still needed to raise enough money to meet their chosen manufacturer's minimum production run. Once again they launched a crowdfunding campaign using Kickstarter. This time they took a slightly different approach, using the platform to presell the kits at a major discount over the anticipated retail price. In the video promoting their campaign, Britta outlines the social benefits of the product itself, which include encouraging people to grow food in their own homes, diverting waste from landfills by using environmentally friendly and recycled materials, and supporting green manufacturing. "We could have done the manufacturing more cheaply overseas," Britta says, "but we wanted to support the development of midlevel, skilled jobs in this country."

Hundreds of people pledged to prepurchase Windowfarms kits during their Kickstarter campaign, which quickly exceeded its $50,000 goal. By the December 2011 deadline, over fifteen hundred people had contributed a total of $257,307 to the campaign, a new record for a food project (which has since been broken again). Windowfarms began manufacturing the new kits in January 2012, when they received the funds from Kickstarter. After experiencing some unanticipated manufacturing hiccups—the norm for many ventures—they missed their March ship date, finally shipping product to the Kickstarter backers in August. In November the new Windowfarms kits went on sale to the general public at a significantly higher retail price.

brief description of your project, including the amount you hope to raise and what you will do with the money. You can also—and you should— post a campaign video (see "Maximizing Crowdfunding Success" section below).

Once your campaign begins, you will have a limited time to raise pledges to meet or exceed your fundraising goal, often only a month or two. Use Facebook, Twitter, e-mail, and any other technique available to you to attract supporters to pledge money to your project. Supporters, usually including friends, family, community members, and existing or prospective customers, can pledge any amount over $1 using a major credit card (though some platforms do have upper limits). You or anyone who visits your campaign page can see in real time how much money has been pledged to the project and by whom. The platforms allow you to update your campaign page during the fundraising period and to send updates directly to your supporters and people following the campaign.

What if you do not meet your fundraising goal by the end of the campaign? It depends which crowdfunding website you use, but most employ either a keep-what-you-raise model or an all-or-nothing model. In the keep-what-you-raise model, you get to keep whatever money you have raised by the end of the campaign, whether or not you have reached your goal. With the all-or-nothing model, backers' credit cards are charged the amount of their pledge if and only if the project reaches its goal by the end of the fundraising period. Kickstarter, one of the oldest and most popular online crowdfunding platforms, operates this way: at the end a successful campaign, it releases the money to you, minus a 5 percent cut, with another 3 to 5 percent cut going to Amazon Payments, which handles the actual financial transaction. If you do not meet your Kickstarter fundraising goal, the platform won't charge anyone's credit cards, and you do not collect any money.

Why take the risk of an all-or-nothing campaign? Yancey Strickler is cofounder of Kickstarter. He believes that having a threshold may assuage the fears of would-be backers who are concerned about what might happen to a project if insufficient funds are raised to get it off the ground, as backers know that they will only be contributing to a project that has successfully met its fundraising goal. With over half a billion dollars pledged to over ninety thousand projects across the entire Kickstarter platform as of this writing ($472 of those pledges were to projects that met their campaign goal), clearly the all-or-nothing model works. [9]

IndieGoGo, the largest crowdfunding platform in the world, offers both options. By far the more popular is the keep-what-you-raise model, even though IndieGoGo charges a higher percent of the proceeds if projects using this model fall short of their goal—9 percent plus another 4 percent to cover payment processing, compared to 4 percent plus 3 percent for payment processing for projects that meet their goals under either scheme. "We chose IndieGoGo's keep-what-you-raise option because we knew that even if we didn't reach our goal, we'd still be able to collect the money we'd raised," Samantha of Emmy's Organics explains, "and we figured that any money at all would be great in helping us redesign our packaging."

Once a successful campaign is complete and you have collected the money pledged to your project (minus the platform and payment-processing fees), you must also deliver the promised rewards to your supporters. If you choose, you can continue posting project updates even after the end of your campaign to keep people engaged in what you are doing, which is a great idea if you anticipate launching another campaign in the future.

—— Choosing a Crowdfunding Platform ——

There are literally hundreds of crowdfunding websites available to help entrepreneurs, artists, musicians, and nonprofits raise money from the masses, with new ones appearing on the scene regularly. Each caters to a specific audience, and each offers slightly different services, terms, and fees. Depending on the characteristics of your business, the specific niche of each crowdfunding service, and whether you prefer the keep-what-you-raise or all-or-nothing model, one platform might be a better fit for your project than the others, so do a little research before deciding which might best help you meet your fundraising goals. Though Samantha and Ian chose IndieGoGo, Kickstarter has hosted a far greater number of successful food-related projects, many of which address social and environmental issues.

Note in particular the eligibility requirements of the options you consider. For instance, Kickstarter has always been intended to serve as a funding platform for creative projects. Charity projects, causes, and businesses seeking general funding violate the site's guidelines, but nonprofits and businesses pitching a specific project are fair game. Indeed, many projects listed on Kickstarter reveal a social conscience and are designed to make money. StartSomeGood, another player in the crowdfunding universe, accepts only those projects with a social mission, making it a good choice if you want to use a platform that is 100 percent dedicated to making the world a better place. IndieGoGo, unlike Kickstarter or StartSomeGood, is not just for creative projects or projects related to a cause but welcomes entrepreneurs and nonprofit causes with open arms. IndieGoGo's application-free process also means you can start raising funds right away.

Newer to the online crowdfunding scene, both Credibles and Three Revolutions cater specifically to food businesses. Both platforms were developed by people who are deeply committed to building robust and sustainable food systems, making them excellent options for socially responsible food entrepreneurs. Credibles (see the section in the previous chapter, "Community-Supported Models," for more details) focuses on the prepayment form of crowdfunding, making it easy for farmers and food producers in particular to both presell product and manage customers' prepaid balances.

As of this writing, Three Revolutions offers entrepreneurs donation-and-reward-style crowdfunding. More exciting, however, are the platform's plans to enable any type of food business to legally solicit loans or equity financing, in addition to gifts, from nonaccredited investors. "We want to offer a full range of financing options, and the crowdfunding section of the 2012 JOBS [Jumpstart Our Business Start-ups] Act made it easier for businesses to raise financing from their communities," says Kevin Lehman, one of the founders of Three Revolutions. "We're waiting to see what the SEC [the U.S. Securities and Exchange Commission] will decide as far as actual rules regarding this type of crowdfunding before we build out the rest of our platform," he adds, noting that it may take years before those rules (as covered in chapter 10) are entirely clear.

—— Maximizing Crowdfunding Success ——

The basic principles for running a successful campaign are the same, regardless of which crowdfunding platform you choose:

- **Use crowdfunding strategically.** "You don't want to go hitting up your family for money all the time. Likewise, you don't want to wear out your welcome in your community's e-mail inboxes," says Windowfarms' Britta, who regularly speaks to audiences around the world on the ins and outs of online crowdfunding. "Find a way to use the cash to produce value and help you—and your business—become financially sustainable," she suggests. "Your social capital and your integrity in your community are more precious than any short-term financial gains."
- **Set a reasonable fundraising goal.** Remember that most food-related crowdfunding campaigns raise tens of thousands of dollars or less. "If

the project is big," Yancey recommends, "fund just one element of it. This can be particularly effective if you can say, 'I've already got it started, and now I want to expand or do this in xyz new way,' and you have a direct plan for making it happen." You can also frame what you're trying to do as a project with a finite beginning and end. "Backers want to have a good sense that the project will be completed as promised," says Yancey. "Don't set a target that vastly exceeds a reasonable, comfortable budget," advises Britta, "as potential backers will sense that something is off."

- **Tell a good story in words *and* in video.** Both the project description and video should include a basic introduction (of both you and the project), a specific request for support, and an explanation of what you'll do with the money and what supporters will receive in return. "It's good to give detail and supporting materials," Yancey says, "but these aren't as powerful as charisma and a good story." If you are tempted to skip the video, consider this: Yancey claims, "There are few things more important to a quality Kickstarter project than a good video." According to Danae Ringelmann, cofounder of IndieGoGo, projects that post a video raise more than double on average than projects that do not. "Of course, you have to have a compelling project, one that can grab people," says Kevin. "Is it important, a big idea? Something that is needed in the marketplace?"

- **Be yourself.** "This is the ultimate, most important thing. Represent yourself as a human being, not a businessperson," says Yancey. "Forget all those rules for job interviews, and don't think about trying to present yourself professionally. Your project and video should reflect what's interesting about you. Your best asset is always going to be yourself."

- **Offer great perks or rewards.** Britta suggests that you choose whether you are appealing to the heartstrings or the purse strings. "If it's the former, don't try to give people a bunch of stuff. Injecting too much of a financial value proposition into a social value transaction can break the social magic. Offer a tote-bag-like reward and focus on your story." On the other hand, if you are using crowdfunding to presell product and want to boost sales, she says, "it makes sense to focus on the great deal they are getting." In either case, make sure to factor the cost of the rewards and shipping into the cost of the campaign. Samantha and Ian of Emmy's Organics, for instance, devised a formula so that the value of their perks never went above a certain percentage of the amount pledged. "Think carefully and creatively about your rewards," Kevin says, "and make sure that they are in alignment with your product." How many different levels of rewards should you offer? Campaigns at IndieGoGo that offered between five and seven raised more on average than projects that offered fewer or more than that, Danae reports. Her other suggestion: "Limiting the number of certain rewards offered introduces a scarcity incentive. Offer personalized perks, such as including handwritten notes or signatures."

- **Choose a short duration for your campaign.** Some platforms allow you to choose how long your campaign will last. More time does not equal more money. "We found that campaigns that set a sixty- to seventy-day deadline raise 100 percent more than those with shorter or longer durations," Danae says. "Thirty days is best," says Yancey of Kickstarter campaigns, adding, "momentum is more important than time. Longer duration encourages procrastination." No matter how long your campaign, concentrating on it for its entire duration is crucial to crowdfunding success.

- **Recruit a few key supporters before the campaign begins.** "Before you launch your campaign, know the names of the first five supporters, and prepare them to pledge the second you go live," suggests Tom Dawkins, cofounder of StartSomeGood. "Never sit on zero [dollars pledged]. You never see a street musician with an empty hat." Britta suggests a complementary strategy: "Have a big backer in your pocket ready to come in about a third of the way into your campaign timeline to help make sure you can quickly communicate the story that you are winning." If you're using a platform with an all-or-nothing policy, identify a donor who will be ready to come in at the last minute to make sure you meet your fundraising goal by the deadline—or be prepared to make up the difference yourself—lest you leave all your pledges on the table.

- **Reach out to your close community first.** Tom cautions entrepreneurs about the myth in online crowdfunding that an anonymous "crowd" will rush in to fund your campaign. "It just won't happen," he says. "I prefer to call it 'peerfunding,' because it's really your close community that will initially support your project." Yancey agrees. "A project's popularity has everything to do with the interest its creators can generate from within their community. If a project has reached 30 percent of its funding goal, in many cases all that money has come from the project's own core audience," he explains. "These early backers publicly vouch for your project; they've shown confidence. When you get to 50 to 60 percent [of your goal], that's when you'll see more strangers getting involved." Danae suggests, "Start the campaign and validate it with your community, and have a plan to go outside by reaching to influencers of groups that would care: bloggers, media people, Facebook groups, people at conferences. Get them on your team to help get the word out."

- **Promote, promote, promote your campaign—using social media, personal outreach, and traditional media.** "Successful projects use Facebook, Twitter, and other social media to get the word out about what they're doing," says Yancey. Samantha and Ian at Emmy's Organics appealed to everyone in their local co-op and even reached out to their suppliers to help promote their campaign. Samantha reminded her suppliers, "If we are successful, it will help them in the long run, too!" And do not forget to get on the phone. "Tweeting [on Twitter] does not equal asking," cautions Tom. "You can tweet about your project and update your Facebook status a hundred times, and 80 percent of your followers will still never have seen your request. They weren't staring at their screen at the exact minute that you posted the tweet. Get them on the phone." "Don't forget traditional media such as the local press and local radio stations," advises Chris Lindgren, cofounder of Three Revolutions, who says that many of their Vermont projects have had great coverage in local papers and on the radio. "These are great stories: the projects themselves are often innovative, and they're raising money in an innovative way." Some entrepreneurs suggest that you dedicate 100 percent of at least one staff person's time to promoting the crowdfunding campaign while it's running. Only you can determine if the potential benefits are worth the expense, but no matter what, you need to take promotion seriously.

- **Use updates to show that both your project and campaign are succeeding.** IndieGoGo's research shows that campaigns that send eleven or more updates raise more than twice as much as campaigns that send fewer than that. Beyond the statistics, there is good reason to send updates: engaged supporters will be more likely to share your campaign with their friends. Visible momentum, in both the project and the campaign, keeps people interested in the campaign. "Let backers and spectators watch your project come to life by sharing the decisions you make with them," says Yancey. Danae suggests that if you fulfill your perks, follow up on your project development, and send contributors some updates even before the campaign is complete, "your impressive diligence and timeliness may prompt someone to pledge again." Once the campaign is over, use updates to thank supporters and continue to give project progress reports.

- **Beware crowdfunding fatigue.** This is particularly important if you are using one of the platforms to support a campaign to raise gift money and your community has already seen a lot of crowdfunding requests. Of course, it can be handy if another group has already gone through the process of educating your audience about what a crowd-funding campaign is and how it works, but it can be a real challenge if yours is just the latest of many requests to come through. If this is the case, think hard about how to offer something truly compelling that will encourage people to open their wallets yet again. Or consider choosing another fundraising technique altogether.

- **Learn from your campaign even if you do not meet your fundraising goal.** Browse the crowdfunding websites and you will notice that quite a few food businesses have been unsuccessful in raising the money they hoped for. Even if you follow all of the tips above, you might not be able to raise sufficient pledges to meet your fundraising goals. Danae points out that this can still be a valuable learning experience. "We've had some people tell us, 'Thank goodness I tried that IndieGoGo campaign, because it helped me understand that my business wasn't a good idea!'" Or you may discover from an unsuccessful campaign that you need to better articulate the benefits of your products or stay more closely engaged with your community before making a request. Perhaps you are overwhelming people to the point of inaction if you have too many simultaneous channels for people to support your project in addition to the crowdfunding campaign. It's also entirely possible that the people you are asking for gifts might be more interested in providing an investment that *does* offer a financial return, in which case the other sections of this book may be more appropriate for you.

For more crowdfunding tips, take advantage of Kickstarter School and the Insights section of IndieGoGo's blog, both of which offer advice and insights that will help inform any crowdfunding campaign. The staff of the platform you choose may also be helpful resources as you craft your campaign, so do not be afraid to ask for help. "There is no point in us putting up projects that won't succeed," says Tom of StartSomeGood. "We're very high touch."

10

......

Investment Offerings and the Law

IN ADDITION TO RAISING GIFT MONEY and preselling products, you can offer people in your community financial returns to reward them for investing in your company—provided that you abide by the appropriate laws. Whether you plan to pursue this form of crowdfunded investment or follow a more traditional investment model, this chapter covers the basic securities laws that you'll need to keep in mind. It also covers the main exemptions that you can take advantage of to avoid the most onerous regulatory requirements and offers tips for working with attorneys and accountants. You'll need to work through the rest of part 2 to choose the type of financing instrument(s)—debt, equity, or something else, such as royalty financing (see sidebar on page 200), that doesn't fall into either category—and specific terms that you plan to offer your investors, but this chapter will help you understand the framework of what is legal to offer to whom, how, and which regulatory authorities you need to alert about your fundraising efforts.

——— Securities Law 101 ———

When you offer people the possibility of financial rewards for their investments, you are most certainly entering into the realm covered by securities regulation, a confusing and rapidly evolving field of law that even the savviest attorneys can find challenging to navigate. Though few entrepreneurs set out to break federal or state securities laws, many inadvertently get themselves into illegal territory. "Before even thinking about raising capital for any type of venture, it is essential to understand the securities laws," warns Jenny Kassan, an attorney with Katovich & Kassan Law Group and CEO of Cutting Edge Capital, a consulting firm and innovation center that works to democratize capital. She has helped a number of companies raise capital from their communities, customers, and fans.

A common mistake people make is to publicly announce that they are seeking investors for their venture. Soliciting for investors via newspaper or radio ads, signs on community bulletin boards or in your retail storefront or farmers' market booth, or posts on any social media sites might seem innocent, but these actions are all illegal unless you have already jumped through the appropriate hoops with your state and/or federal regulators. "There are restrictions on public solicitation," explains attorney Ken Merritt. "It's a trap for the unwary. Particularly on the Internet, people feel that they can just post something about their offering on social networks like Facebook or LinkedIn," he reports.

What you can legally say depends on the amount you are hoping to raise and which state the investors are in. "If securities regulators get a complaint, someone is soliciting investors in California for investment in a Vermont company, for instance, there can be some very serious consequences," Ken warns. "You can be fined for violating securities regulations and, in the most extreme circumstances, face imprisonment." The safest bet is to avoid asking anyone to invest, including any public announcements about your intentions to raise investment, until you are certain that you understand what is legal in your case. Even then, make sure to get your attorney's blessing on the particular language that you plan to use to promote your offering.

The first thing to determine is whether or not state or federal regulators would consider the investment opportunity that you are offering to be a security. While it's tempting to believe that you can avoid securities law because whatever it is that you are doing to raise money is not actually a security, here's the bad news: securities law applies in almost any situation where you are raising money from investors. "Even some of the most experienced business attorneys make the mistake of assuming that securities laws don't apply to small, isolated transactions, to loans, to investments by friends and family, to nonprofits," says Jenny. "This could not be further from the truth, as the definition of a security is quite broad."

So what is a security? "A note, a stock, a bond, a warrant, a put option, any promissory notes in corporate setting, derivatives … these are all securities," explains John Friedman, an attorney in the Hudson Valley region of New York who works with food-related sustainable businesses. In other words, most promissory notes or loan agreements in the name of the busi-

IDENTIFYING SECURITIES

///

According to the federal Securities Act of 1933 and subsequent cases tried in federal court, a security is any sort of investment contract, transaction, or scheme where someone invests money in a common enterprise (i.e., an enterprise whose success or failure determines the amount of the investor's return) and expects to profit based on the efforts of the promoter or another third party (i.e., the investor expects to profit from the efforts of someone other than the investor).

The information that you include in the promotional materials associated with an investment opportunity affects whether or not it might be considered a security in the eyes of the law. If your materials promise things like great returns or guaranteed income, the court will almost certainly find the instrument to be a security. A court is also more likely to consider your financing instrument a security (and therefore subject to securities regulations) if it offers the right to receive payments based upon the company's profits, if it can be transferred between people, if it comes with voting rights in proportion to the number of shares owned, if it can increase in value, if there are plans to offer the instrument to the public, or if there is any risk that someone can lose money through the instrument.

Some states use the risk capital test, which asks:

- Are the funds being raised for a business venture or enterprise?
- Is the transaction being offered indiscriminately to the public at large?
- Are investors substantially powerless to affect the success of the enterprise?
- Is investors' money substantially at risk because it is inadequately secured?

If the answer to each of the above questions is yes, then the state will likely find your offering to be a security. Note that if your state uses the risk capital test, the law might consider some of the financing mechanisms described in chapters 8 and 9, including community-supported models and presales, to be securities.[10]

ness (there are exceptions to this rule for short-term or secured loans; see chapter 11 for more information about different types of debt), any equity investment offer, any revenue-sharing agreement, or any other fundraising instrument you might devise where the investor gets a financial return is a security. If you draft a document or contract that outlines, for instance, the terms of a loan agreement that you plan to shop around to a number of

FEDERAL SECURITIES LAWS

//

The Securities Act generally requires companies to give investors "full disclosure" of all "material facts," the facts investors would find important in making an investment decision. This act also requires companies to file a registration statement for securities offerings that includes information for investors. The SEC does not decide whether the securities offered are "good" investments. Rather, the SEC staff reviews registration statements and declares them "effective" if companies satisfy their disclosure rules.

The Exchange Act requires publicly held companies to disclose information continually about their business operations, financial conditions, and managements. These companies, and in many cases their officers, directors, and significant shareholders, must file periodic reports or other disclosure documents with the SEC, and in certain cases companies must report directly to investors.[11]

people for the purposes of raising capital for your business's growth and development, that document is a security, as is any offer to sell stock in your company to anyone who doesn't have any role in managing the company. Certainly, if there is a possibility that someone could lose money if your company doesn't succeed, it's a security.

Not every attempt by every venture of any kind to raise money will be subject to securities laws. For example, a nonprofit 501(c)(3) soliciting donations will need to be aware of laws related to gifts, but it is not subject to securities laws. Debt notes that mature within nine months are usually not securities. In the 1990 *Reves* case, the Supreme Court recognized that some small business notes that are secured by assets or accounts receivable are not securities.[12] You will want to consult a securities law professional to be sure either way.

If your investment offering is a security, state and/or federal laws require you to register the offering with the appropriate authorities *before* you even start recruiting investors or shopping the investment opportunity around. A registration (called a qualification in some states) includes a prospectus, which contains important facts about the business operations, financial condition, and management, along with attachments such as organizational documents, specimens of the security being sold, financial statements—anything that might help an investor understand whether or not to invest. Sometimes the laws also require that you regularly file post offering reports with federal and state securities authorities (and sometimes to all investors) disclosing pertinent information about business operations, financial conditions, and management. You will probably need to enlist the help of an attorney—preferably one with securities expertise—and maybe also an accountant to prepare all of the necessary paperwork and registration documentation. This can be costly, depending on how complicated your investment offering is.

After you've compiled the appropriate information, you send it to the federal and/or state regulators, along with payment for any necessary fees. You may have to go back and forth with them several times, making adjustments to your offering until everything meets the regulators' requirements. Once everything is in order, they will send you a letter to say that your submission is "effective" and you have permission to begin offering it.

"Any capital-raising activity will need to comply with both federal *and* state registration requirements in all states in which capital raising is taking place," Jenny explains. So, for example, a venture in California that is soliciting investors in Oregon and Washington will have to be concerned with four separate securities law regimes: California, Oregon, Washington, and federal. The initial process for filing at the federal level alone, including hiring professionals to put the documents together, can cost hundreds of thousands of dollars, plus hundreds or even thousands of dollars in filing fees. Fortunately there are several exemptions that your security may qualify for at the state level that might allow you to avoid filing at the federal level at all (see below).

Even if you do not qualify for one of the exemptions discussed below, you can make the decision *not* to register your security (at the state and/ or federal levels) if you are prepared to face the risks associated with this choice. In a number of cases, especially if nobody files a legal claim related to your investment opportunity, there may be no consequences to breaching securities laws. "I'm not actually aware of any cases where an entrepreneur has gotten in trouble for not filing, but that doesn't mean it doesn't, or couldn't, happen," says John. If someone ever does discover that you have violated securities laws and takes you to court and/or reports you to the regulators, you may face serious fines and be personally responsible for paying back your investors. "Some of my clients want to offer their investment opportunities without filing them," John reports. "Sometimes I agree and sometimes I don't that we need not register them. It depends on the circumstances if the particular deal is an 'offering' or not," he says. "Even if it is, there are legal exemptions from filing that may apply. How to proceed depends on management: some people are more risk adverse than others." So it's important to learn the basic securities laws, consult an attorney about your unique situation, and make an informed decision about whether to take the risks associated with not filing.

Despite the time-consuming and often complex nature of registering your investment opportunity, it's important to remember that securities laws have been designed with a noble goal in mind: to ensure investors have all the information necessary to make an informed choice about whether or not to invest in a company. And this can also be valuable to the entrepreneur. In John's view the process of registering is beneficial in much the same way that writing a business plan can be. "In addition to having a sort of insurance against claims that you didn't warn your investors about potential risks, you also get the value of actually having thought about and identified those risks. This increases the likelihood that you'll be able to minimize the damage should any of those things actually occur," he argues, adding, "It's business planning and strategic thinking in the guise of regulatory compliance."

—— Exemptions —— Make It Easier to Sell Securities

Few people actually attempt to do a fully registered investment offering at the federal level. Fortunately, there are several exemptions to the general filing requirements for companies and offerings that meet certain criteria. These exemptions make the legal filing and compliance process a bit simpler and less expensive than a full federal registration. A few of them allow you to make public announcements that you are seeking capital (this is known as "public solicitation"), making it much more efficient to reach potential investors. There are still strict requirements that you must follow: for instance, you must still comply with any applicable federal laws, and you must file at the state level in every state where you plan to solicit investors, unless you also qualify for state exemptions in those states. "It is possible that something that is not a security under federal law can be a security under state law," Jenny warns. "Because the definition of a security can vary

THE SEC DEFINES ACCREDITED INVESTORS

1. a bank, insurance company, registered investment company, business development company, or small business investment company;
2. an employee benefit plan, within the meaning of the Employee Retirement Income Security Act, if a bank, insurance company, or registered investment adviser makes the investment decisions, or if the plan has total assets in excess of $5 million;
3. a charitable organization, corporation, or partnership with assets exceeding $5 million;
4. a director, executive officer, or general partner of the company selling the securities;
5. a business in which all the equity owners are accredited investors;
6. a natural person who has individual net worth, or joint net worth with the person's spouse, that exceeds $1 million at the time of the purchase, excluding the value of the primary residence of such person;
7. a natural person with income exceeding $200,000 in each of the two most recent years or joint income with a spouse exceeding $300,000 for those years and a reasonable expectation of the same income level in the current year; or
8. a trust with assets of in excess of $5 million, not formed to acquire the securities offered, whose purchases a sophisticated person makes.[13]

so much from state to state, it is essential to look carefully [or ask your attorney to look carefully] at the relevant states' statutes, regulations, and judicial and regulatory opinions on the subject." You will still need to pay professionals to ensure that you are doing everything within the bounds of the law, but it's a far less involved process than a federally registered offering.

In these exemptions, the SEC distinguishes between two different categories of investors: accredited investors and nonaccredited investors. Individuals qualify as accredited investors if they have a net worth of at least $1 million, not including their primary residence, or if they currently have an annual income of at least $200,000 and have had income at that level for the previous two years. (The combined income requirement is $300,000 for couples.) Certain institutions and company executives also qualify as accredited investors (see sidebar above for the full SEC definition). Depending upon which exemption you conduct your offering under, the SEC places limitations on the number of nonaccredited investors you can bring onboard. Furthermore, there may be additional requirements if you want to offer your investment to nonaccredited investors at all.

The reason for drawing a distinction between accredited and nonaccredited investors is fairly straightforward: the law assumes that the more money you have, the more you can afford to take the risk of losing money you invest in a security. The SEC also considers accredited investors to be more sophisticated in terms of making investment decisions. Whether or not this is actually true, as a capital-raising entrepreneur, expect to disclose a lot more information about your company if you plan to solicit nonaccredited investors.

Depending on the exemption, it's not always legal for your investors to resell your company's securities (e.g., sell their shares of your company's stock to anyone else). Having the option to resell the security to a third party provides a way for investors to get their money out of the investment if they need to, and this can help encourage investment in the first place. That said, there isn't much of a secondary market for securities from companies that are not publicly traded on stock exchange platforms, which includes most small food companies and other small businesses. This means that although it is theoretically possible to resell securities, there isn't an easy way for investors to find buyers for their equity shares or debt notes.

The exemptions from the federal registration requirements include

- the intrastate offering exemption, helpful if you plan to offer securities only to residents in the state where your business is incorporated and does most of its business
- Regulation A, which is almost as onerous as a full federal registration but might work for you if you're raising less than $5 million (though the SEC is expected to raise this maximum to $50 million, as directed by Congress in the JOBS Act of 2012; see below)
- Regulation D, Rule 504, which allows you to raise less than $1 million from accredited investors only and permits general solicitation under certain circumstances
- Regulation D, Rule 505, which allows you to raise less than $5 million (and perhaps up to $50 million under the proposed 2012 JOBS Act) and allows you to include up to thirty-five nonaccredited investors in addition to an unlimited number of accredited investors (but you

cannot do any general solicitation, and if you bring in even one nonaccredited investor, the compliance rules become much more onerous)

- Regulation D, Rule 506, similar to Rule 505 and also known as the "private offering safe harbor," which allows you to raise an unlimited amount from accredited investors and up to thirty-five sophisticated nonaccredited investors but does not allow for general solicitation.

The exact details of some of these exemptions are changing in ways that should make it easier for small businesses to raise money, thanks to the JOBS Act of 2012. As always, check the SEC rules or consult with your attorney for the specific requirements if you plan to offer a security, whether or not it is based on one of these exemptions.

—— Direct Public Offerings ——

As noted above, many of these federal exemptions ban general solicitation, which means that you cannot make any announcements to the public that you are seeking investors. Again, this includes but is not limited to newspaper ads, radio announcements, and posts on Facebook or Twitter. The law does allow you to talk directly with people you know, provided that you keep these communications private. A private meeting, phone call, or letter is okay; a public conversation via Facebook wall posts that everyone can see is not. A special announcement to the members in your CSA program would be acceptable, as long as you have a significant relationship with these people. An e-mail blast to everyone who subscribes to your e-newsletter would be pushing it. Do check with the specific requirements in your state or in any state where you plan to solicit investors. California, for example, has extra requirements for private offerings to unaccredited investors.

Clearly, private offerings severely limit your pool of investors, since you can solicit only people you already know or whom you can contact privately through a registered broker. But it is possible to offer your securities publicly. This does not mean that you are "going public" with your company; "going public" refers to an initial public offering, or IPO, making it possible to offer stock publicly to anyone. It takes quite a bit of time and money to accomplish the mountains of paperwork required, which adds up to hundreds of thousands of dollars in attorney and other professional fees. A company doing an IPO probably also paid an investment banker, also known as an underwriter, hefty fees (or a percent of the capital raised) to prepare all the documents and help find investors. The total costs can easily reach $1 million, which means that an IPO really makes sense only for established companies that expect to raise more than $25 million in capital. In addition to being out of reach for most businesses, an IPO isn't the best route if you're trying to raise capital from members of your close community, since the first investors in an IPO are usually institutional investors or wealthy individuals that your underwriter knows; the actual public won't get a chance to invest until after your business is listed on a public exchange such as NASDAQ or the New York Stock Exchange, at which point the share prices will be at the whim of the market. Furthermore, if you "go public," you will be subject to very onerous reporting requirements and other rules that apply only to public companies.

Another option for soliciting investment from the people in your community, whether or not they are wealthy, is through a direct public offering, or DPO. With this method, you skip the investment banker or underwriter and offer your security directly to the public, without an intermediary. This is not technically considered going public, because you do not become a public reporting company. You still need to work with an attorney or other professional to help you prepare and file certain documents with the states in which you plan to seek investors and with federal regulators. The filing and reporting requirements are much less onerous compared with those necessary for an IPO. Once you file, you can legally solicit investors on your own rather than rely upon an investment banker to find investors, unless of course you choose to enlist a broker to help out. Whether your company has yet to open its doors or has a long track record, if you have legions of adoring fans you believe would be interested in being part of taking your company to the next level, a DPO might be an option for you.

There are several ways to do DPOs, including the federal Regulation A and Rule 504 exemptions mentioned above. In most cases it will be necessary to do a state-level registration. Many states accept a form called the Small Company Offering Registration, or SCOR.[14] This form is meant to reduce the regulatory burden for state registration of a public offering. But as Jenny explains, "Some states, even though they do accept the form, are considered 'SCOR unfriendly.' The best practice is to look at the options available in each state." Again, that the offering is a DPO does not refer to the *type* of investment you offer your investors but rather the way in which you solicit, or find, those investors. If you decide to do a DPO, whether to raise debt or equity or some other type of security, you will still need to create and legally document a formal offering for your investors.

Here is an example that illustrates why one (rather famous) company decided to do a DPO, in this case to raise equity financing. In 1984 Ben & Jerry's ice cream company had grown to the point where its founders were concerned that it was starting to contradict their deep social values. "We had grown the business to $4 million in revenues, and we were bursting at the seams," cofounder Ben Cohen recalls. "It felt like our business was just another cog in the economic machine that was oppressing people, communities, employees, and the environment." They even considered selling Ben & Jerry's rather than continue down what Ben calls "the slippery path" of corporate success. "Instead, we decided to keep the company and see if it was possible to use it as a force for progressive social change," Ben explains. But they needed to build a new manufacturing plant to take the business to the next level, and that was going to require some cash.

The normal course of action would have been to raise venture capital at this stage. In fact, Ben says that several firms approached them to see if they'd consider an equity investment. But this route didn't sit right with the founders either, as it would have resulted in further padding the pockets of a few rich investors. Instead, Ben and Jerry decided to use the business's need for cash as an opportunity to help build the wealth of their community, by allowing them to become co-owners in the company. "That way," Ben explains, "as Ben & Jerry's prospered, so would the members of our community." They also made a conscious decision to spread ownership in the business—and therefore the wealth that the business generated—to a large number of people, particularly those who were not rich, as opposed to concentrate ownership in the hands of the few already rich people. "The way we did this was to hold what became the first ever in-state Vermont public stock offering," he says. Their intention was to sell stock in Ben & Jerry's to Vermonters: their neighbors, the people who had supported them from the very beginning. "All the lawyers and financial and accounting consultants that we were using, they were all saying we were crazy and we shouldn't do it," he recalls. "They said things like, 'There aren't enough people in Vermont to buy the offering'; 'they don't have the money.' But we made our equity offering available to nonaccredited investors, with a minimum investment of only $126, because it was important to us to make ownership available

THE FUTURE OF CROWDFUNDING ONLINE

//

I predict that the near future will bring several new online platforms that will make it easier for entrepreneurs to offer debt and/or equity investment opportunities to nonaccredited investors, so keep your eyes peeled for those. As Three Revolutions plans to do (see chapter 9), other businesses will likely take the new crowdfunding laws resulting from the JOBS Act of 2012 and turn them into legal, user-friendly, web-based fundraising tools. As of this writing, there are already several websites that help streamline the process of raising money from accredited investors; successful companies are usually tech-related, though some food manufacturers have successfully raised funds on these platforms, as well. We'll probably also see more options for streamlining the process of raising money through the existing exemptions listed in this chapter.

to people regardless of their economic class." Ben & Jerry's advertised the offering in the local newspapers, in addition to hosting road shows around the state. "When we sold out the $750,000 offering, one out of every one hundred families in Vermont had bought stock in the company," Ben reports.

In addition to this money raised from the public, Ben & Jerry's received a grant through a local Urban Development Action Grant program (a precursor to the Community Development Block Grant program) and was able to raise low-cost debt through an industrial development bond. "We were able to open our first real plant, which allowed us to continue to grow the business," Ben reports. "The people who had invested in the company did so mostly because they loved the company and what it stood for, and they thought that maybe this would pay for college for their kids somewhere down the line."

—— Working with ——
Attorneys and Other Professionals

Sooner or later when you embark upon any major fundraising effort, you will need to hire people to provide legal, accounting, or other professional services. The original owners of Ben & Jerry's were not the first socially minded entrepreneurs to be called crazy by an attorney who just isn't used to working with innovative people who are passionate about their values.

Unfortunately, this continues to be a common and frustrating experience. It might take you some time to find professionals whose values and fee structures match your priorities, but it's worth putting in this extra effort up front. Just like your investors, these are business partners that you might have for a very, very long time, and if these relationships are good ones, you'll be much better off.

Where can you find good professional service providers? Word of mouth through your networks is likely the best source of leads. "Talk to other people about their experiences with lawyers or accountants," recommends attorney John Friedman. "The main issue is understanding what is being done, why it's being done, the value it provides, and what needs to be done by professionals and what doesn't," he says. Take, for example, the process of setting up a corporation. You can pay an attorney to do this for you, or you can do it yourself with some paid guidance, or you can do it entirely on your own. "If your lawyer doesn't tell you when not to have a lawyer do something for you, that's not the right lawyer," John warns. The same advice holds for accountants. You probably want one to help you set up your bookkeeping system in the first place, but the relative value of hiring one to do your regular bookkeeping may not be worth the expense.

Make sure you understand how the professionals you interview price their services. Some charge by the hour and others by the job. Some may be willing to wait until your fundraising campaign is complete before collecting payment, and others may need to be paid monthly. Don't be afraid to negotiate, even to the point of offering product for payment, in part or in full. Depending upon your cash flow situation, one arrangement might work better for you than another. Just be careful if you plan to pay your professionals out of the proceeds of your capital raise, as this may prompt a conflict of interest. If your attorney or accountant starts trying to find investors for you in order to make sure she gets paid, she is starting to act as a broker-dealer, another role formally defined by the SEC, and one that comes with its own set of compliance laws.[15]

Once you have found a good attorney, there is the issue of how you will work together. Joel Solomon is chair of the Renewal investment funds, which invest in green and organic consumer-facing products. He is also entrepreneur in residence at RSF Social Finance and serves on the boards of both Tides and Tides Canada, both of which offer financial services to the charitable sector. "Don't go to your attorney with a very specific plan and ask if it is legal," advises this veteran of many, many socially responsible investment deals. "Instead, explain what goals you are trying to accomplish, and ask for the best way to make it happen." Then your attorney can explain your options, plus the costs and risks associated with each one. "When you are innovating, there is always some risk involved," Joel explains, "so I find it more effective to find out what the risks are and then decide for yourself whether or not they are worth taking."

PART THREE

Borrower Be:

DEBT FINANCING

ASIDE FROM GIFT MONEY, WHICH USUALLY COVERS ONLY A SMALL portion of a business's expenses (if you are able to attract any gifts at all), debt and equity are the two main sources of financing. These chapters cover the advantages and disadvantages of various forms of debt, including how they work, understanding the different terms involved in debt agreements, where to find different types of debt, and how to work successfully with different types of lenders and lending platforms.

At its simplest, debt means that someone, or an institutional lender such as a bank or credit union, offers you or your business a certain dollar value of credit. You receive some or all of that money up front, and you pay it back at some point in the future, in full or in part, usually with interest. Debt comes in many flavors: loans, mortgages, lines of credit, microloans, and credit cards. Some kinds of crowdfunding covered in the previous section (such as subscriptions and other forms of presales), are in essence debt agreements. If your vendors or suppliers let you make purchases now and pay later, that's also a form of debt. There are also a wide variety of lenders. You might make a personal loan to your business, making you the lender. You can raise debt financing from friends, family, and community members. Banks and credit unions offer credit to individuals and businesses, as do various government programs. Increasingly, other institutions, including microlenders, foundations, and nonprofits, offer loans to entrepreneurs and businesses that meet certain criteria. The chapters in this section cover all of these options.

When might debt be a good choice for you? It's tough to state any hard-and-fast rules because there are now so many different types of debt available, from a wide variety of sources. Which of those might be a good fit for you will depend on how well your values match those of your lenders and the forms of debt that you can access given your situation. That said, there is one very important factor for social entrepreneurs to keep in mind that makes debt financing more appealing than equity: when you raise equity financing, you sell shares of your company, which has traditionally meant some loss of control, and it definitely means sharing a portion of the business's financial success—potentially a large portion—with equity investors. Although there are ways to keep your values intact and limit investor returns while raising equity (see chapter 17), using debt avoids these issues altogether, and you have the final say over how you run the business. Other advantages to debt financing include the fact that any interest you pay on loans or other forms of credit is usually tax deductible and that you have a much better sense of exactly how much you owe your creditors and when the payments will be due. Most debt agreements are much less complicated than equity agreements, making them easier for you and your investors to understand; their relative simplicity also means that debt agreements are cheaper to set up, with or without the help of an accountant or attorney. If you have made a personal loan to your company, lenders tend to be more lenient about using new debt to pay yourself back, whereas equity investors will probably expect to see their money put to use in growing the company.

On the other hand, there are some disadvantages to using debt rather than equity to finance your business. It can be challenging for brand-new ventures to set aside the cash to make regular debt payments (that is, if you cannot negotiate a delayed payment start date; more on that in the following chapter). No matter what stage your business is in, the money you use to repay debt is money you can't use to invest in the business in other ways. The more debt you have, the harder it is to access additional debt *or* equity financing. Many entrepreneurs seek out a combination of debt and equity to raise all the money they need for their businesses. As you read through the following chapters, you'll get a clearer sense of what combination of financing tools might make the most sense for you.

11

......

How It Works:
Debt Concepts

HOW WILL YOU KNOW what kind of debt, also known as credit, is right for you? It will depend on the specifics of the credit in question. This chapter covers the various types and elements of a debt or credit agreement and how changing each element will affect your experience as a borrower. It also touches on key requirements for securing debt from professional lenders.

If you're receiving a loan from a friend or family member (see chapter 13) or if you are the lender, making a loan to your business (see chapter 12), you'll have the opportunity to work together on the specifics associated with each element of the loan. The good part about such a situation is that you may be able to negotiate terms that are in excellent alignment with your values *and* business plan. The downside is that it may take a lot of time and energy to negotiate mutually agreeable terms with each of your individual lenders. Banks, credit unions, and other commercial lenders often have strict policies that determine the debt terms they offer you, and negotiating special treatment will likely be out of the question (see chapter 14). Still, the more you know about the nature of debt, the better you'll be able to assess whether or not the debt terms work for you.

Term loans are the simplest form of debt: you borrow a certain sum of money once, and you pay it back over time. Common examples include mortgage loans, construction loans, and loans to purchase major equipment and machinery. These examples all involve capital expenditures or expenses that a business incurs only once and that will enable it to generate revenues over time.

The **borrower** is the person or entity that is receiving the assets of the loan. Keep in mind that when you're financing a business, the borrower could be the business itself, but it could also be you as an individual. You may have friends or family members that feel more comfortable lending to you directly rather than lending to your business. (The assumption in this chapter is that we're talking about a loan made to your business, but if you are documenting a personal loan *from* you *to* your business, then you are the lender and the business is the borrower.)

The **lender**, or **creditor**, is the person or institutional entity—such as bank, credit union, or other commercial lender; a foundation; or even another business—that offers certain assets to another party for a period of time.

The **loan amount**, also known as **principal,** refers to the value of the assets that the lender offers the borrower. For the purposes of this book, we'll assume that the loan is in the form of cash. How much should you borrow? In addition to whatever money you have calculated that you need to spend, consider the following:

- All other factors being equal, the higher the loan amount, the higher your payments will be, and the more you will pay in interest over the life of the loan.
- The more debt your business carries, the harder it will be to convince lenders to loan you more.
- Most institutions charge fees that may eat up some of the loan proceeds.
- You may not have revenues right away to cover the repayment of the principal and interest, so the loan may need to cover the earlier repayments in addition to whatever else you planned to use the loan proceeds to pay for.
- Commercial lenders may not lend you the full amount that you request. If they have reason to believe that you will be unable to make the payments on a larger loan or you don't have sufficient collateral (see below), they may give you a loan only for a smaller amount. In this case you will need either to find the rest of the money you need elsewhere or make do with less.

The **loan term** refers to the length of the loan (in other words, how long you have to repay it after receiving the money). Shorter terms mean that you will pay less interest over the life of the loan, but you will also make higher regular loan payments because you will make fewer of them. You may not have a choice about the loan term that a lender will offer you, and it may depend on the purpose of the loan. For instance, commercial lenders commonly offer thirty-year mortgage loans, but you may only get a five- or ten-year term for loans for equipment. **Short-term debt** is money that you must pay back in less than a year; **long-term debt** has a term of a year or more.

Interest is the percentage of the loan amount that you pay to the lender in exchange for the use of the money loaned. A **fixed interest rate** is the same throughout the term of the loan. A **variable interest rate** (also known as a **floating interest rate**) changes over time, usually based upon international or federal indices such as the London Interbank Offer Rate (LIBOR) or the federal funds rate. For borrowers and individual lenders, loans are much, much easier to keep track of when they have fixed interest rates. Because the payments are the same every month, it is easy for you as the entrepreneur to project the effect of your loan and interest payments on your cash flow. Many commercial lenders often prefer to charge variable rates because it is easier for *them* to make cash flow projections, since their depositors usually earn interest calculated at variable rates.

If you have a fixed interest rate and variable rates go down over the term of your loan, you will end up paying more interest than you would have with a variable rate. On the other hand, if you have a fixed interest rate and variable rates go up, you'll pay less than you would have with a variable rate. Sometimes interest is described in terms of basis points rather than percentage points, but they are related: one basis point equals one one-hundredth of 1 percent of the principal amount (e.g., 25 basis points = .25 percent).

Many entrepreneurs sweat the interest rate, and of course it's true that the higher the interest rate, the more you will pay toward the loan-plus-interest over time. Lest you get too bogged down by this detail, however, it can help to think in terms of the payments themselves rather than the percentage rate. A difference of a few percentage points of interest may not make a noticeable difference in the repayment amount; this is especially true with smaller loans. As an example, if you borrow $100,000 over five years at a 5 percent interest rate, your monthly payment will be $1,887. If your interest rate were 8 percent instead, your monthly payment would be $2,028 a month, a difference of only $141. In other words, the amount you borrow and the loan term, not the interest rate, will have the biggest effect on the size of your payments. Meanwhile, a higher interest rate may go a long way toward attracting lenders who have other options for putting their money to work.

The **interest accrual period** is the time over which the interest is calculated. If you do not pay this interest before the end of the next accrual period, it may be compounded, or added to the principal amount you owe to your lender. If the terms say that interest is "compounded monthly," this means that the interest accrual period is a month. The shorter the interest period, the more interest you will pay over the term of the loan. This is because accrued interest is added to any remaining loan principal, and you will owe interest on the new total as well.

The **payment period** describes the time you have between payments. This period might be bimonthly, monthly, or quarterly (every three months). For instance, if your interest rate on a $100,000 loan is 10 percent, and you pay quarterly, you would pay $2,500 (one quarter of 10 percent of the principal) at the end of every quarter. The payment period may be the same as the interest accrual period, but it may very well be different.

Repayment and interest start dates are when you must start paying back the loan principal and/or interest. In most cases these dates will be at the end of the first full payment period after the loan is disbursed and you have received the money, but you may also negotiate a situation in which you start paying back the principal and/or interest at some date in the future. (An **interest-only loan**, for instance, is when you pay only interest until the repayment date.) Even though the interest clock usually begins ticking the moment you receive your loan, delaying the repayment start date could be helpful in avoiding cash flow problems if you do not expect your company to begin to earn revenues for some time. The trade-off to choosing later repayment and/or interest start dates is that you will ultimately pay more interest over the life of the loan than if you started making payments right away.

The **maturity date** is the end date of the loan. With a **fully amortizing loan**, the borrower pays down the principal over the life of the loan and also pays interest at each payment period; the payments are usually the same every period, even if the proportion that covers interest versus principal varies over time. But you can also structure a loan such that you pay back none of the principal or interest until the maturity date, at the end of the loan term; this is known as a **bullet loan** or **balloon loan**. Alternately, you can choose to structure an interest-only bullet or balloon loan in which the borrower does make regular interest payments but pays all of the principal at maturity. If you are considering bullet or balloon loans, just be careful about making sure you can have cash on hand to repay these types of loans (plus whatever interest you owe) at the end of the term.

You are more likely to encounter the following terms when you are dealing with commercial lenders:

Collateral refers to the business or personal assets that lenders generally require you to offer as a form of security in exchange for the money they lend. If you cannot pay back the loan, lenders will take the collateral in lieu of money. Lenders usually accept land, buildings, and equipment, and you can sometimes put inventory or even accounts receivable up for collateral. A loan that is backed by collateral is called a **secured loan** (as opposed to an **unsecured loan**). Sometimes you can negotiate better terms, including a lower interest rate, if you have good collateral.

Revolving credit, also known as a **revolving loan** or a **line of credit**, is debt with a certain **credit limit** (a maximum amount you can borrow), against which you can borrow as much or as little as you choose. You pay interest only on the amount you borrow. Like term loans, revolving credit can be secured with collateral or may be unsecured. The main variables in a line of credit are the credit limit and the interest rate. Many lending institutions charge fees if you don't borrow up to your credit limit; these fees are known as **unused line of credit fees**. Like early repayment fees, you could think of these fees as an insurance policy in the event that you need more than you thought you might when you originally applied for the credit. In the event of a default, the lender will likely refuse to lend any additional funds, in addition to requesting immediate repayment of the outstanding balance.

A **guarantee** (or **guaranty**) is an assurance that you or another party provides to the lender that a loan will be repaid. Whether or not you have collateral, most commercial lenders require a **personal guarantee** for business loans. In essence, this is like signing your receipt when you pay for a meal using

COLLATERAL AND NATIVE COMMUNITIES

//

Since land is so often used as collateral for business loans, many Native Americans face serious challenges when it comes to accessing commercial credit. Fortunately, there are quite a few community development financial institutions, or CDFIs, that specialize in providing financial training and credit services in Native communities. The CDFI section in chapter 14 includes information on how to find such institutions.

your credit card; you are personally promising that you will pay back the business loan. What this means is that if your business cannot repay the loan for some reason—even if you've registered your business as an LLC or corporation in order to limit your personal liability— the lender can come after your personal assets: your house, your car, the antique grandfather clock that has been in the family for generations. In addition, commercial lenders will probably report any late payments to your personal credit record if you personally guarantee the loan. Needless to say, many entrepreneurs are nervous about signing a personal guarantee. Keith Kohler of the K2 Group often advises fundraising entrepreneurs. "If the lender you're talking to does not ask for a personal guarantee," he advises, "don't bring up the subject!" Every owner of the business, plus any family members that might be affected in the event that a bank comes after the personal assets of the guarantors, needs to be aware of what's going on when you sign a personal guarantee. In certain cases lenders will also accept guarantees from third parties (i.e., from an entity that is neither the borrower nor the lender), including other individuals, businesses, foundations, or government entities such as the USDA.

A **cosigner** is an additional person who pledges to a lender that a loan will be paid back. If your credit score is low or if you do not have good collateral, a commercial lender might ask for this extra assurance.

When you're dealing with commercial lenders, expect to pay **fees** in addition to interest. You will likely pay an **origination fee** to cover the cost of underwriting and processing your loan; your lender will usually subtract this fee from the amount of money you receive for the loan, though this amount is still part of the total loan amount, and the lender will charge you interest on the total. Sometimes commercial lenders will waive fees up to a certain limit—it can't hurt to ask.

Your borrower may charge you **late fees** if you do not make payments on time. There may also be a specified **grace period**, meaning that you can be late up to a certain point without incurring late fees.

If you pay back your loan early (in other words, before the maturity date), a commercial lender may charge you **early repayment** or **prepayment penalties** to cover the interest that you didn't pay over the time remaining in the loan term. If a lender offers you a loan without a prepayment penalty or with a modest one, try to borrow money for the longest term that you possibly can. If your business doesn't do as well as you expect, you'll be grateful for the low payments. If your business does better than expected, you will certainly be able to find ways to put the "extra" money to good use. Even if you expect to be able to pay your loan back early, you might think of these fees as the premium on an insurance policy against future cash needs; they could be relatively cheap compared to the cost of scrambling for cash later.

Representations and warranties provide lenders with written assurance that certain things about your business are true before they'll give you a loan. Representations and warranties can be part of the written loan agreement. As an example, a lender may ask you to include a representation that all financial statements you have provided are accurate, that you are current with all taxes you owe, and that there are no legal suits against your company. In other words, are you being honest about everything you have told the lender?

Covenants, similar to representations and warranties, are promises the borrower makes about how the business will be run and when it will update the lender about business developments. **Affirmative covenants** refer to things that the borrower will do, such as maintain appropriate insurance and records of financial accounts. **Negative covenants** describe things that the borrower shall not do, such as taking on additional debt, selling to or merging with another business, or substantially changing the nature of the business. Often covenants are related to financial ratios, which may appear either as affirmative covenants (e.g., you must maintain a debt service ratio, or the amount of cash you have on hand to repay a debt compared to the amount of your regular payment, of 1.1 to 1) or negative covenants (e.g., you must not let the net worth of the business fall below $100,000, measured quarterly).

Reporting requirements specify how frequently the borrower must deliver financial statements to the lender (e.g., borrower shall deliver a balance sheet, income statement, and statement of cash flow within forty-five days after the end of the fiscal year). Reporting covenants may also require the borrower to let the lender know of any events that might make it difficult to repay the loan, such as substantial damage to the business facilities or any legal action brought upon the business. Be careful about what you agree to in the representations and warranties or covenant sections, and make sure you're thinking about all possibilities that may exist for the entire term of the loan. Of course, you want to make your lenders comfortable lending you the money, but you don't want to have your hands tied if something unexpected comes up. For instance, if your business isn't able to meet its revenue projections before your seasonal slow period and you need a bit more cash to get through a couple of months, but you've agreed not to take on any more debt, you might find yourself in a sticky situation.

While of course nobody wants to think about not being able to pay back a loan, sometimes it happens. In their loan agreements, commercial lenders will spell out **events of default**, or what constitutes a loan default on the part of the borrower. These might include late payments, filing for bankruptcy, or failing to meet any of the conditions laid out in the covenants. If your company defaults on the loan, the borrower may demand early repayment in full. If you do not have cash on hand to repay the loan, the borrower may repossess the business collateral and pursue your personal assets.

Subordinated debt (also called **mezzanine debt**, **unsecured debt**, or **junior debt**) is a more expensive form of commercial debt that you might use after you have pledged any available collateral to other lenders. If you have concerns that selling equity might jeopardize your ability to manage your company in accordance with certain social values, subordinated debt can be an excellent alternative to equity financing. Or you might use subordinated debt as a bridge loan to help you close a cash gap between the time you receive a commitment for another type of financing and the time you actually receive the check. Because it holds a lower repayment priority relative to other debts and the lender is taking on a higher risk—you repay subordinated debt only after you have repaid other debts in the event of bankruptcy or in any other situation where you are liquidating your company's assets—lenders charge much higher interest rates than with secured, or senior, debt. In addition to pledging to pay back subordinated debt, your lender may also expect you to provide a "kicker" in the form of warrants to purchase stock at a predetermined value at some point in the future or to contribute a share of your revenues for a time. (See chapter 17 for more information on how equity financing works; that's also where you'll find an explanation of **convertible debt**.)

—— The Cs of Lending ——

Particularly when you begin to work with commercial or government lenders such as credit unions and banks (see chapter 14) or the Farm Service Agency (see chapter 15), the following Cs of lending will definitely come into play. Some sophisticated individual lenders may also pay very close attention to them. Familiarize yourself with what they are and how they work, and you will be ready.

1. Character. I list this one first because no matter how well you measure up to the following Cs, if a lender has any reason to doubt your personal character, you might not get a loan. Yes, it's a very subjective thing to measure, but lenders want to feel that you are trustworthy and likely to make good on any debts. Attitude is crucial. You want to project confidence, but you also don't want to seem so relaxed about a loan that you run the risk of sending the message that you don't take debt obligations seriously. Personal connections and referrals can go a long way; remember chapter 1? If you found a lender through one of their clients, tell them that. Your lender may ask you for personal references or people who can vouch for you. Even if your lender does not ask for personal references, you can offer to provide them.

2. Credit. Chapter 4 covered how important it is to build and repair your personal credit rating. When you start applying for loans, you'll be glad you did this work, as your credit score (and that of your busi-

ness, if it has already established a credit rating of its own) is one of the first things that a lender will look at. The higher your credit score, the more likely you are to get a loan, the bigger the loan your lender might consider, and the lower the interest rate you will be able to find.

3. Collateral. As described above, collateral can be any asset that a lender might take in place of cash in the event that you cannot repay your debts. You can put buildings, machinery and equipment, inventory, and even accounts receivable up as collateral. If you have no business collateral, commercial lenders may insist that you put personal assets up instead. The stronger your collateral, the larger the loan you will be able to qualify for.

4. Capacity. Can your business generate enough cash to repay the loan? Lenders will want to see your cash flow statement (in addition to other financial statements; see chapter 5) to feel confident about your capacity to make repayments associated with any credit they might provide to you. Assessing capacity includes an examination of your business plan. Expect lenders to check your assumptions. Lenders may also look into your personal ability to repay a business loan and even whether or not your spouse has a steady job and therefore might be able to repay your business loan should things go awry.

5. Capital. In some cases lenders may require that you put up a certain amount of the total funds needed for whatever the loan is meant to cover, much like a mortgage loan in which you must put 20 percent down up front. Sometimes "capital" also refers to the strength of your company's balance sheet relative to the amount of the loan you are seeking. In general, the more capital you have, the better.

6. Conditions. This can mean one or both of two things. The first refers to the general conditions under which the lender is considering extending credit to you, which could include the conditions of your industry, where you are positioned within it, your relationships with suppliers and customers, the state of the credit markets in general, or all of the above. It can also refer to conditions the lender might place on a loan or line of credit depending upon how you measure up with the other Cs.

12

......

Investing in Your Own Business:
Sources of Personal Debt

THIS CHAPTER COVERS SOURCES of personal debt that you can use to finance your business. These options include personal loans and lines of credit (including mortgages and other debt that use your home as collateral), credit cards, and peer-to-peer lending. Chances are high that you will be your venture's first investor, both in terms of the time and energy you commit and in terms of cash that you bring to the table. If you have invested your own money into your business, other potential lenders, including your friends, family, other individuals, and lending institutions, will be far more likely to do the same. They might also be more interested in investing in something that they can see is already under way, and it will take some cash to get to that point: your cash. If you've been poking around to see about getting a loan for a new business from a bank, you have probably already discovered that very few commercial lenders will give a loan to businesses without a track record, period. So you'll need to look into other means of raising money in the beginning.

If you have good credit, there are many more options for obtaining personal debt than there are business credit options for new businesses. With that in mind, this chapter is about financing your business in a somewhat roundabout way: by borrowing money or obtaining credit for yourself rather than your business, then using that credit for business purposes. (As we learned in chapter 3 you and your business are separate entities, except in the case when you choose to operate as a sole proprietorship.) This might be the way to go in your situation if you have a good credit rating yourself and one or more of the following are true:

- Your business is just getting started and therefore cannot qualify for loans from banks or other business lenders because it has not yet built a credit record of its own.
- You would prefer to work solo rather than put a lot of effort into rallying your community to support your fundraising efforts.
- There are other reasons why you cannot or don't want to raise money using other methods (for instance, you might not want to sell equity in the company under any circumstances).
- You are not afraid of putting your personal credit rating or personal assets at risk.

While the assumption is that your ultimate goal is to use money you find from the following sources for business purposes, don't forget the lesson from chapter 4: keep your personal finances separate from your business finances. Also remember that you personally, not the business, are responsible for repaying debts described in this chapter. This means that both your personal credit score and any personal property that you have offered as collateral are at stake if you fail to repay these debts. Finally, make sure that you properly account for all transactions involving personal debt. Consider any monies "raised" using these methods as personal funds, and draft a formal agreement between you and the business to account for any investment you make to the business from your personal funds.

—— Personal Loans and Lines of Credit ——

On the surface there is not much difference between taking out a business loan or line of credit for which you must sign a personal guarantee and taking out a personal loan or line of credit. When your business is new, however, you may personally qualify for credit while your business almost certainly will not. Another difference is that personal loans and lines of credit are in your name rather than the name of the business. This means that any credit that you take on for business purposes may negatively affect your own credit score—and your ability to qualify for future credit—even if you do make sure that you make all payments on time (see chapter 4 on the factors that influence your credit score). But many an entrepreneur has used personal loans or personal lines of credit to finance a business during its early years.

Personal loans, mortgages, or home equity loans, if you qualify, can help you cover your business's start-up costs or the cost of onetime capital improvements. Examples include renovating your storage warehouse with a new cooler, building a new barn for your farm, or purchasing your new food truck. A personal line of credit might make sense if the business is already up and running, but you need a way to handle regular cash flow shortages, such as paying for monthly ingredient orders, purchasing seeds ahead of the growing season, or placing the order for boxes to ship out your holiday orders before you've received payments from your customers.

When shopping around for loans, consider the interest rate and loan term (which are the main factors that will affect your monthly payment), as well as any fees or penalties; refer to the terms in the previous chapter, "How It Works: Debt Concepts," for guidance. Also carefully consider the risks: if you fail to pay off your loans according to the bank's schedule, your personal assets, including your home, will be at risk. It's a good idea to discuss the risks involved with your spouse or any other family members that may be affected in the event that your business does not fare as well as you may hope and you are unable to pay back the loan. Is financing your business worth losing your home when the bank comes to collect its debt?

When evaluating whether or not to give you a mortgage loan, home equity loan, home equity line of credit, personal loan, or personal credit card, lending institutions will look at:

- The Cs of lending covered in chapter 11.
- The loan-to-value ratio: how much you want to borrow, compared to the value of your home or other collateral (or, if you do not yet own your home outright, the value of your current equity in the home). The more you want to borrow compared to the value of the collateral you put up, the higher the interest rate you can expect to pay.
- How much other debt you are carrying, including any outstanding balances on student or automobile loans.
- Your earning power. If you are planning to leave a job to run your new business full time, Ted Levinson, director of lending at RSF Social Finance, recommends taking out a home equity or personal loan while you are still employed. "It is much easier to qualify for loans with steady employment income than it is once you've joined the

ranks of the self-employed," he explains. Of course, you need to make sure you can make the payments after you have left your employer.

See chapter 14 for more details about working with banks, credit unions, and other lenders.

——— Credit Cards ———

Many entrepreneurs have financed a new business using personal credit cards. Historically, they have been the fastest and easiest way to access cash. Today there are far more financing options available to entrepreneurs, some of which are either less expensive than credit cards or do a better job of engaging your customer base or both. Make sure you consider all of your options before deciding that using personal credit cards is the way to go.

A credit card is essentially a line of credit: a bank offers you a credit limit, and you can borrow as much as you need against that limit, paying interest only on the amount you borrow. They are quite convenient, allowing you to immediately make purchases, take out sums of cash (cash advances), or even transfer balances from other creditors. You make payments against these purchases just once a month. If you pay your monthly balance on purchases in full, you can avoid paying any interest at all; in essence, you get up to a month of free credit for anything you buy with your credit card. Whether you view this as a good or a bad thing, the banks that issue credit cards like to make it easy for you to open new accounts (particularly if you have good credit to begin with), so getting started with a credit card is much easier than accessing other forms of debt. Chapter 4 outlined two different techniques for using a personal credit card to pay for business expenses; one requires you to open a separate credit card to use for business purposes, and the other requires more complicated accounting of the specific charges related to business versus personal purposes.

In 2008, Zoë Bradbury's first year of farming in a rural Oregon town near the coast, her expenses quickly outpaced her own savings. By April she found herself needing to raise another $10,000 to finance an irrigation system for her berry crops. She had expected to receive a loan through the USDA's Beginning Farmer and Rancher Program. "Based on the name of the program, I thought that would be a good fit," she remembers. Unfortunately, it turned out that she didn't qualify for a loan, since she leases, not owns, the land that she farms. Not even the fact that she was leasing the land from her family or that neither party had any plans to go anywhere could convince the USDA that this was a good investment. Even if she had been able to get a loan from one of her local banks, Zoë didn't want it at an interest rate that she figured might be near 18 percent.

Ultimately, her choice to apply for a credit card boiled down to timing. Since she'd had no idea that she wasn't going to qualify for the USDA loan, Zoë had already begun paying for the things that she needed to farm, so she found herself scrambling for cash. She successfully applied for a credit card that was offering a twelve-month interest-free promotion and started charging all farm expenses to that, including the irrigation system, hoping that she'd be able to pay off her balance before the 18.9 percent interest rate kicked in. Thankfully, her growing season and sales that year were enough to pay the bill. "It really was miraculous," she remembers. "I literally had the money to pay off the card right when the promotional period expired."

With no free credit to count on the following year, Zoë started a CSA program, collecting payment from her members before the growing season. "It makes all the difference financially to get an influx of cash at the beginning of the season, so you can make it to the time of year when cash is flowing again. Otherwise the September to June period is too long," she says. "The CSA checks start coming in at the end of February. At first we had an April 1 deadline for people to pay for their shares, but now that we're more solvent, we've moved it to May first."

Zoë was fortunate to have found a credit card offering such a generous no-interest promotion period. Given more recent economic trends, you might be hard pressed to find such a deal, particularly if you don't have good credit to begin with. Be wary of short-term promotions that offer no or very low interest for only a month or so, after which an unusually high interest rate kicks in.

When shopping around for loans or credit cards, keep in mind that your local credit union may charge members much lower rates and fees than the big multinational banks. If you are self-employed or have less than stellar credit, you may be more likely to qualify for credit from a credit union, even if banks turn you down. Credit unions are less likely to send you slick offers through the mail, so you'll have to be a little more proactive, visiting a local branch or website to discover just how much you can save by becoming a member. You can learn more about the benefits of choosing to work with credit unions in chapter 14.

—— **Peer-to-Peer Lending** ——

If you are looking to borrow $50,000 or less that you plan to pay back within one to five years, so-called peer-to-peer (or P2P) lending can be an excellent alternative to credit card debt. P2P lending occurs via online platforms that connect borrowers with lenders, and despite what the name implies, the "peers" that loan money to you are not likely to be people you know at all. In fact, an increasing number of institutional lenders are the ones putting up the money for P2P loans. The application process is no more complicated than applying for a credit card, and the interest rates can be much lower. If you have less than excellent credit, you might be able to qualify for a P2P loan even if you don't qualify for a credit card. The worse your credit, the higher your interest rate will be, but sometimes high-interest credit is better than no credit.

Since people tend to understand credit cards already, and since peer-to-peer lending is a newer (and arguably, better) debt alternative, I think it's important to describe in detail how it works. There are two major peer-to-peer lending platforms: Lending Club and Prosper. Both connect would-be borrowers with lenders who are willing to take a chance on one or more of the many loans seeking funding. To apply for a loan, you fill out an online application, and the platform checks your credit rating. If you qualify for a loan, they will assign you an interest rate based on how risky they deem your situation (which, again, is based on how other borrowers with similar credit ratings have performed in the past). Then they post the description of your loan and the financial information you provided with your application on their website, where people are constantly looking for loans to fund. If enough people choose to invest in your loan, the money is automatically deposited into your bank account (minus an origination fee), and monthly payments are collected automatically.

Compared to a credit card, you'll likely pay much lower interest rates with a peer-to-peer loan. "On average, we charge 20 to 30 percent less than with credit card alternatives," says Scott Sanborn, Lending Club's chief marketing officer, of the company's interest rates. Plus, peer-to-peer lending rates are fixed for the life of your loan, so you won't experience the kind of nasty surprises that occur when your credit card company suddenly jacks up your rates.

In addition to low, fixed interest rates, there are several other reasons peer-to-peer is an increasingly popular way to raise money for business purposes:

- **The whole process is very simple and very fast.** The initial application process takes place online, and in most cases you will know within one business day if you qualify. If all goes smoothly (i.e., you are a qualified applicant, you respond quickly to any requests for additional documentation, and your loan attracts investors), you could have your money within a week of filling out the initial application, which is a lot faster than most other forms of financing. Even if your loan takes the maximum time to fund, you'll wait only two weeks after your application and verification process is complete. "We even see some people using Lending Club as an alternative to a home equity loan," Scott says. "It doesn't make sense from a rate perspective, but if you think about the length of time it takes to apply, the number of forms you need to fill out, and the very small difference that a higher interest rate makes on a monthly payment of a few hundred dollars, ... people are saying, 'I just want to get my business started!' and going for it."

- **You don't have to put up any collateral.** "We don't require collateral, a business track record, or financial statements," says Jim Catlin, Prosper's executive vice president of acquisition and risk management. "Unlike other alternatives in small business lending, we enable entrepreneurs to get access to credit through their personal credit history."

- **You gain access to a vast pool of potential lenders.** Despite its name, the majority of peer-to-peer lending does not actually involve loans from people you know. Most people's P2P loans are funded by a number of complete strangers who are turning to P2P lending platforms as a way to access higher rates of return than they can get from other forms of investment. (Increasingly, P2P loans are being funded by institutional investors who come for the same reason.) "We even have some investors who come to Lending Club solely to invest in small businesses in their area," Scott reports.

- **Your friends, family, and other community members can invest in your loan.** Anyone who is signed up to invest in loans posted on your P2P lending platform can choose to invest in your loan, and there's no reason your contacts couldn't sign up (so long as they meet the site's guidelines). "The real value of P2P lending is we're able to connect interested investors to worthy borrowers in a way that's great for both parties," says Jim. "We love it when our borrowers invite people they know to bid on their listing," he adds. "It's a manifestation of our whole ethos of bringing community into lending, supporting small businesses and individuals."

During the early days of P2P lending, there were many more companies offering borrower and lender matchmaking services online, but when the SEC asked them to start registering their securities, many P2P sites closed up shop. Both Lending Club and Prosper register their notes (i.e., the loans that they offer on their websites) with the SEC, so you can rest assured that everything they do in their current operations is perfectly legal.

Peter Renton has been studying P2P lending since 2010 and shares his knowledge through his blog, the Lend Academy. His primary interest is encouraging more people to invest through P2P lending sites, and his insights are valuable to prospective P2P borrowers as well. "P2P is going to explode, particularly if you want to raise small amounts of money," he predicts. "Lending Club is growing tremendously," confirms Scott. "Since we started lending in 2007, the volume of loans through our site has been more than doubling every year, and in 2012 our lending volume actually tripled compared to the year before."

Tips for succeeding as a peer-to-peer lending borrower:

- **Consider using a P2P loan to improve your personal credit situation before seeking a loan for business purposes.** If you can refinance other personal debt at a lower rate than what you're currently paying to a credit card company or other lender, you'll be in a better position to qualify for additional debt for your business in the future. And you might be eligible for lower interest rates on a Prosper or Lending Club loan to refinance existing credit compared to the rate you'd get for a loan for business purposes. "Small business is inherently risky from the investor's perspective," explains Peter. P2P investors can—and do—filter the loans they consider by category, and people borrowing money in this category have defaulted at higher rates than people borrowing for other reasons, at both Lending Club and Prosper, hence the higher interest rates.
- **Submit your P2P loan application before you apply for other forms of debt.** "If you've applied for three or four loans or credit cards in the six months before you come to Prosper or Lending Club, that's a black mark on your application," Peter warns. Since potential P2P

lenders can see your credit inquiry history on your borrower profile, a high number of such inquiries can indicate that you've been turned down for credit before coming to the P2P site, which may prompt the platform to choose not to fund your loan.

- **Second (or third) time's a charm.** If you do want to borrow up to the peer-to-peer lending platform's limit, consider borrowing a smaller amount first and maxing out your second loan. Borrowers who have a perfect history of paying back their first loan on Prosper are eligible for significantly lower interest rates than first-time borrowers. "Peer-to-peer investors love to fund loans from repeat borrowers who have shown they are trustworthy," Peter observes. "You can use this to your advantage if you don't need your whole slug of money at once."

- **Tell your story effectively.** "What we find is that small business listings quickest to get funded are the ones where they share information about the type of business they're launching and provide evidence that they've thought through the business plan," Jim says. "It's not the level of detail but the logic: why they think their business is going to work and why they'll be able to pay back the loan." But it's also about telling your personal story. "Good stories foster emotional resonance," Jim says, "and more emotional resonance means you will get more lenders."

- **Don't necessarily ask for the maximum loan amount offered just because you can, especially if you are in a hurry.** Smaller loans are more likely to fund than larger ones, and you'll get a better interest rate with a smaller loan. There are exceptions to this rule per the previous tip: if you need the money, you are sure you can manage the monthly payments, and you have already been successfully paying back a loan, by all means ask for the maximum your second time around.

- **If you have anything unusual (such as delinquencies—i.e., late payments) showing in your credit history, explain them in your public profile.** In other words, explain why you were late in making payments on any historical debts, describe the steps you have taken to remedy the situation, and make a clear case for why it won't happen again. Your explanation won't necessarily help you attract investors who are automatically ignoring loans that show any questionable credit history, but it may convince investors who are handpicking their loans that yours is worth funding.

- **Publicize your loan opportunity to friends and family.** If your friends and family invest in your loan, it shows other lenders that your loan is worth checking out. You can also ask your friends and family to write recommendations for you, further encouraging other lenders who might not know you personally. Scott reports that Lending Club actually created one of the very first Facebook apps, one that allows people to promote their loan. "Not that many people seem to be that excited to talk about the fact that they're borrowing money," he notices, "but a few Lending Club borrowers have successfully funded loans to expand their operations by promoting this investment opportunity to their existing customers and community. They said, 'We'd rather pay interest to you, our customers and friends, than to the bank.'"

- **When lenders ask you questions, answer them promptly and update your profile accordingly.** Prompt responses to lenders' queries (or even "canned" questions from the platform itself) help lenders feel more comfortable lending to you, but only the person who asked can see the answer you provide. Chances are if one prospective lender asked the question, others may be wondering the same thing. This is why it works in your favor to update your profile to reflect the responses to any questions lenders have asked you.

- **Submit your P2P loan application while you can still show W2 income.** In other words, apply while you are still earning income from an employer. This maximizes your chances of qualifying on the platform at a lower interest rate.

- **Make sure you have sufficient funds in your linked bank account to make all loan payments on time.** If you do not make your payments on time or at all, this will negatively affect your credit rating, making it more difficult to access other forms of credit in the future. "If things start to go wrong and you're having trouble making your payments, contact your P2P lending platform to see about going on an adjusted payment plan," recommends Peter. Scott says that the most common fix is to change a borrower's payment date so that it falls at a more flush time of the month. "We try to work with the borrower. If that doesn't work, then we resort to a collections agency," he explains. "After four months, then your loan goes into default, … which destroys your credit record."

13

......

Loans from
Friends, Family, and Others

AFTER YOU'VE DUG AS DEEPLY as you comfortably can into your own cash reserves and personal credit, loans from friends and family are the next most likely source of debt for your business. Beyond your friends and family, other members of your community may be willing and able to make loans to support a new or growing food business, particularly one that offers goods or services they enjoy. Don't forget to consider the businesses that purchase your products, from which you purchase supplies and ingredients, or that are located near your retail location. Refer back to the list of prospects you made in chapter 7 to identify potential lenders. Remember that these same people or businesses may also be interested in making an equity investment by purchasing stock in your company; again, I suggest you read through this entire book before beginning to make your requests so that you can walk potential funders through all of their options for helping finance your business.

The first part of this chapter describes the particulars of loans that you negotiate directly, one at a time, with each of your lenders. This includes choosing an appropriate—and legal—interest rate in each case. It also covers some ways to get creative about how you offer to repay a portion of the loan principal, interest, or both, in product rather than in cash. The end of this chapter covers methods for streamlining the process of soliciting loans, including loan offerings that apply the same terms to all prospective lenders and using peer-to-peer lending platforms to raise money from your community.

Although entrepreneurs frequently use friend and family loans without complying with securities laws and don't suffer any consequences, we're now getting into territory where the securities laws covered in chapter 10 apply. There certainly are risks, and these laws were originally put into place to protect everyday investors, particularly those who don't know you or your business very well. If you need a refresher on the relevant securities laws, refer back to that chapter so you can make sure you're in compliance or at least understand the risks if you choose not to comply. As always, this book makes no attempt to provide legal advice and is not meant to replace professional counsel from an attorney or accountant.

—— Direct Loans ——

Alexis Koefoed and her husband, Eric, used to raise pastured chickens for meat and eggs at Soul Food Farm in Vacaville, California. "We turned sunlight, grass, bugs, and high-quality domestic feed into animals that lived a healthy and humane life, which then became delicious and healthy food," she says. "We are driven by the belief that you are what you eat, and what you eat eats. This informs everything we do, from the way we managed our pasture to how we managed the birds' health and the general care of the farm." In a major departure from the factory-like conditions under which most meat and egg chickens are raised, Soul Food Farm's chickens were moved around to different areas of the fifty-five-acre farm so that they could access fresh pasture during the day. "Our chickens were free to roam in fresh air and peck and take dust baths," says Alexis, adding that the chickens were kept safe from natural predators inside the mobile chicken coops at night.

In 2010 it came time to replace the original chicken coops, and Alexis figured this would cost her about $30,000. She had heard through the grapevine that the then nascent Slow Money Northern California chapter was researching the needs of local food businesses seeking financing. Someone Alexis had already spoken to about raising money introduced her formally to the group. They decided Soul Food Farm would be a good project to consider for investment because of the combination of several factors: the business was easy to understand; Alexis could explain clearly how the money would be used; she had a track record of sales and consistent customers; she was unable to access capital elsewhere; and the amount of money being requested was a good fit with the Slow Money investors' capacity to invest. Alexis wrote up a two-page summary of Soul Food Farm and its current needs, a document that included the basic elements of a business plan (see chapter 6).

Marco Vangelisti is an active supporter of sustainable food system entrepreneurs, and he brings over twenty years of experience in the realm of finance to this work. Northern California boasts one of the most active Slow Money chapters, thanks in large part to Marco's infectious enthusiasm and leadership. He has been involved in some of the most innovative approaches to capitalizing food businesses in his Northern California foodshed. His role in the Soul Food Farm story is one such example. Marco helped draft an e-mail to the Slow Money California chapter's investors letting them know that there was an opportunity to learn about Soul Food Farm's capital needs; he also made sure that this e-mail did not include a solicitation to invest, which he knew would violate securities law. It turned out several people were interested, including Marco himself, and the group gathered more information from Alexis regarding the business's operations, the potential risks it faced, and of course the financials.

Meanwhile, Alexis worked closely with a consultant to develop a simple promissory note with specific terms that she could offer interested investors. The two of them figured the process would be much smoother if Alexis presented something to the investors rather than waiting for them to make an offer; they also wanted to keep the offer as simple as possible to avoid any unnecessary work on her part. They did decide to offer investors some choices, however. People could choose to invest $2,500 or $5,000, and they could choose an interest rate within a certain range. "I set the maximum interest rate that I would accept at 6 percent," Alexis reports, "and I hoped that some of the investors would be willing to accept less than that." They also proposed a delayed start date for loan repayment. "Unlike factory-farmed chickens, whose natural cycles are disrupted with artificial lighting and hormones, pastured chickens do not lay as many eggs in the winter as they do in the summer months," Alexis explains. This made sense to Marco, who reports, "The loan was set up so that Alexis wouldn't have to start repayment until June. At that time she would have more product to sell and therefore more cash with which to repay the loan."

The consultant Alexis worked with served as an intermediary, fielding the investor questions, passing them on to Alexis, and passing her responses back to the investors. He believes this significantly reduced the amount of time Alexis needed to spend answering redundant questions. "But he was most instrumental in translating my world to the investors," Alexis says. They hosted a tour of Soul Food Farm so that the investors could see the operations for themselves and meet Alexis and her husband in person, an important gesture designed to build personal relationships between the farming couple and their prospective investors. "We walked around the property, we saw the chickens in the pasture, and we shared a meal on the farm," Marco recalls. What Alexis didn't realize is that people would be ready to write a check right then and there; fortunately, the consultant had brought his laptop on the tour, along with the promissory note files, and they quickly printed up hard copies. Alexis signed individual promissory notes with most of the investors that very afternoon. "Eventually," Marco reports, "nine of us each signed notes with Alexis, investing a total of $37,500," several thousand dollars more than she had initially asked for but money she knew she could use to improve her business without, she thought at the time, running into trouble in terms of making the monthly payments.

When you're working directly with individual friends, family, community members, or other businesses, you have the opportunity to work with each lender to agree upon terms that meet the needs of both parties. It's much easier if you can present your lenders with specific terms for them to consider, even if you are willing to negotiate with them. You need not come up with an agreement that includes all of the terms covered in chapter 11, but at the very least you will need to agree upon the principal amount of the loan, an interest rate, a payment schedule (including a payment start date), and a maturity date.

——— Choosing an Interest Rate ———

There are laws preventing interest rates above a certain limit, which vary state to state. When you're working with lenders to choose an appropriate interest rate, there are two laws to keep in mind. The first has to do with usury, or excessive interest. Every state specifies a maximum legal interest rate that can be charged for loans, and it is illegal to charge an interest rate above this limit. Sometimes there are exceptions to the general state limits. For instance, some states allow higher interest rates when the loan itself is above (or below) a certain amount, when the loan is secured with real estate, when the loan is made to a certain type of entity, for certain types of loans, and/or when the loans are for specific purposes. If you want to be sure that you're using the most up-to-date information while taking into account all available exceptions, be sure to consult an attorney or accountant.

There is no law to prevent you and your lender from choosing a very low interest rate or even an interest rate of zero (in other words, a no-interest loan). But things can get very complicated for your lender if you decide upon an interest rate below the Applicable Federal Rate, or AFR, which is set by the IRS as a benchmark for market-rate interest. In the case of below-market loans, the IRS could determine that the lender did in fact charge the difference between the chosen interest rate (known as "imputed interest") and the AFR—even if this interest was never received—and "gave it back" as a gift to the borrower. The lender would have to report this interest income on her tax return. The imputed interest may also be subject to gift taxes, depending on how much the lender has already gifted to the borrower in that calendar year and whether or not the total gifts exceed the annual gift exclusion amount (see chapter 7 for more information on gift taxes).

Your loan might qualify for one of two exceptions to these rules. If the loan in question is $10,000 or below and is between individuals (i.e., the loan is to you personally rather than to the business itself), then below-market interest rates are allowed. For loans of $100,000 or below, imputed interest laws apply only if the borrower's net investment income (as reported on her tax return) is $1,000 or less.[16]

You can also avoid any potential risk of encountering unexpected gift-tax or income-tax issues related to below-market interest rates by choosing an interest rate above the AFR published at the time the documents are signed. Check the IRS website for current AFRs, which are published monthly. As always, it would be wise to consult with an attorney or accountant on this point.

Before even beginning to negotiate an interest rate with your lenders, you need to know what you can afford to pay per your repayment schedule. If your loan is fairly simple (i.e., you'll be making monthly payments that start immediately), you can use one of the free online amortization calculators to see how your payments will change with different interest rates. Just be prepared to wade through advertisements offering mortgages. Most amortization calculators will figure your monthly payment if you provide the principal amount, the annual interest rate, and the number of payments per year. Some will allow you to specify other customizations, such as a set payment amount or a balloon payment. If you want to know exactly how much of each payment applies to interest versus principal on your loan, you'll need to find a calculator that shows you the actual amortization table or schedule.

If you expect that you'll want to tweak the details for multiple loans or test out multiple different scenarios that you want to keep for reference, search for an amortization schedule in Excel or another spreadsheet format.

Interest in Kind

At the request of certain investors, Alexis of Soul Food Farm offered interest-in-kind as an alternative to cash interest. "Most of the investors chose a flat payment schedule, which means that I credit their PayPal accounts by the same amount every month for the term of the loan, [with] each payment covering both interest and a portion of the principal at the same time," she explains. "But some of them take their interest in the form of chicken meat or eggs." Arno Hesse (see chapter 8 for more information about the Credibles crowdfunding platform he helped develop) loves to eat good eggs; he and Alexis calculated that the value of his monthly interest payment was roughly equivalent to the value of two dozen eggs, so he collected a dozen every other week from Soul Food Farm rather than cash interest.

If you want to offer your investors the option of taking interest payments in the form of product, here are a few decisions you will have to work through:

- **What types of interest and/or principal repayment options will be available?** Will you offer your investors a choice of interest in cash or interest in product or just one or the other? If you do offer a choice, will you offer a discount for choosing interest in product? (As with any debt offering, you will need to choose a basic interest rate or a range of rates from which your lenders can choose.)
- **How will you determine the value of the product offered as interest payments?** You have several options here: you can offer product at the retail price at the time you sign the agreement, the retail price at the time the "interest" is delivered, or at a discount over either price.
- **How flexible is the interest payment schedule?** If your products are available only seasonally, how will you handle paying interest during times when you have no product to offer?
- **How will all parties keep track of what has been paid?** You should include the value of the interest in kind in the 1099 reporting form you will submit to the lender at the end of the calendar year, though the onus is on your investor to report all interest income, whether received in the form of cash or product, on her tax return.

- **How will the interest in kind be collected or delivered?** You can specify in your agreement that the investor must pick up interest at your place of business or at one of your farmers' markets' locations, for instance. Depending on your stomach for adding degrees of complication, you may be able to work with one of your wholesale customers to hold investors' interest-in-kind payments on your behalf, particularly if they see value in having people stopping in regularly and shopping while they collect their interest. Alexis worked out this sort of arrangement with a couple of her wholesale customers.

The interconnected financial relationships that Alexis fostered between her farm, her investors, and her wholesale customers show that the sky is the limit when it comes to structuring loan terms. Unfortunately, even the most creative credit arrangements cannot fully protect against the risks of doing business. In July 2012, after having faced months of rising feed prices thanks to the drought in the Midwest, Alexis and Eric decided to shut down their chicken operation. "In hindsight, I think the Slow Money Northern California investors and I would agree that we didn't talk enough about the 'what if' scenario if things went wrong," Alexis says, adding that they could have spent more time talking about what she calls "hard truths," or all the different pieces of the puzzle that must be in place for farming to be successful. "Crop failures, the unexpected, the fight for price points in the market," she lists; "farmers have to deal with things of that nature."

And this is where the importance of fostering strong personal relationships really comes to the fore. Alexis never would have received these loans without the sense of shared trust that had developed. She and her investors are working out arrangements to modify their loans as she shifts the farm's attention to lavender and olive oil production, and she is doing everything possible to honor their good faith. "Even though I have stopped raising chickens, I take these loans very seriously, and I am paying everyone back," she explains, grateful that "they have been very patient with me while I get back on my feet." Alexis suspects that Soul Food Farm may one day return to the egg and poultry business, but as a part of a more diversified farm business that is less susceptible to shifting conditions in one sector. "This was really a reality check on the risks of investing in this space," Marco says. Arno agrees, noting that he believes Alexis will make good on her loans, but it may take longer than initially expected.

"Funding for food businesses is not all sunshine," he says. "There are risks. But we're learning how to make it work."

—— Formalizing Direct Loans ——

There are many benefits to ensuring that your friends, family, or other individual lenders understand—and can easily review—the exact terms, payment schedule, payment dates, and current balance remaining on loans they have made. Formally documenting the loan and having a good tracking system in place clears up potential misunderstandings before they arise, maximizing the likelihood that you will stay friends with your friends and avoid any loan-related awkwardness at family gatherings. When it comes to soliciting lenders in the first place, having these systems in place may give your prospective creditors more confidence that you are serious about paying back your loan in a timely manner. A good loan-tracking system will save you time and energy, too, reducing the amount of record-keeping work you have to do to ensure that you're paying back your loans on schedule. On the flip side, if you do not carefully document all activity associated with your loans, there is the risk that the IRS will unfairly tax your lender for money that was never actually lent to you or have the lender pay taxes on interest she never received. To complicate matters further, the IRS could view your loan as a gift if you haven't tracked repayments, potentially subjecting your lenders to gift laws.

To formally document a loan, you draft and sign formal documents that outline the various details of the loan that you and your lender have agreed upon. Remember that you personally, not the business, may be specified as the borrower. Especially when you are just getting started, friends, family, and others may be more willing to give you a personal loan rather than making a loan to the business.

You can document very simple loans (relatively small amount, fixed interest rate, simple repayment schedule with equal payments, no collateral) with a promissory note. In order to fill out a promissory note, you'll need to identify the lender and the borrower and specify the principal loan amount, the annual interest rate, the payment start date, the final payment due date (maturity date), the number of monthly payments, the amount of each payment, the payment method (e.g., check, online transfer, cash), and the length of the grace period for late payments.

If the loan is large or the terms are more complicated, you will need to draft a full loan agreement in addition to the promissory note. Again, both parties need to sign this document. This would be the case if you plan to include representations and warranties, covenants, events of default, or guarantees, for instance (see chapter 11 for explanations of these terms and how they might affect you as the borrower). You will also need a loan agreement if the loan is secured (i.e., you plan to offer certain assets as collateral). In the case of a secured loan, make sure to check your county and state for any filing requirements related to collateral.

The Finance for Food website offers free promissory notes and loan agreement forms that you can use to document your loans. There are also several online services that document and keep track of friends and family loans, including LendingKarma, LoanBack, LendFriend, and ZimpleMoney. Depending on the company and which of their services you choose, they'll help you do everything from create simple loan forms such as promissory notes, create more complicated loan documents with custom terms, calculate repayment and amortization schedules, send you automatic reminders when loan payments are due (and e-mail lenders when you've made payments), and keep records of all activity related to the loan. The free and least expensive plans usually cover self-service creation of basic loan forms. ZimpleMoney is slightly different from the other services mentioned above in that it allows you to automate the payment, collection, and management of financial agreements that you have already documented (by yourself, using another service, or with an attorney).

If you do choose to use one of the aforementioned services, for each loan you set up, expect to pay a flat-rate setup fee (fees vary based on the platform; some charge different fees based on the amount of the loan) and possibly also a monthly fee. ZimpleMoney also charges fees for automated payments, such as setup fees and monthly or "per transaction" fees (i.e., if you make monthly payments, you would incur one "per transaction" fee each month). Either the borrower or the lender has to pay these fees. It may be worth it to the lender to pay a little extra for the peace of mind of loan documentation, tracking, and automated collection. Or you may choose to cover these fees as a gesture of goodwill toward your lender. Since the fees for these services are for the most part independent of the size of the loan, you may decide that these services are worthwhile only for larger loans.

It is important to note that while loan tracking and automated collection systems make documenting a loan much easier, you and your lenders may also want to hire an attorney to verify that all the specifics of your loan documentation are consistent with both your state's loan regulations and the tax preferences of your lender.

—— Loan Offerings ——
and Other Streamlined Debt Approaches

There are certain downsides to negotiating multiple direct loans from friends, family, or other community members. Although you do have a lot of flexibility when it comes to structuring each loan, it may seem like a hassle to you and your lenders to figure out all the details. Even when you can reach agreement about terms, you could find yourself in a position of documenting and tracking several loans, each with different terms, which might become a distraction from the hard work of actually taking your business to the next level. If you want to offer multiple lenders the same terms, consider drawing up a single loan offering and recruiting people to lend to you at the terms you specify. Don't forget to refer back to the laws covered in chapter 10 to make sure you're complying with the appropriate securities regulations, whether you choose to go with a private or public offering.

If the disclosures and costs required for a private loan offering or direct public offering are too much, there is a much simpler if less flexible option. Peer-to-peer lending platforms do save you the time and trouble of having to work through the details of direct loans from friends and family with a lot less hassle, but you'll also have a lot less control over the terms, repayment schedule, and the type of loan. As described in chapter 12, the P2P lending platform chooses the interest rate for you. Although not as up close and personal as direct loans, this streamlined approach might be preferable to you—and to the people who could lend you money, particularly if you're finding it hard to agree on an interest rate. Another advantage is that P2P lending lets you raise debt not only from people you know but from anyone who finds your loan on the P2P lending website.

14

······

Take It to the Bank . . .
or to Another Commercial Lender

AS YOU'VE PROBABLY GATHERED from the stories featured so far, it's really difficult to get a bank loan when you're first starting a food business. But that doesn't mean that you should give up on commercial debt altogether. To begin with, not all banks are the same. Furthermore, there are several alternatives to banks, known as (surprise!) alternative lenders.

When you're just getting started, borrowing from a microlender or revolving community loan program might be a better fit. An increasing number of organizations offer loan programs specifically for farmers or other food entrepreneurs, either those that are just getting started or those that are expanding. Later on you might consider bank credit, but don't forget credit unions, which can offer much better rates. It's even possible that your customers or vendors might have credit or loan programs designed to serve businesses like yours. The trick is knowing which lenders are likely to consider lending to your food business and which steps to take to maximize your chances of successfully accessing credit.

The first section in this chapter covers tips for working with commercial lenders in general, and the following sections cover the different types of lenders and how to find one.

Although I have organized the chapter by categories of lenders, note that the lines between them are not hard and fast. For instance, many CDFIs and all Farm Credit programs are in fact credit unions. You'll also notice that many of the federal programs listed in chapter 15 behave a lot like the microcredit or commercial lending programs covered in this chapter because these are in fact the lenders that administer these programs on behalf of the federal government. The bottom line, as always, is to consider all of your options and go with the ones that make the most sense for you and your business.

—— Tips ——
for Working with Commercial Lenders

When seeking commercial credit, you should first identify a short list of potential lending institutions in your area that seem like a good fit based on the descriptions in this chapter. Chapter 11 covered the importance of character when it comes to finding credit. If you or other family members already have a relationship with a specific bank or credit union, whether it's from personal or business banking experience, approach those institutions first for your lending needs. You can also consider opening business accounts at a lending institution that seems appropriate for your future lending needs before you actually need a loan so that you can start to get to know people there. At any stage of this process, you can visit a lender in person to ask questions and begin making a personal impression, but this will obviously be easier if the office is close to you.

You'll need to study each lender's website and talk to an actual person there to determine if your business is in their sweet spot. Take care to find a lender that specializes in loans or credit of the appropriate type and magnitude before going through the entire loan application process. Not all lenders like to make all sizes of loans, and if you need a $75,000 loan, it doesn't make sense to invest a lot of time and energy into building a relationship with lenders that, regardless of what it says on their websites, really only make loans of half a million dollars or more. Likewise, you don't want to ask for a working capital line of credit at an institution that concentrates on real estate lending for business. If you can find one, you'll have an easier time working with a lender that has experience working with socially responsible food businesses similar to yours. Otherwise, expect extra scrutiny into certain details of your business plan. For instance, be ready to explain why your cost of goods sold is higher than for conventional businesses they have more experience with, and be able to show evidence for the higher margins you expect to be able to achieve with your differentiated products.

While you're searching for a lender that's a good fit, begin compiling the information you'll need to fill out credit applications, which are notoriously time-consuming to complete. Many of the people I interviewed for this book mentioned the mountains of paperwork required, particularly for bank loans, so the more legwork you can do ahead of time, the better. If the loan application is easy to get hold of online or in person, go through each lender's application as completely as you can, noting any questions you have about it. If it asks for any documents you don't already have prepared, start putting those together. The applications will probably ask for personal and business financial statements, credit reports and tax returns, your business plan (make sure to include an executive summary and clearly state what you intend to use the loan for), accounts receivable or sales contracts and accounts payable, incorporation documents and business licenses, leases, and any other contracts. If you're working with an agricultural lender, it doesn't hurt to prepare a copy of your crop plan as well. Ask any vendors or service providers that offer you credit terms if you can use them as trade references. If you do business with a company that is a current client of a particular lender or if you personally know someone who has a relationship with a lender, ask if she would be willing to serve as a character reference.

Only after you've determined which lenders are most likely to work with you should you start actually filling out the applications. It doesn't hurt to make an appointment to talk to a lender in person to answer any of your questions, but don't miss this opportunity to make a good impression. Have as much as you can already in order to clearly demonstrate that you are on top of things. Showing up promptly with an application that is mostly filled out and a concise list of questions is much better than showing up with a completely blank application and no supporting documents and asking, "So how do I fill this thing out?" When your credit application package is complete, definitely make an appointment to present it in person. You may even want to prepare a brief presentation or slide deck. See chapter 16 for some tips on making presentations, but keep in mind that lenders tend to be more numbers oriented than story oriented. If you have packaged products, you can bring along samples.

Once you have submitted a completed application package, you may be asked to submit additional information. The lender may send someone to do a site visit to your home or place of business to inspect your operations and assets you have pledged as collateral. The lender's underwriters will use all of this information to determine whether or not they will give you credit and, if so, how much and at what interest rate. This will all depend

APPLY FOR CREDIT BEFORE YOU NEED IT

///

Don't underestimate the power of timing when it comes to applying for credit. If you wait until you actually need the money, you can find yourself in trouble for a few reasons. For one, applying for credit takes time— either to apply for credit or to wait for lenders to respond —which you might not have if you're also trying to manage a cash flow crisis. Perhaps more important, when cash is tight, your financial statements won't be as strong, and you'll be less likely to qualify for credit. If you are in a good financial position and anticipate needing credit in the future, start the application process as soon as you can. If your business follows seasonal patterns, apply for credit when you're in a position of financial strength to present the best face to potential lenders.

on your personal credit rating, the business model itself, the strength of your collateral, the experience of the people running the business, or other aspects of your "Cs of lending," as outlined in chapter 11. If you have more than one offer, fantastic! You'll have the opportunity to choose the credit terms that are most favorable for you. Don't forget about the values you identified in chapter 2; the "cheapest" loan might not necessarily be the best one. Consider what type of organization your interest and fees are supporting, what kind of fit the lender might be for your future capital needs as your company evolves, and what kind of relationship you can expect to have with the person who will be working with you over the life of your credit relationship.

—— Microfinance ——

For many people, the concept of microfinance conjures up images of small loans made to the very poor in developing countries. Indeed, the practice of making such loans overseas has been a powerful force to lift people, particularly women, out of poverty. But the formula also works closer to home, though in this country microfinance—also known as microlending or microcredit—usually refers to loans of up to $50,000. When your business is just getting started, a microloan can make a huge difference, so a microlender is likely to be your first stop for a business loan. "It all begins with micro," says Claudia Viek, CEO of the California Association for Micro Enterprise Opportunity (CAMEO), which has over 160 members that provide assistance to very small businesses; those with with five or fewer employees are sometimes known as microenterprises. CAMEO's members include lenders, training programs, job creators, agencies, and individuals dedicated to furthering microbusiness development in California. "Eighty-five percent of businesses [in the United States] have fewer than five employees, and self-employment is now a significant labor market trend," Claudia reports. "Also, 97 percent of all businesses in rural America are micro, and the vast majority of those are solo entrepreneurs."

Most commercial lenders choose not to make microloans, and it's hard to blame them. No matter how big or small the loan, a lender has to go through the trouble of determining whether or not the borrower will be able to repay the money owed, and that takes time and energy. Every loan requires the same amount of energy to evaluate, so most lenders prefer to make larger loans. Not only is this more efficient for them, but there's a financial incentive: lenders collect more interest over time for larger loans. So what are you supposed to do if you need to borrow $50,000 or less? Microlenders to the rescue!

Microlenders will check your credit score to see if they are willing to lend you money, though acceptable scores can be much lower than those that banks or other commercial lenders would consider. This is good news for people with little credit history or low scores. In addition to the capital itself, microlending organizations, many of which are nonprofits, usually provide a range of support services, such as business and credit assistance. Thanks to growing recognition of the role that very small businesses play in generating jobs and boosting the economy, new programs are making it easier for lending institutions to make microloans. As a result, more and more entrepreneurs are tapping into this source of financing, which is a great fit for home-based businesses and other early-stage food ventures that don't need a lot of capital to grow.

In addition to general microbusiness support organizations (see the Resources chapter), more and more agricultural organizations have begun to offer microloan programs, either on their own or in partnership with one or more commercial lenders. These programs usually serve a single state or a small geographic area and, like most microlenders, often provide a range of services in addition to capital. Examples include the Carrot Project (serving farmers and farm-related businesses in Maine, Vermont, the Greater Berkshires—Dutchess and Columbia Counties in New York, Litchfield County in Connecticut, and Berkshire County in Massachusetts), Financing Ozarks Rural Growth and Economy (serving individuals, small businesses, and small farms in Northwest and North-Central Arkansas), the California FarmLink, the New Mexico Farmers' Marketing Association (in association with the Permaculture Guild and Permaculture Credit Union), and the Maine Organic Farmers and Gardeners Association. The Equity Trust loan program considers applications from projects nationwide that assist in the permanent protection of land and/or buildings for agriculture, affordable housing, community economic development, or other community needs; support the economic vitality of CSA farms or the economic success of projects protecting the affordability and use of land and/or buildings for community benefit; or directly or indirectly enable land reform and promote alternative ownership models. The easiest way to find out about agricultural microloan programs in your area is to ask your local Extension agent or contact local organizations that serve farmers.

As of this writing, the USDA had also launched a new microloan program for farmers and ranchers through its Farm Service Agency (FSA). For more information about working with federal programs, refer to chapter 15.

—— CDFIs ——

Community development financial institutions (CDFIs) are specialized financial institutions that work in market niches that most financial institutions ignore. They provide a range of financial products and services in economically distressed or low-income areas, including commercial loans and investments to small start-up or expanding businesses. There are over eight hundred CDFIs nationwide that are certified by the CDFI Fund, a division of the U.S. Department of the Treasury that works to ensure that all people have access to affordable credit, capital, and financial services. According to the Opportunity Finance Network, a national network of CDFIs, they are "100 percent dedicated to delivering responsible, affordable lending to help low-income, low-wealth, and other disadvantaged people and communities join the economic mainstream."[17] If you fall into one or more of these categories or if you or your business is located in a distressed area, start your credit search with a CDFI. Even if the first one you contact is not a good fit, they should be able to refer you to other institutions that can help.

CDFIs can be community development banks, community development credit unions, community development loan funds, community development venture capital funds, microenterprise development loan funds, and community development corporations. Although few CDFIs have experience specific to food businesses, this is changing for the better. In 2010, as part of the Healthy Food Financing Initiative (HFFI), the CDFI Fund began a program to provide specialized training and technical assistance to CDFIs seeking to finance grocery stores and other businesses that deliver healthy food options to food deserts. The program was based on the success of the Reinvestment Fund in Philadelphia, which (among its other programs) provides financing for supermarkets, grocery stores, and other healthy food retail operators that plan to operate in underserved communities where infrastructure costs and credit needs cannot be solely filled by conventional financial institutions. Nessa Richman of Brightseed Strategies played a role in designing the first training and education program to help CDFI leaders understand how to best serve entrepreneurs in the healthy food space. "In the first year there was a series of eight workshops. When the invitation went out for the first workshop, more than double the number of CDFI leaders applied than the workshop could hold," she reports. "Those that did attend represented a wide array of types of CDFIs from around the country."

In 2012 HFFI awarded a number of CDFIs a total of $25 million. This is a very modest amount of money when you consider the vast needs for financing food-based businesses around the country, and the scope of financing that other programs provide; Farm Credit, for instance, provides $225 billion in financing annually across the country to producers alone. Still, it is encouraging to see an entirely new federal agency show an interest in supporting food financing. "There is a wide scope for CDFIs and their partners to use these funds to finance the full spectrum of healthy food system enterprises, from farms and ranches to food hubs to direct-to-consumer retail venues, like CSAs and buying clubs," Nessa explains. "These funds are not limited to finance of conventional retail stores by any means." Like many other people who have been working on this effort, she is hopeful that in the future every interested CDFI will be able to access training and financial resources to help them provide better services to food-based businesses. "CDFIs that are part of HFFI want to see projects that have both an economic benefit to low-income communities and that provide better access to healthy food to low-income individuals," Nessa advises. "If you can hit both of those, then you can be more attractive to them."

The CDFI Fund maintains a searchable database of certified CDFIs that have received funding from the CDFI Fund; you can even limit your search to CDFIs that have received funding through HFFI. Alternately, you can download a full list of certified CDFIs by state. If you're looking for resources and capital for food businesses and other projects in Native communities, the First Nations Oweesta Corporation (http://www.oweesta .org/) can connect you to Native CDFIs (plus other financial organizations that are in the process of getting their certification) and other tools for Native community development.

—— Credit Unions ——

Samantha and Ian of Emmy's Organics (we heard more of their story in chapter 9) had always had an account at the local branch of a federal credit union. "A lot of the people there had seen how fast our business had grown. When we first started, they let us do a little tasting demo in the credit union lobby," she remembers. "They made us the business of the month; that was in the very beginning. And we know people from the community that work there." Samantha and Ian had reached the point where they were hand-scooping more than sixty thousand macaroons a month—between two and three thousand per day—using little ice-cream scoops. "We were always racing to see who could go faster! Ian got carpal tunnel syndrome. We thought, 'We can't ever ask an employee to do that,'" Samantha recalls. "How were we ever going to grow?"

They were able to show, between their financials and their growth trajectory and their plans, how a forming machine would make a huge difference in their ability to generate additional revenues. All they needed was a $20,000 loan. "They did ask us to have someone cosign the loan," Samantha explains, "so Ian's mom was our cosigner. It's great because we're building good credit for our business by making our payments every month." The whole process felt comfortable because they were already familiar with the institution, and having the local connections made it much more approachable. Samantha says she and Ian will absolutely consider approaching the same credit union again for a loan, possibly for a new packaging machine next time.

Credit unions are cooperatively run, not-for-profit organizations that are owned and managed by their members. This allows them to offer higher interest rates on deposit accounts and lower interest rates on loans than banks.

Membership eligibility varies depending on the credit union, but for most you must show that you live or work in the area or organization that the credit union serves. A small deposit finalizes your membership, and then you can access the credit union's services. You can also vote on credit union issues.

After the events of the fall of 2008 and the subsequent economic fallout, many people mobilized to move their money out of the too-big-to-fail banks and into local credit unions, arguing that while big banks prioritize their own profits, credit unions focus on the needs of their members. The logic is that anyone can vote for their values with their dollars, literally moving their checking and savings accounts away from institutions that serve their shareholders and into organizations that serve their communities. In addition to checking and savings accounts, many credit unions offer business loans and other credit services. The downsides to credit unions for credit-seeking entrepreneurs is that if they do offer business lending services at all, they likely do not offer as many different options as banks, and credit union online banking options tend to be a little less sophisticated than banks', making administration a bit less convenient for you. But what credit unions do offer usually comes at much better rates than what you can find at a bank. It is also possible that a credit union will give you a business loan even if your credit rating is not quite stellar, something a bank is less likely to do; during the post-2008 recession, credit unions increased their lending even as big banks reduced theirs. Credit unions are also more likely to make "smaller" loans (i.e., loans less than $1 million). If supporting your local community is important to you, a local credit union is the way to go.

—— Farm Credit ——

If you're a farmer, rancher, producer, or harvester of aquatic products—or a cooperative of one of the above—and are looking for a traditional loan, the Farm Credit System (Farm Credit) may be your best bet. Chartered by the federal government in 1916 to lend to agricultural producers, Farm Credit consists of eighty-four locally owned, independently operated farm credit cooperatives—commercial lenders—across the country. Farm Credit's sole reason for being is to provide financial services and make capital available for farmers, ranchers, and their value-added agricultural ventures at competitive rates. Farm Credit also provides financing for purchasing rural homes, communication, and energy and water infrastructures and to support agricultural exports.

And they handle quite a bit of the lending in this space. "Farm Credit provides about 40 percent of all commercial ag financing, including loans to smaller operations. Half of all the loans in Farm Credit's portfolio are for less than $50,000, and 88 percent of them are for $250,000 or less, so we really are a small farm lender," says Gary Matteson, vice president of Farm Credit's Young, Beginning, and Small Farmer Programs and Outreach. "Farm Credit makes over sixty thousand new loans, totaling $10 billion, every year to farmers who have fewer than ten years of operating their own farm. By comparison," he continues, "USDA's FSA Beginning Farmer loan program annually originates about fifteen thousand loans totaling $2.5 billion."

Every local Farm Credit Association is cooperatively owned and operated by the farmers and ranchers it serves, which means that every borrower is an owner and has a stake in the system. This is good news if you don't like the thought of paying interest to some big bank. Farm Credit's ownership structure and mission also affect how they're willing to work with their borrowers. "Farm Credit loan officers will brag about how long they were able to stick with a farmer that was going through a rough patch," Gary explains. "You'll hear stories like this one: That farmer had a total crop failure and was able to continue farming because Farm Credit worked with her to figure out how to reschedule payment of her loans over a longer period of time."

Farm Credit is an excellent option for newer or smaller-scale operations that may have difficulty getting credit from other lending institutions. Every local Farm Credit lender has a Young, Beginning, and Small Farmer Program designed to meet the unique needs of farmers who are thirty-five years old or younger, have ten years or fewer of farming experience, and/or whose operations produce less than $250,000 annually. Gary says, "There is technically no minimum size for a Farm Credit loan, but a farmer seeking a small loan should recognize that as a cooperative Farm Credit is interested in establishing a long-term working relationship and not just a quick transaction." Farm Credit also works with larger agriculture-related ventures. For instance, they finance some of the largest agricultural cooperatives in the country, such as Sunkist and Ocean Spray. On this larger side of the spectrum, loans can run into the hundreds of millions of dollars, often in cooperation with commercial banks.

Like all institutional lenders, Farm Credit loan officers may use a score-card process to determine whether or not to give you the loan. This quick method will consider factors such as your credit record, revenue history, and length of time as a homeowner. For loans that depend on repayment from farm business operations, how much of their own money borrowers propose to invest becomes important. "The local Farm Credit Association's Young and Beginning Farmer Program may allow a reduced amount of owner's equity to give a break to those just starting out who haven't had time to build up their savings. That might mean if the typical borrower has to put up 30 percent equity, the young/beginning farmer may only be asked to put up 25 percent," Gary explains. "But recognize that some types of farm businesses, such as dry-land wheat farming, are inherently riskier and may require 50 or 60 percent equity."

Farm Credit and commercial banks often work closely with USDA's FSA to improve the credit quality rating of a loan by seeking a loan guarantee from FSA's Beginning Farmer loan program. FSA loan guarantees are something that the lender, not the farmer, applies for. Even though you may not apply for an FSA loan guarantee yourself, you should ask your lender if you are eligible and if getting a guarantee will help you get the loan.

They'll also carefully review your business plan. "We're doing a lot more outreach to sustainable farmers and those that are doing nontraditional, smaller-scale, and more diversified agriculture," Gary reports. "In some places, such as the Northeast, we're already working with a lot of organic, sustainable, and direct retail farmers." But this is not universally true, so you need to be prepared for the likelihood that the loan officer you encounter may be unfamiliar with some of the more innovative business models that are at the forefront of the sustainable food movement.

Banks

Banks are usually the first lenders that people think of when they need credit, but you can't just walk to the nearest one and expect it to be the right lender for you. As I mentioned earlier in this chapter, not all banks are the same, so you'll need to do your homework to find a bank that's a good fit, if a bank is even the best option. There are several factors that make working with traditional banks, particularly the larger ones, challenging. The big national (and even multinational) banks prefer making larger loans. "Lenders actually think $250,000 and under is a small loan!" says Rebecca Thistlethwaite in her book *Farms with a Future: Creating and Growing a Sustainable Farm Business*. Their strict lending policies mean that it's harder for them to be flexible to accommodate your needs, especially if your credit rating isn't fantastic. Even if you find a sympathetic person in your local office, they'll still likely have to forward your loan application to a regional or national office. There's nothing worse than being weeks into the process, only to learn that the regional office rejected your application. Ask up front how frequently the bank makes loans or extends lines of credit of the size you're looking for before you waste too much time. You can also ask whether the underwriters in your branch are the ones making the ultimate decisions or whether they need to run things by another office.

Smaller, locally owned community banks, if there are any left in your area that haven't been purchased by larger banks, have many of the same characteristics of local credit unions. Depending on the banks, these can include a willingness to make smaller loans, more flexibility with loan terms, lower fees and interest rates for credit (and higher interest rates for deposits), and a commitment to supporting local businesses and other local causes. Compared to credit unions, they may offer a wider range of business services, and their online banking systems are likely more sophisticated. The Independent Community Bankers of America website features a community bank locator: http://www.icba.org/consumer/BankLocator.

Given the trend of consolidation in the banking industry, however, there is no guarantee that your small local bank will stay that way, which can be a problem. I spoke to one food business owner who had a loan from a small, community bank that ended up being bought by a larger, national one, which had different lending policies. When the new bank decided to terminate his loan, he quickly had to come up with an alternative.

Particularly in rural communities, many banks have specific programs for farmers or other agricultural businesses, though the types and sizes of farm businesses they specialize in vary. Very few banks focus on socially responsible or green businesses, but one such institution is New Resource Bank in San Francisco, which supports local food systems and lends only to businesses that commit to improving the sustainability of their operations.

—— RSF Social Finance ——

"Today's capital markets can be described as complex, opaque, and anonymous, based on short-term outcomes," says Don Shaffer, president and CEO of RSF Social Finance. "But along with our many partners, we are working to create a world where financial transactions are direct, transparent, and personal—based on long-term relationships." Don leads an organization that isn't quite a bank, isn't quite a credit union, isn't technically a CDFI, and isn't exactly like any other lending institution I've ever encountered. And if you're looking for a commercial lender that has a deep social mission in its very DNA, you need to know about it. RSF is a pioneering nonprofit financial services organization dedicated to transforming the way the world works with money. In partnership with a community of investors and donors, RSF provides capital to nonprofit and for-profit social enterprises addressing key issues in three focus areas: food and agriculture, education and the arts, and ecological stewardship. (Full disclosure: I worked there for three years and continue to invest in their Social Investment Fund.)

RSF's social enterprise lending program offers mortgage loans, construction loans, equipment loans, and working capital lines of credit, ranging from $200,000 to $5 million. RSF also offers mezzanine finance for businesses seeking growth capital. Borrowers must meet strict social criteria related to the organization's management structure, the products and services offered (including how they are made and packaged), workforce relations along the entire supply chain, and existing capital partners; all must reveal a commitment to social good and environmental sustainability. For-profit borrowers generally have $1 million or more in annual revenues, plus three or more years of operating history, strong collateral, and excellent repayment history on any debts and are either profitable or can show a path to profitability in the next twelve months.

In addition to capital, RSF provides their lenders with technical support and connections through their deep relationships in the fields of finance and social enterprise (they have financially supported many of the networks mentioned in chapter 1 since those networks came into being). In an unprecedented demonstration of both transparency and a commitment to fostering community, rather than calculate interest rates based on obscure international banking benchmarks (as most commercial lenders do), RSF convenes quarterly meetings of borrowers, RSF staff, and RSF investors to discuss how rates affect all three parties. They also include a list of all their borrowers on their website (try getting that list from any other lender!). I cannot recommend RSF highly enough. Tell them I sent you.

——— Whole Foods Market ———
Local Producer Loan Program

In some cases your biggest customer might be the lender you are looking for. Many socially responsible food businesses hope that one day Whole Foods Market will pick up their products, and this benchmark is often a turning point in a food company's growth process. Recognizing that access to capital is an issue for many of their suppliers, and as part of their interest in supporting local producers, this national retailer introduced the Whole Foods Market Local Producer Loan Program (LPLP) in 2006. "We found there are a lot of small companies with wonderful products, and we want to bring those products to market," says Heather Kennedy, senior administrator of the Whole Foods Market LPLP. "We saw this program as fitting exactly the need of our vendors, who need straightforward, easy financing," she continues. "Our LPLP takes down the barriers and layers of bureaucracy that other financing methods might have." If you already have a relationship with a Whole Foods Market regional buyer and offer a product that is unique and local to your region, if you need money for a capital expenditure rather than working capital, and if you have equipment that you can put down as collateral, a loan from the Whole Foods Market LPLP might be a good match for you.

Gene Mealhow is one food entrepreneur who was able to take advantage of this unique program. In the early 1990s Gene was working as a consultant helping farmers implement more sustainable practices when he encountered a very rare variety of popcorn. The farmer who had hired Gene to help him improve his yields suspects that the Native Americans who lived near Cedar Rapids, Iowa, had introduced the variety to his great-great-great-grandfather when he settled in the area in the 1850s, but nobody knows for sure where it came from. Its kernels are tiny, and when they are popped the tough hull all but disintegrates, making it easier to eat and digest than other varieties of popcorn. It is also harder to propagate, grow, and process than other varieties, and besides the farmer Gene was helping, hardly anyone was interested in this heritage popcorn. A few years later, however, Gene and his wife, Lynn, launched a business to bring Tiny But Mighty Popcorn to the public and rescue this rare treasure from obscurity.

In the beginning Gene and his wife got Tiny But Mighty Popcorn into the local Hy-Vee and Fairway grocery stores, but they always saw Whole Foods as a huge opportunity. "We thought, 'We're non-GMO; we're a local farm; we fit with their philosophy; we're a great match," Gene says. "So we put together these nice little sample packets, which included popcorn and information about what we do, our customers' testimonials, and things like that, and sent them out to the offices of all eight Whole Foods regions. And we got eight of the nicest rejection letters you've ever seen in your life!"

Not being the kind of person to take no for an answer, Gene tried contacting individual Whole Foods stores in the Chicago area. When he finally got someone from the Willowbrook store on the phone, Gene says, "I told him, 'I know Whole Foods is supposed to get local products from local farmers,' and he said, 'I tell you what: I'll give you a shot.'" The Whole Foods buyer said he'd put Tiny But Mighty Popcorn on the shelf, and if it sold, he'd buy more. If it didn't, Gene would have to buy it back. "So we mailed him three cases, and maybe ten days later he called back, asking for three more," Gene reports. "I told him I'd bring him ten cases! I said I'd drive into Chicago and do an in-store demo until I sold five cases, and then I'd leave five with him. He says, 'That's great. What day are you coming?'"

Gene sold five cases in three hours the day he did the demo in the Willowbrook store, and the buyer not only bought the other five cases but also told Gene to take a case to "his buddy" in the nearby Yountville store. "That guy also tells me it's the best popcorn! He offers to buy a few cases, and I offered to do demos," Gene says. That summer Gene and his son did demos all across Chicago, showcasing and selling not only their own brand but also Whole Foods' own 365 brand oil and 365 brand salt. "You have to have good demo people that really talk about your product. Plus I'll tell customers that I love working with Whole Foods because they support me as a farmer," says Gene. "You keep pushing the whole package, and you are creating a win-win situation for Whole Foods. They *love* that." Soon Tiny But Mighty Popcorn was selling so well that Gene and his wife started using a distributor to get their product to Whole Foods and other grocery stores.

In 2009 Gene had a booth set up at a children's event and met Jim Slama of FamilyFarmed.org (see chapter 1). Jim agreed that there was something compelling about Tiny But Might Popcorn. He decided to help Gene and Lynn take the company to the next level, and with Jim's help they developed a new business plan, which included an expanded production facility and plans for popped and flavored products in addition to kernels that customers pop at home. This is when Gene started looking into the Whole Foods LPLP, six years after his relationship with the retailer began.

When he first applied, Gene had heard that a lot of people approach Whole Foods without really understanding how that business operates. "People looking at LPLP should do a little research on Whole Foods to really understand how their business model works. Where I learned a lot about how to approach them is by talking to the grocery buyer. Talk to whatever buyer is in the department that your product would be in," he suggests. Heather agrees, saying, "If you are already a Whole Foods vendor, talk to your buyer to learn more about the LPLP and the application process." Because each of the twelve regions manages its own loan program separately, the details of each program are unique, though Heather says the average loan size is about $50,000, and the average interest rate is about 5 percent. "We really try to cover capital expenditures rather than marketing, demo costs, or first production runs," she says, "and we prefer to take equipment as collateral. We won't use land as collateral because we would never put someone in a position to possibly give up their farm."

When you apply to the Whole Foods Market LPLP, be prepared to submit a business plan and the usual financial statements. "Touch on all the points that match up with their marketing and business philosophies," Gene suggests. "They support companies that make money for them." According to Heather, they also like to make loans to vendors who meet the higher tiers of Whole Foods' quality standards. "For example, we have a program to help customers identify ratings of animal products and animal welfare where a vendor will get a certain number of stars out of five," she explains. "One of the loans we're most proud of was to a North Carolina pork producer who was able to get to five stars through using an LPLP loan to process his pork on site. He was the first to get to five stars." The program offered Gene a $25,000 loan at 5.9 percent, which he will pay back over five years, and Whole Foods looks forward to carrying the new popped and flavored Tiny But Mighty Popcorn products as soon as they are ready.

In 2012 Whole Foods lent out $2 million through their LPLP, and Heather says the volume is picking up. "The LPLP will continue to develop, and it will remain important because one of our core values is creating win-win partnerships with our suppliers."

—— Factoring ——

One rather expensive option for companies in a cash flow crunch is factoring, also called invoice factoring or accounts receivable factoring. A factor is an organization that will buy your accounts receivable, usually at much less than they are worth. You get immediate cash, and then the factor takes over the responsibility of collecting the money your customers owe you. When researching this section, I couldn't shake the feeling that factors are a lot like payday lenders. Both charge very high fees for services you can usually avoid, but when you really need one, they can be a godsend. One such situation would be if you receive an unusually large order that you would not be able to fill without an immediate influx of cash. If your business has very high margins and you are confident your customers will promptly pay their bills, and if you have no other options, then you might still make some money on the large order even after you take the factor's fees into account. But if you find yourself repeatedly in a situation where you need to consider factoring, you should carefully examine the conditions that got you into that place to begin with and do everything you can to avoid getting there again.

"Not many businesspeople are capable of calculating the actual interest rate that factors charge," says Ted Levinson of RSF Social Finance, which extended a line of credit to an organic food company that had been using a factor prior to working with RSF. "There are several tricks of the trade," he explains. Ted described a few of these to me using a hypothetical example: ABC Factor charges 1 percent per fifteen days with a six-day "float" on the face amount of the invoice. You deliver an order and send a $1,000 bill to XYZ Company and factor it. ABC Factor advances your company 80 percent and charges a $100 collateral maintenance fee. Twenty-five days later, your customer XYZ pays the bill to ABC Factor, who treats it as outstanding for forty-five days (twenty-five days + six-day float = thirty-one days, which ABC Factor rounds up to forty-five). That means you pay 30 percent interest on $1,000, or $300, even though you got only an $800 advance. With the $100 fee, the factor has earned $400. The effective annual percentage rate (APR) on this is over 600 percent, but the ABC Factor will swear you're paying 1 percent per fifteen days.

In addition to slightly shady fee structures, keep in mind that with factoring you're letting a third party come between you and your best customers. The factor, not you, will be contacting your customers to collect the bills and in the event that these bills become overdue. If you must use a factor, make sure to check references to confirm that it is professional in its dealings with both its clients and its clients' customers. And as Ted recommends, make sure you have an accountant review the paperwork before entering into an agreement with a factor.

15

......

Federal Grant and Loan Programs

WHO WOULDN'T WANT FREE GOVERNMENT MONEY for their business? All you have to do is find a federal grant program that you're eligible for, fill out an application, and the check is in the mail, right? If only it were that easy. This idealized view of federal financing programs leaves out many of the details: that it's a serious challenge to sort through the many available programs—some of which may have been changed, cut back, or, worse, discontinued in the last round of legislative decision making—to find one that might work for your business; that many of them are actually loan programs rather than grant programs, meaning you will have to pay the money back over time, plus interest; that the people administering the programs (and reviewing the grant proposals) are often much more familiar with traditional business models than some of the newer models that are part of a more sustainable food system; that the programs are fiercely competitive, some much more so than others, either because of the sheer number of applicants or because of scant dollars available in the first place; that you may need to provide matching funds from somewhere else in order even to receive certain grants; that there can be significant delays in receiving the money once you've been approved for a grant; and finally, that very few businesspeople are prepared for the amount of work it takes to do all the reporting required of government grantees.

Nessa Richman is the founder and president of Brightseed Strategies, a consulting firm that provides information and resources for people and organizations working to build healthy food systems. She has helped several organizations provide training and technical assistance around federal grant and loan opportunities to their food system stakeholders, including businesses, nonprofits, and government agencies. "Most community-based organizations and small food businesses have very limited resources," she observes. "They lack the internal capacity needed to learn how to apply for federal programs. It's generally quite complicated. But people still want to pursue all possible pots of fundraising."

Clearly, there is no such thing as free money, even in the case of grants. But I also feel it is important to dispel the myth that grants are the most prevalent source of federal funding: it is far more likely that the majority of food businesses would be able to access a government loan rather than a grant, which is why I included this chapter here in part 3 about debt financing. The good news is that there are in fact many federal programs that can benefit food-based businesses. The Small Business Administration, or SBA, offers many programs for "small" businesses of any type (and by "small," they really mean most independently owned businesses). For farmers, ranchers, and rural businesses, the USDA offers many programs as well. Several factors are making it easier to survive the entire government funding process: pioneering "intrapreneurs" in government offices around the country are taking it upon themselves to help sustainable food businesses find and apply for their programs, and they're also working hard to streamline the reporting requirements once the businesses have received government funding. An increasing number of nongovernmental organizations are not only lobbying for better funding of these and new programs but also helping farmers and food entrepreneurs successfully apply for grants and loans.

Receiving federal funding has important benefits beyond the funding itself. Nessa explains, "It provides a stamp of credibility for an organization or a business. And it provides a national platform for talking about your work that you wouldn't have otherwise." It can also give other types of investors more confidence, encouraging them to invest additional funds in your venture. If you're willing to dig into the morass of options, challenging odds, complicated application processes, and onerous reporting requirements associated with federal funding programs, and you are convinced that it makes sense to devote some of your energy to obtaining federal dollars in addition to building your local customer base with, for instance, a crowdfunding campaign, read on.

If you haven't already visited Grants.gov in an attempt to find a funding program that's right for you, save yourself the trouble. It's a notoriously difficult site to navigate for that purpose. Even if you did manage to find all the programs there that might be appropriate for what you're trying to do, you'd still have to read through pages and pages and pages of fine-print governmentese and acronyms to figure out whether or not you are actually eligible. However, as soon as you know that you do plan to submit an application for a government grant program that uses Grants.gov to receive them—most do—go ahead and register for the site (see the section "Applying for Federal Programs" below).

SBA Programs

For most small businesses, whether or not they are related to food, the Small Business Administration is the most appropriate place to start. SBA has a wide range of programs, and it's highly likely that you will be able to find one or more that will be relevant to your business at some point during its evolution. The 7(a) SBA loan program, for instance, offers loans to support employee stock ownership plans (ESOPs); implement pollution control mechanisms; help businesses develop export programs; support rural businesses; purchase businesses; purchase equipment, machinery, supplies, or materials; and purchase inventory, as well as help refinance existing debt that is not under reasonable terms, seasonal financing, and construction financing. Veterans are eligible for express loan servicing and extremely low rates. The SBA prohibits certain uses, such as refinancing bad debt or reimbursing a business owner for any debt or equity investments she has made in her business. The SBA also has a program that offers microloans for many of the above purposes.

Finally, the CDC/504 loan program offers loans in partnership with commercial lenders and community development corporations, or CDCs. A combination of senior debt (provided by a commercial lender), subordinated debt (provided by the CDCs on behalf of the SBA), and funds that you must put up yourself, this program provides long-term, fixed rate loans for fixed assets such as land, land improvement, buildings, construction, renovation, and machinery. You cannot use a 504 loan for working capital or inventory, consolidating or repaying debt, or refinancing (except in certain cases involving expansions).

The SBA website has a grant and loan search tool that allows you to find programs that might work for you, depending upon what kind of business you have and what type of financing you are looking for: http://www.sba.gov/content /search-business-loans-grants-and-financing. It is important to note that the SBA itself does not administer any of these loan programs. Instead, they partner with commercial lenders, providing loan guarantees while the commercial lender actually reviews loan applications and administers the loans.

HOW SMALL IS SMALL?

//

The SBA does have guidelines for determining whether or not your business is "small"; these take into account the average number of employees over a twelve-month period, average annual receipts, and the industry that you're in. Unless you plan to apply for a government contract as a small business, you really don't need to worry about these guidelines. But if you're curious, here's how they affect producers. The majority of fruit and vegetable operations can have average annual receipts of up to $750,000 to be considered "small businesses." Cattle feedlots can have average annual receipts of 2.5 million, and the upper limit for "small" chicken egg producers is $12.5 million. Remember that if you process the majority of your fruits or vegetables beyond what is necessary to sell them in your local market, this is considered manufacturing; in 2012 the SBA considered most food manufacturing business "small" if they had five hundred or fewer employees. For manufacturers of cookies and crackers, the maximum number of employees went up to seven hundred fifty, and for a few specialties, including breakfast cereal manufacturing, it was one thousand. The full list is available at http://www.sba.gov/sites/default/files/files/Size_Standards_Table.pdf

If you think you might qualify for an SBA loan, you can contact your local SBA office for referrals to preferred lenders in your area. Alternately, when you are interviewing commercial lenders, you can ask if they work with the SBA.

In addition to federal programs, many states offer small businesses financial assistance through grant or loan programs. The SBA website or office staff can also connect you to your state's economic development agencies (also known as EDAs), which offer assistance in applying for state grant, loan, and tax-exempt bond programs in addition to providing other technical assistance for business owners. See http://www.sba.gov/content/economic-development-agencies.

—— USDA Programs ——

The USDA administers the vast majority of the federal grant and loan programs that are relevant to farms, ranches, and other rural food-based businesses through its many subprograms, which include the Agricultural Marketing Service (AMS), the FSA, the National Institute of Food and Agriculture (NIFA), the National Resources Conservation Service (NRCS), the

Risk Management Agency (RMA), and Rural Development (RD). Rural Development in particular has a wide range of programs to support business development in general; eligible businesses need not be related to agriculture. That said, all rural development projects must be located in an area that has a population of no more than 50,000 (no more than 20,000 for some programs).

In 2009 the USDA launched its Know Your Farmer, Know Your Food initiative (KYF2), with a mission to strengthen the critical connection between farmers and consumers and support local and regional food systems. This was in part a response to some of the contextual barriers to getting federal funding to small-scale, diversified agricultural ventures. One of these barriers is momentum: for many years USDA funding programs were used primarily to finance large-scale, commodity crop operations. This meant that the employees administering the programs didn't necessarily realize they could use those same funds to support smaller farms or other locally oriented businesses that didn't look like the types of projects that had historically benefited from federal dollars. For instance, the FSA offers loans for storage facilities, which many program staff historically interpreted as *grain* storage facilities. It took some time for word to spread that storage facilities also include *cold* storage facilities, such as walk-in coolers, which play an important role in a wide range of food-based businesses.

KYF2 aims to correct some of the confusion about which USDA funding streams can be used to support sustainable food businesses, in part by educating program staff, in part by changing the language in some of the outdated program materials and expanding the diversity of operations included in examples, and in part by making sure that marketing and outreach of the programs is extended to a wider diversity of food system entrepreneurs.

How can you find out which USDA program might be right for you? You could spend the rest of your life digging into the program descriptions on the USDA website and trying to figure out which ones you are eligible for and how to apply, but I don't recommend this path. In 2012 the USDA released an online tool called the Know Your Farmer, Know Your Food Compass Map (the Compass) as a first step in identifying which USDA financing programs might be appropriate for your food business. The Compass showcases dozens of examples of local and regional food projects, including businesses that have received federal support. You can access information by navigating through interactive documents that you can download from the website or by using its interactive map. Both are organized by themes, including Local Meat and Poultry, Local Food Infrastructure, Healthy Food Access, and Farm to Institution. Search around for projects like yours, then take a look at how much funding they received and from which program. The Compass, which is updated on average once every three months, even includes information about projects that have received funding from federal sources outside the USDA (see section below), so you can get a sense of which programs you might research further.

If the online format of the Compass doesn't suit you, try *Building Sustainable Farms, Ranches, and Communities: Federal Programs for Sustainable Agriculture, Forestry, Entrepreneurship, Conservation and Community Development.* Published by Sustainable Agriculture Research and Education (SARE; see sidebar on page 175) in 2009, this comprehensive, 188-page book gives overviews of dozens of programs, including contact information, case studies, matching funds requirements (if there are any), and application information for each grant program covered. It is available in pdf format for free. If you would prefer a much more abbreviated digest, try the *Guide to USDA Funding for Local and Regional Food Systems,* published by the National Sustainable Agriculture Coalition in 2010. Though some of the specific details are no longer accurate (such as figures related to total dollars available for each program and application deadlines), this succinct document does a great job outlining the landscape of USDA programs. You will still find a treasure trove of well-curated information in its thirty-six pages.

What these guides don't necessarily reveal are the reporting requirements associated with particular grants. Make sure you know what you are getting yourself into, in terms of what is expected, in what format, and under what time line. I heard a consultant's story of a client business that went through quite a bit of trouble to apply for a certain USDA grant and even got to the point where they were approved to receive the award. Still, they ultimately decided not to accept the grant because the reporting requirements would have taken so much of the organization's time and energy that it just wasn't worth it.

Once you've identified one or more potentially appropriate programs to help fund your business, you can head to the USDA's program websites to learn more about the details. Many of them feature lists of previous grantees, guidelines for requesting applications, and sometimes more detailed case studies of one or more grantee projects. A quick look at these can help you assess whether your business is a good fit for the program in question: is your business comparable to those on the list in terms of purpose, size,

MATCHING FUNDS REQUIREMENTS

//

Sometimes federal grant or loan programs require that you match the amount of federal assistance with funds from other sources. Sometimes in-kind contributions, such as pro bono legal support or other donated technical assistance, count as matching "funds." Sometimes the value of your inventory can count toward the matching requirements. Often it means that you have to show that you already have cash in hand for or at least committed to the project. Make sure you can meet the matching requirements before you apply for a program that includes them.

location, and social or environmental benefits? Keep in mind, however, that your business might be eligible for a program even if no grants have been made to similar projects in the past.

At any point during this process, you can talk to a real person about your intentions to apply for a grant or loan. I heard this over and over during my research. "If you're interested in a particular USDA program, don't be afraid to actually call the contact person on the phone," Nessa says. "USDA grant program officers are interested in seeing the best possible applications come through the door, and they're happy to give you all the information that they can." The last thing you want to do is waste time and energy applying for a program your venture isn't eligible for, as Zoë discovered in chapter 12. In cases where programs have both state and local offices, contact the state office first; it's more likely that you'll reach someone there who fully understands the range of possibilities available to you.

Keep in mind that many federal employees will pick up the phone or answer voice mail, even if they are completely overwhelmed with e-mails. Try not to get too discouraged if you have a difficult time finding someone who understands your particular business and where it might fit into the puzzle of funding programs offered. If you think that it's frustrating to navigate federal agencies with all their idiosyncrasies, imagine working for one. The people in local and state offices have the capacity to be very helpful to you, so it's in your best interest to recruit them onto your team, so to speak.

Once you have a potential ally on the phone, introduce yourself and give a brief description of your venture. Here are some good questions to ask:

SUSTAINABLE AGRICULTURE RESEARCH AND EDUCATION GRANTS

//

USDA's SARE program offers grants to agricultural businesses in each of their four regions: western, north central, southern, and northeastern. Each region's program varies slightly, but for the most part the grants are available for farmers, ranchers, and producers who want to test out a solution to a particular agricultural problem their region faces, often in partnership with a local extension agent or representative from another agricultural or educational group; the partner organization may also qualify for a grant to participate in the project.

White Oak Pastures is a multigenerational, family-owned farm in Georgia with a fifty-member CSA and an intention to become a zero-waste operation. They are using a SARE grant to test the viability of using black soldier fly larvae to break down livestock processing by-products into valuable compost. The larvae also serve as a high-protein supplemental feed for the farm's chickens. Although the farmers are still figuring out the best ratio of flies to waste, it seems promising that black soldier flies align perfectly with the one-thousand-acre farm's sustainable agriculture practices of organic production, multi-animal rotational grazing, environmental stewardship, and animal welfare.

Maximum SARE grant sizes for producers vary depending upon which region you are in and how many different farms or ranches apply together for a specific grant. The maximum grant at the time of writing is $25,000, which is available to groups of three or more farmers or ranchers in the western SARE region; groups in other regions are eligible for slightly less than that, and individual grants max out at $7,500 to $10,000.

- Which funding programs that you work with might be a good fit?
- Are there other programs that my project might be eligible for?
- Can you provide me with a list of people or organizations that have submitted successful applications in the past?
- Do you know of any webinars, other online resources, organizations, or people that can help me develop applications for these programs?
- Is there anyone else I might talk to for financing advice, either at the USDA or elsewhere?
- What are the reporting requirements?

Don't be afraid to ask your state representatives about previously funded projects similar to yours. For example, if you are in Alabama trying to raise money for a value-added project to create jam out of produce and you stumble upon a description in the Compass about a similar project in another state, it's OK to bring that to the attention of the local USDA officer as an example of how programs can be used—in a nonconfrontational way, of course.

Earlier I mentioned that many USDA programs are in fact loans or loan guarantee programs, not grants. While some loans may be administered directly by the USDA division itself, many are actually managed by commercial lenders. Staff at the banks or credit unions that administer the loans can be of great help in assessing eligibility for these programs, so ask the USDA contact you're speaking with to refer you to those institutions near you.

—— Other Federal Programs ——

In addition to those offered by the SBA and USDA, there are other federal funding programs that might be appropriate funding sources for your socially responsible food venture. This section lists several to give you a sense of what is available, but keep in mind that there might be other obscure programs that could conceivably work for your project. Check the Compass for other potential sources of funding.

The same advice offered above for USDA programs holds true for the other federal funding: your best bet is to talk to a real, live person in one of the program offices to see if a particular grant or loan program is appropriate. Better yet, seek out a good contact at a nearby community entrepreneurship center or agricultural support organization who can help you get your head around the government programs that might be most suitable for your specific business. This way you can focus your research on only the programs you have a chance of accessing rather than wasting your time trying to learn about dozens of programs, most of which probably won't apply in your situation.

Many government agencies offer grants for Small Business Innovation Research (SBIR) and Small Business Technology Transfer (STTR), including USDA, the Environmental Protection Agency (EPA), the National Oceanic and Atmospheric Administration, the U.S. Department of Energy, and the U.S. Department of Transportation. As far as I am concerned, these grants definitely fall into the combined categories of hard to find, challenging to apply for, deeply competitive, not likely to be appropriate for the vast majority of food businesses, and annoying to report against if you do manage to receive one. But if you want to leave no stone unturned and think your business might somehow be eligible, search away: http://www.sbir.gov/.

If you are in the market for property upon which to launch an urban agricultural venture, you may be able to benefit—albeit indirectly—from certain programs run by the EPA's Office of Brownfields and Land Revitalization. The EPA defines brownfields as properties where there are (or may be) hazardous substances, pollutants, or contaminants present, making expansion, redevelopment, or reuse more complicated. There are former brownfields sites around the country that are now farmers' markets, supermarkets, urban farms, or community gardens. The grants offered through the Office of Brownfields and Land Revitalization are available to governmental groups (such as towns, cities, counties, tribes, or states) that are interested in assessing or cleaning up brownfields sites. Little of the money in these programs is available directly to entrepreneurs, so you'll have to work with your city or county to gain access to this money. Also of interest to entrepreneurs is the revolving loan program administered by the Office of Brownfields and Land Revitalization, which grants federal dollars to certain local agencies so that they can in turn offer loans to individuals, businesses, or nonprofit organizations in order to develop brownfield sites. Each community determines the loan terms, such as interest rates and repayment periods, and these programs frequently charge rates that are lower than you would be able to find elsewhere. Visit the urban agriculture portal at the EPA's brownfields website to learn more about their programs to benefit food-related ventures: http://www.epa.gov/brownfields/urbanag.

The U.S. Department of Housing and Urban Development's Community Development Block Grant program, or CDBG, can also indirectly benefit fundraising entrepreneurs in eligible areas. In this program certain cities, urban counties, or even states receive grants for activities such as expanding economic opportunities for low- and moderate-income residents. These entities in turn might be using those funds to provide grants or loans to support local businesses. At the same time they did their DPO (see chapter 10), Ben & Jerry's ice cream company received funding through the precursor to the CDBG program. To find out if your business is in an eligible area and to find out which CDBG grant recipients might have grant or loan programs available, contact your local Community Planning and Development office: http://www.hud.gov/offices/cpd/about/staff/fodirectors/.

Green for Greens: Finding Public Funding for Healthy Food Retail (http://changelabsolutions.org/publications/green-for-greens) is a helpful guide for healthy food retail project entrepreneurs. Published by ChangeLab Solutions in 2012, it provides tips on how to approach economic development agencies. It also gives an overview of how local, state, and federal economic development programs have been or could be used for healthy food retail projects.

—— Applying for Federal Programs ——

Some federal grant programs have rolling application deadlines. Other programs accept applications only once a year, but the application period may not fall at the same time every year, depending on how the internal program review and approval process goes. For some programs, you may have to submit a letter of intent, which will need to be reviewed and approved before you can submit a full application by a later deadline. You will need to find current information about the program in question, either by contacting the point person or searching the program's website. Beware outdated information from years past, which seems to linger indefinitely on the web.

If you know that you intend to submit an application, the most foolproof plan is to have it prepared ahead of time so that you will be ready to submit it once the program announces that it is receiving applications. You will usually have only a few weeks to submit an application from the time it is announced, and it usually takes a lot longer than that to pull a federal application together. Farmers and other food entrepreneurs whose business cycles depend on the growing season might be frustrated to learn that many USDA grant applications are due in the summer or fall, when they are right in the thick of things. Another complicating factor is that many people wait until the last minute to submit their applications, and the resulting traffic often brings down the whole Grants.gov system, causing many would-be applicants to miss the deadline, with no recourse. Fortunately, program eligibility requirements and application details do not change much from year to year, so you can plan ahead to complete your application at the right time.

If you can get hold of an application from a business or organization that has received funding from the same program in the past (the program websites often list previous awardees), this can be a great opportunity to learn what works well. If you can't, it would still be a great idea to look to someone who has experience putting together winning applications. Ask the program officer to provide a referral or check with your local agricultural organization.

PART FOUR

....

Selling Equity:

THE GOOD, THE BAD, AND THE UGLY

AT ITS SIMPLEST, RAISING EQUITY FINANCING ENTAILS SELLING investors shares of your company. These investors take a risk by giving you money up front for a financial return at some point in the future. Equity financing has some attractive benefits compared to most forms of debt. The majority of lenders expect you to begin paying off your debts right away, and it can be difficult to grow your business when you have to set aside cash every month to pay off your debts or at least put a payment toward the interest. When you sell equity, you receive the money in advance and have some time, usually several years, to build your company before your investors expect to see a payoff; this can be quite helpful in the early stages of your business because you can put all the money you have (and earn) during this time into additional improvements. When it comes down to it, the actual differences between debt and equity depend on the specific terms that you can work out with your investors, and if you want to grow to a national scale, you'll likely need a combination of both equity and debt. This means you'll need to evaluate which aspects of each type of financing fit with your needs and values and do your best to craft investment agreements that match up accordingly.

Selling equity used to be synonymous with taking on a few very wealthy individual investors as well as maybe one or two professional investment firms relatively early on in a company's development cycle. These investors expected positions on your company's board, where they could monitor progress and exert control when major decisions came up that might affect their financial returns. In this traditional model, equity investors took a gamble that your company would grow, preferably very quickly, to the point where it could either go public through an IPO or be bought by another company. It was at this point, known as the liquidity event because of the sudden influx of cash, that traditional equity investors counted on getting their return.

There are several aspects of this traditional model that have made selling equity to raise capital either impossible or unappealing for sustainable food businesses. Many food businesses simply do not have the growth trajectories and return prospects that make them interesting to traditional equity investors, particularly if the business intends to serve its community with local food rather than, say, seek national or even international distribution with a product sourced from ingredients from anywhere. If you have founded your business upon certain strong values, it can feel very dangerous to cede any management control to outsiders who may not always agree with those values, especially if your company's stock price doesn't grow as quickly or as much as those investors might hope. If you are incorporated as a worker- or producer-owned cooperative in order to increase the wealth and authority of these owners, having outsiders buy stock and gain any level of management control might be completely antithetical to your very reason for existence.

Still, some food companies with very deep social values do meet the profile that traditional equity investors are looking for. These include companies that offer technological solutions to food system problems and organic and/ or fair trade food manufacturers whose branded products have very broad consumer appeal. Usually, the vision of success of these companies includes achieving sales at a massive scale (i.e., national distribution through a variety of channels). They have aggressive plans for rapid growth, and managers with the experience to make it happen. Founders may not mind if outside investors or a multinational company owns the majority of the company if it means that they can multiply the impact achieved through, for instance, their sourcing standards or the health benefits of the product itself. Even if your company does not meet this profile, the good news is that there are an increasing number of options for raising equity financing in creative ways that do support a wide range of food entrepreneurs' values and priorities.

The following chapters will give you a sense of the key features of an equity offering, how you might structure one (or at least negotiate with your investors to structure one) to best suit your goals, and how to work with different types of equity investors. Chapter 16 comes first because in all likelihood you will begin the process of identifying and cultivating potential investors long before you will need to draft a term sheet that includes the various elements covered in chapter 17. Chapter 18 covers professional investment entities, such as venture capital and private equity firms and family offices.

Foundations are unique in their ability to make grants, loans, and equity investments in businesses that meet their strategic goals. Because I hope you will be able to make the most appropriate pitch to a foundation that might be able to help your venture—in other words, do not assume that grants are the only tool at their disposal—chapter 19 appears in this part of the book. And finally, chapter 20 covers several ways you can transition out of your venture while keeping its values intact.

16

......

Individual and Angel Investors

WHO MIGHT INVEST by buying equity in your company? The first place to look is (surprise!) the list of your family, friends, and anyone else that you started putting together in chapter 7. Beyond that list, you may find other people who might be interested in investing in your company by buying shares, including angel investors. This chapter covers the ins and outs of working with individual investors, including where to find them, how to get them to notice you, and what the typical cultivation process might look like once you've got their attention.

George Weld, owner of Egg restaurant in Brooklyn, New York, is passionate about shifting the restaurant business from what he calls "a dead-end industry" to one in which people want to spend their whole lives working. Although many people have had jobs in restaurants, he notices that most people move on to other work if they can. "Almost half the money that Americans spend on food gets spent in restaurants," George says, adding, "Ten million people work in restaurants, which is seven times the number of people in our armed forces. If we're serious about changing the food system, we've got to get restaurants right." George believes that people who run restaurants, work in them, and fund them have the responsibility to demonstrate that a business that takes the triple bottom line— people, planet, and profit—seriously can be a viable business. "That's what we've been proving at Egg, a highly principled, mission-driven business that sources from human-scale purveyors, since 2005," he says. According to George, Egg puts over $200,000 a year into the pockets of small and organic producers. "We've also created a work environment that makes it clear that we believe working with food is one of the most important jobs that a person can do," he says. "We pay our staff well and offer benefits to everyone. We pack the house every day with people who love our food and love eating someplace where they can know the food was prepared by people who care." The business also operates a small farm in upstate New York. "Not only does this help in a tiny way to stimulate the economy there, it supplies the restaurant with some of the best produce we've ever tasted," George explains. "It also gives our staff the opportunity to work with the food from beginning to end, and helps reduce the alienation between urban and rural that plagues the food economy."

In 2011 George and his team decided to launch Parish Hall, a sister restaurant to the tiny Egg, managed by the same principles and staffed by people who trained there. "More room means more opportunities for our cooks and consumers. Growing will allow us to be more efficient and flexible," he says. "It will also allow us to be profitable, which will let us do more of the important work we're privileged to do: develop employees, nurture community, and educate students." But first they needed to raise the money to make the new restaurant a reality.

George initially considered raising money by doing a convertible debt note. "That's what a lot of people in the restaurant business do, but either they aren't thinking it through that well, or I am too cautious," he says. He was nervous about having a fixed payment, which would have been hard to pay back while the new restaurant was just getting started. "Thank God I was nervous, because we'd be in big trouble if I had done a convertible loan [with payments starting immediately]."

Egg, the farm, and Parish Hall are each single-member LLCs, wholly owned by an LLC holding company. George decided to raise money by selling membership units in the holding company, which is roughly equivalent to selling shares of equity in a corporation. (Make sure to consult your attorney for the specifics of selling membership units in an LLC, as there are some important differences compared to selling stock.) Because he didn't want to end up in a position of having to force a liquidity event, George structured his offering in such a way that investors would receive a percent of the restaurant's profits indefinitely. Initially, he offered a straight ratio: investors would receive 1 percent of the available payout for every 2.5 membership units of the LLC they owned.

"We had this really successful restaurant, feeding thousands of people a week," George says. "The easiest way to raise money would have been to put a card on the table, 'Hey we're opening a new restaurant! Help us grow!' Not being able to do that without violating the law was so frustrating." But

George had chosen to do a private offering, available only to accredited investors. (By the time he heard about DPOs, he'd already raised some money with this offering and didn't want to go back to the drawing board. Plus, George had also just been through a five-month process to get an SBA loan, which he says "required hundreds and hundreds of pages of paperwork that needed to be notarized upside down and all over," and so the thought of the new DPO paperwork just did not appeal to him.) Instead, he decided to look for accredited investors. "I realized fairly quickly whether someone was being led by numbers or mission," says George of the process of meeting with prospective investors. "If someone was only focused on numbers, my hunch was that if things got hard, they would be difficult people to have in the mix," he explains, adding that he suspected his restaurants' mission was not worth it to them. It took him a year and a half to raise the first half of his $500,000 goal from people who understood what his restaurants were all about.

Meanwhile, George submitted an application to Slow Money and was chosen to present at their National Gathering in San Francisco in October 2011. In the months that followed, the Slow Money NYC chapter organized a collaborative process to help investors assess George's restaurant investment opportunity, with several angel investors choosing to participate. He says, "I tried barking up a couple other trees to try to get money before the Slow Money NYC group coalesced, but it seemed like such a con game." Some people were evaluating Parish Hall against nightclubs and restaurants that would draw celebrity crowds, and George felt as if he were trying to have a different conversation from the one the numbers-oriented investors were having. "We wanted to talk about creativity and community building. The nice thing about working with the Slow Money group is we can have the *same* conversation," he says. George advises other socially responsible food entrepreneurs to find investors with whom you don't have to be on guard so you can talk about what really matters. "It might take you longer, and you might end up with a fairly large group of investors [each of whom invests less per person], but if they're good people, it's not a burden," he says.

The Slow Money NYC group of investors did request a few changes to George's initial offering. "They all seemed reasonable, and when it came to discussing changes, it was a really collaborative process," says George of the experience. "It didn't feel competitive at all, as they clearly wanted to come to an agreement that worked for everyone. I came away from that negotiation feeling really great about it." There were some sophisticated investors in the group, and George says he learned a lot from them, particularly around what they expected in terms of a rate of return. After the negotiations were complete, they made only one substantive change to the offering, giving the Slow Money NYC investors a preferred rate of return. "Now someone who owns 2.5 units of the LLC receives 1.5 percent of the payout, instead of 1 percent, until they have made their initial investment back," George explains, "and then it goes back down to 1 percent."

Thanks to Slow Money NYC, George closed with $468,000 in hand, having raised a quarter of a million dollars in three short months, an uncharacteristically quick equity fundraising time line. Ultimately, twenty-four different investors purchased LLC membership units at $10,000 apiece (some buying more than one unit). This is a large number of investors to manage, and in a situation like this, it's important to develop a plan for setting expectations lest you wind up spending all of your time answering their questions. "There are not many things written into the LLC agreement that require member sign-off, but for those few major issues, we created an investor advisory committee of four people who are empowered to speak for the group," George says. "We also hold calls with the advisory committee once a quarter. I think that's pretty key so that you're not fielding panicked phone calls from twenty-four people all of the time."

Based on the valuation of the company, the new investors owned 20 percent of the membership units in the LLC, with George owning the remaining 80 percent. "My accountant and I valued the company based on a wild guess," George admits. "The valuation models for restaurants in particular are all over the place. One standard method would give it a $300,000 valuation, another $3 million," he says. Though some of his investors were skeptical about his number, he got around the issue by focusing on the actual returns that the investor would receive rather than the valuation itself. "If your projections show that your investors will earn a decent return, the valuation isn't that important," George says. He was fortunate that his investors felt this way, as it means that he maintains the vast majority of the LLC's membership units and the voting control that goes with them.

The Spectrum of Individual Investors

Individual investors run the gamut from those having zero experience in equity investing (this might include your wealthy aunt Gina) to those who are equity investment experts, including retired entrepreneurs who now spend most of their waking hours investing in and advising new companies, even if they aren't "professional" investors per se (this title is usually reserved for the managers of investment funds, covered in chapter 18). There are pros and cons to working with people at all points on this spectrum, and it's dangerous to make sweeping generalizations about them as a whole. With that caveat, here are some considerations.

When it comes to less-experienced investors, you may need to spend a lot more time educating them about how equity investing works. They may not understand how start-up businesses differ from the more established, publicly traded companies whose stock they may already own. It's important to be very clear with any prospective investor that they would be taking a risk to invest in your business. Don't forget that the securities laws requiring you to disclose information about your business are there to protect the unsophisticated investor, and if somewhere down the road one of your investors feels that you misled her about the risk, this is where you can find yourself in legal hot water. Many food entrepreneurs have found that inexperienced investors need a lot more hand-holding after the offering has closed, too. If someone has never experienced the ups and downs of a new business, they may get a little bit more worked up than seasoned investors during periods when your business isn't doing as well.

"The least experienced investors can be really tough to work with, but it goes both ways," observes Pam Marrone of Marrone Bio Innovations. She recommends looking for investors who have already run a business. "That's really important. It's common to run into investors who have an MBA, they've done consulting or worked for the government, but they've never run a company," she says. "Bad luck happens. There's weather, people get sick, whatever. But this kind of investor has never been in a CEO's shoes, and they just don't have a context for what you're going through." In Pam's experience these are the first people who will blame the company's management: you. "This happens much more quickly with someone who has never run a business," she observes.

What exactly are angel investors? Contrary to popular belief, they are not limitlessly wealthy people who magically show up at the right time with all the capital you need. In the most traditional sense, angel investors are wealthy people who invest their own money at a very early stage in a company's development in exchange for a portion of the company's equity. (Note that "very early" is relative—a recent report found that the median valuation of a company prior to an angel-only fundraising round was $2.7 million for the first quarter of 2012, though food and beverage companies represent a very small proportion of the deals examined.[18]) Quite often angel investors have been successful entrepreneurs themselves, and they usually invest in industries they know well. In addition to cash, they frequently bring a wealth of expertise to the table, providing entrepreneurs with advice, mentorship, and introductions that can help a business succeed. Levels of risk tolerance vary. Depending on the person, an angel might be willing to be the first investor in a company. Some will take the plunge only after others have done so. An angel might invest a relatively small amount at first, waiting to see if you meet your projections before investing more money. Of course, the size of an investment will also vary widely from person to person and from deal to deal, but you shouldn't expect an angel to invest more than a quarter to half a million dollars, and usually they'll invest much less than that. In general, angel investors tend to be more patient than venture capitalists or private equity firms, but they generally want to see an exit at which they can reap a financial return.

Angels who work on their own can be very difficult to find, and you'll have to ask around in your networks to see if you can identify anyone who might be a good match for your company. Fortunately, there are many angel groups (either formal entities or informal groups) around the country that have systems for generating deal flow (the process of finding companies to invest in) on behalf of their members. If you meet their criteria, submitting an application to a group of angels will streamline your search process. While few angel groups explicitly seek out companies founded upon principles of social responsibility, they won't necessarily turn them away if the company meets their general criteria.

Angel groups usually accept applications only from those companies that have the potential to exploit a large market niche, plan to grow quickly, have experienced management teams, and offer investors a clear path to earning a financial return, also known as an exit plan (see below). Depending on the angel group, members may not necessarily have a lot of money to invest in companies that make it through their competitive selection process. "Angel groups behave in the same way as venture capital firms, with high bars to get over and lots of hoops to jump through," says Pam Marrone of Marrone Bio Innovations of her experience working with three different angel groups to raise her company's first round of financing. "They're good, but it's very little money for a lot of work." But if you believe your company is well suited to an angel investor, and your only alternative is to spend weeks, if not months, seeking out solo angels, it certainly is more efficient to try your luck with angel groups. "Early money raised will most likely come either from someone you know or through local connections," reports Michael Burgmaier of Silverwood Partners. Because most people—angels and otherwise—prefer to invest in companies that are located near them, your best bet is to find a local angel group.

—— Investors' Circle ——

Finding a values fit is always important, and the most relevant angel group for socially responsible businesses is **Investors' Circle** (IC), a national network of angel investors, professional venture capitalists, foundations, and family offices (professionally managed entities set up to manage one or more wealthy families' finances) that are using private capital to promote the transition to a sustainable economy. IC also recently launched a local network program; as of this writing, there are active groups in Philadelphia and North Carolina with plans to support the development of additional groups in New York, San Francisco, Boulder, and Chicago.

One of the most active angel networks in the United States,[19] IC's formal membership consists of approximately one hundred fifty investors, two-thirds of them individual angel investors and one-third institutional investors (including investment funds, foundations, and family offices). They are all accredited investors (see sidebar on page 111) actively seeking out investment opportunities in companies that are solving social and environmental problems. Since 1992 IC has helped over two hundred fifty businesses raise $166 million, plus $4 billion in follow-on investment (and that number will probably have gone up by the time you are reading this book). In 2011 IC merged with the **SJF Institute**, an organization that helps positive-impact entrepreneurs—and by extension, the communities they live in—thrive. The institute has provided direct technical assistance to over fifteen hundred impact entrepreneurs and has helped hundreds of others through its programs, which include Getting Ready for Equity workshops, networking events, and the Green Jobs Award. Additionally, a number of nonmember investors participate in IC's activities that connect capital-seeking companies to prospective investors.

What makes a company a good fit for IC? Food-based or sustainable agriculture businesses have been accepted into the organization's Community and Economic Development and Sustainable Consumer Products tracks. The latter category is the most competitive, but it also attracts the most interest from investors, according to Justin Desrosiers, IC's director of strategy & operations. Most IC members make investments only in companies they expect will get to a significant scale, both in terms of impact and potential for generating revenues. "We will, for instance, consider a submission from a company that sells organic coffee to retailers across the country," Justin explains, "but not from a company that is launching a single, local, organic coffee shop." Companies that are successful at IC expect to achieve $5 million in annual revenues within the next five years. Though IC considers private companies at early, expansion, and growth stages, they accept applications solely from fully formed companies; individuals or technologies are not eligible. "Appropriate businesses are well beyond the concept stage," Justin says. "We strongly prefer companies that have already gone to market and achieved some degree of traction, as evidenced through revenues, contracts, strategic partnerships, retail distribution, et cetera." You also need to have a very clear plan for generating a windfall of cash to repay your investors at some point in the future, as IC members will want to have this kind of assurance that there will be a way for them to get their money back. Historically, most companies that attract investment are looking to raise less than $3 million, and on average the successful companies raise more than $500,000 through the IC network.

Engaging with Angel Groups

If you decide that Investors' Circle or another angel group is in accord with your business, it's important to have the right expectations regarding the process for pitching your investment opportunity. Although the exact experience will vary from group to group, you'll likely encounter some version of the following:

- First, you submit some kind of online application form. IC, along with more than seven hundred fifty other angel groups, uses the online angel start-up funding website Gust (see Resources) to handle this part of the process.

- Next, the group reviews your application. If your company meets the basic criteria, the brief business plan you submitted with your application will be distributed to members for initial consideration.
- If there is enough interest from a substantial number of members, the group will invite you to make an in-person presentation. This will usually be around ten minutes, with a few more minutes to answer questions.
- If a sufficient number of investors respond positively to the presentation and express further interest in investing, they will organize a due diligence process to fully vet the opportunity. During this phase, you will be expected to answer quite a few questions about your company and eventually your investment terms, often through a representative of the group (see the section on the due diligence process below).
- If all goes well, interested investors will individually commit to investing, each signing your investment documents. At your first close, you will receive the money.

Most angel investors have seen a lot of business plans and get hit up for money all the time. If you can find an interested angel investor, you'll need to make a very good impression to get to the point where she will consider investing in your business, a process that might even take years. "We really appreciated the feedback we got from Investors' Circle on our business plan and on our presentations," says Chris Mann of Guayakí, an organic yerba maté beverage company on a mission to steward and restore two hundred thousand acres of South American Atlantic rain forest and create over one thousand living-wage jobs by 2020 by leveraging their market-driven restoration business model. He submitted his first application to IC in 2001 and gave a presentation at the fall conference that year. "That was the first time we had really gotten good feedback," he says. "It's not just investors that are helpful; it's contacts, advice." It's a good thing he found these extras valuable, because in Chris's case that was all he got from his early experience with IC. "We didn't have a single [investor's] name after our first presentation," he remembers. In fact, it wasn't until two years later, after he had given his third IC presentation, that a longtime IC member finally decided to invest. "She said to us, 'I like your presentations, you're still around, and I've seen the product in my local store,'" Chris recalls. "Only then was she ready to invest."

——— Elevator Pitches and Presentations ———

Making a good first impression is a critical facet of attracting the attention of investors you don't already know, especially if they are being bombarded by fundraising entrepreneurs—and you should assume they are. Your goal is to pique investors' interest to the point where they will agree to meet with you, and your key tools in this effort are an elevator pitch and a visual presentation. Your elevator pitch should be short, certainly less than a minute and ideally only thirty seconds. It should succinctly cover what problem your company solves, what its products or services are, why they are unique, who buys them, and how many more people could be buying them if you had more capital (what is the potential market?). Try to include some kind of hook that will make you or your business stand out from the dozen other pitches the investors may have heard that same month, week, or day. Always make sure to include a follow-up request: "Would you be willing to meet with me so that I can tell you more about how we're making it easier for CSA farmers to increase their profits without adding new customers?" Use simple language, not jargon, and tell a story rather than spitting out more numbers than necessary; there will be time for all the numbers later, if you can capture the investors' attention. Write down and practice several versions of your elevator pitch that might appeal to different kinds of investors. For example, if your company manufactures gluten-free, shelf-stable, heat-and-eat entrees featuring grass-fed beef, you might write one pitch for people who want to support those with celiac disease, one for people who are investing to combat climate change, and one for people who want to benefit financially from trends in natural and organic grocery sales.

Your presentation, or slide deck, is a visual version of your business plan summary, often in PowerPoint format. While this presentation is another excellent tool for getting a first meeting—you might even have a chance to bring it out during your proverbial elevator ride—it will most likely be the centerpiece of a meeting. How many slides should you show? Of course, it depends on the context. The slide deck you use during a live presentation should be different from one you leave behind after the meeting. The latter can be longer and include more text and numbers; too much information on your slides could distract from information you plan to convey in person (do not read from your slides!). Legendary venture capitalist Guy Kawasaki stands by his 10-20-30 rule for one-hour meetings: use no more than ten slides, delivered in twenty minutes or less (to leave ample time for people being late, technological difficulties, and most important, discussion afterward), and use at least a thirty-point font.[20] Go with a presentation style that is most comfortable to you; humor and personality can work, so long as you also cover (briefly) all the pertinent aspects of your business plan. As with your elevator pitch, remember that the main point here is to convince potential investors that you are offering a valuable investment opportunity worth learning more about.

When making your pitch or presentation, be prepared for the very real possibility that investors will not be interested in your opportunity. Don't waste this situation by being frustrated or incredulous but rather use it to learn what you can for the future. Sheryl O'Loughlin is executive director of the Center for Entrepreneurial Studies at Stanford University. She is also cofounder and CEO of Nest Collective, a family of mission-driven foods, and for nearly ten years served as CEO of Clif Bar (see chapter 20). "Ask for advice and listen," she advises for those situations when investors say no. "Find the thread that connects everyone's feedback. It doesn't mean don't do it, but it means watch out," she says, adding that you can then take this advice to mitigate any risks that have been uncovered.

The Due Diligence Process

When someone is sufficiently interested in making an equity investment in your company, they'll start what is known as the due diligence process. Some inexperienced investors might not realize that this is the formal name for "kicking the tires," but you'll definitely hear more sophisticated investors and venture capitalists talk about it. Equity investing is a fairly complicated proposition, and it carries the risk that investors might never see their money again once it is invested. So it makes sense that someone considering an equity investment would want to do her homework to understand what exactly she's getting into.

Just how involved the due diligence process will be depends upon several factors, including the investors' level of experience, how much they are investing (relative to both their net worth and how much they have earmarked for such investments), and how risky they deem your venture. At the very least, equity investors will want to see a leakproof business plan, financial statements showing past performance and projections into the future, business licenses, trademark documentation, contracts, and other materials. They'll check all of your assumptions, look for any weaknesses, and ask about what would happen under different scenarios. (In this sense investors are looking for the same sorts of materials that commercial lenders ask for; see chapter 14)

Expect that investors will want to talk to your management team plus key customers, suppliers, and even other lenders and investors. They will probably want to see your operations firsthand. They will want to learn as much as they can about the market you're in, especially if it is a new area for them. They'll put your products through their paces, too, comparing them to the competition's and making sure they are every bit as great as you claim.

Pay careful attention to how you and your key teammates conduct yourselves during the due diligence process. Interested investors will be closely watching how—and how quickly—you respond to requests for information, and they may even be testing to see how you perform under pressure. Ideally, you should know your numbers cold. If you don't, make sure to include your CFO in all investor calls and meetings. Answer questions confidently and without hesitation, even if it's to say, "That's a great question. I'll get that information to you within twenty-four hours." If you get defensive or flustered, they will wonder if you're cut out for the job or if there is something you're hiding.

You might be concerned about what investors will do with the information you give them during the due diligence process. The main concern is that a person or firm may be considering an investment (or have already invested) in a similar company and will use the information you give them to boost your competitor's performance. Many entrepreneurs would prefer investors to sign nondisclosure agreements, or NDAs, before they share sensitive information; in theory these documents prevent people from passing along that information in a way that might hurt your business. Unfortunately, while some people will sign your NDA, many of the more sophisticated investors will refuse, and there's not much you can do about this. Sometimes this is because of a blanket policy, but it also might be because they are in fact probing you for information that will increase their knowledge of your field for reasons that have nothing to do with any interest they have in investing in your company. You'll have to decide how important the NDA issue is to you and whether you're willing to let an investor who appears to be interested walk away over it.

If it sounds as if the due diligence process takes a lot of time, that's because it usually does. "It can take anywhere from eight to twenty-four months," says Michael Burgmaier of Silverwood Partners, "and investors are very good at monopolizing, or even wasting, people's time." The more prepared you can be ahead of time, the better. Get all your materials together before you actually need them. Don't forget that the whole time your prospective investors are scrutinizing you, you will also need to continue to run your company in such a way that you are hitting the goals you have set out in your business plan.

While an investor is conducting due diligence on your company, don't forget to do due diligence on her. This is your opportunity to learn more about your investors' values, gauge whether or not they really "get" your mission, and decide whether you want to have these people on your team for the foreseeable future, for better or for worse. Do you want active investors who will mentor and support you, or would you prefer passive investors who will sit back and let you run the show? How patient do you think investors will be if your venture doesn't do as well as you have projected within a certain time frame? What is their level of risk tolerance? Do you share a vision of how and when they will receive their return on investment?

If you're not sure about where investors stand on a particular point, don't be afraid to ask them about their expectations or investment history. If you can, talk to other entrepreneurs who have received investments from the same investors. What have their experiences been like? Don't underestimate the importance of good chemistry. If you've got a strong feeling in your gut that this person or firm just isn't the right fit, it's better to end the relationship before any money has changed hands than to wait until some bad experience confirms your hunch.

Eventually, if all goes well, you and your investors will decide that you want to work with each other. Congratulations! Now it's time to start negotiating the terms of the equity investment deal. The following chapter offers tips for that part of the process.

17
......

How It Works:
Equity Concepts

AS WITH DEBT, there are many different variables that come into play when you're raising equity financing. The first sections of this chapter cover the basic concepts you'll need to know before you sell any of your company's stock. It goes on to describe some specific equity financing structures that socially responsible food-based businesses can consider.

The moment you start thinking about selling equity, you should consult with an attorney to ensure that you meet your fundraising goals in a way that is within the bounds of securities law (see chapter 10). Remember, it's all too easy to find yourself on the wrong side of these laws, and ignorance is no excuse. This book covers the most basic legal considerations in a very general sense, but it is not meant to be a substitute for professional legal counsel; only a qualified attorney will be able to guide you through the specific options that are both available in your state and appropriate given your unique situation. The first decision for you and your attorney will be whether or not to do a public offering. As described in chapter 10, these are the only offerings you can advertise publicly, and you'll need to file various documents with the appropriate authorities. If this is what you decide to do, which exemption will you use? Or will you do a fully registered offering, complete with a full prospectus? Alternatively, a more limited private placement might be the right option for you, particularly if you plan to sell equity only to a small number of accredited investors, whether they are individuals or professional investment firms. The important point to remember is that you should not start advertising your offering to anyone before you get a green light from your attorney.

——— Exits and Liquidity Events ———

Probably *the* most important thing to keep in mind if you plan to raise money for your business by selling equity is that your investors will want their money back, plus a return on their investment. It is in the scramble to repay equity investors that so many socially responsible food entrepreneurs have ended up losing control of their companies. This is why it is so crucial to spend the time and energy to find equity investors who share your values and are willing to discuss terms that match your intentions for how quickly the company needs to grow. No matter how patient your investors, you need to have a good answer to the question of how they will **exit**, or get their money back out of your company.

From the perspective of an equity investor—or any shareholder, for that matter—shares in a privately held company are illiquid, meaning that for the most part they cannot easily be sold for cash without incurring some loss of value. Traditionally, most entrepreneurs pay back their investors (and reap the financial benefits resulting from any shares they hold themselves) either by taking the company public through an initial public offering of shares in the company or by seeking to have the company acquired by a competitor or strategic partner. These are the most common examples of **liquidity events**, both resulting in an infusion of cash for shareholders and an exit, if they decide to sell those shares and get out of the game altogether.

Liquidity events also result in a significant shift in who owns, and therefore controls, the company that was once completely yours. In the case of an IPO, institutional investors and members of the public become the owners of a significant portion of the company, with a proportional number of votes. In the case of an acquisition, the management of the acquiring company (and their majority shareholders) will be in control. While it's impossible to predict exactly how the change in ownership and control will affect the specific operations of your company, it is safe to assume that the new owners are unlikely to see eye to eye on 100 percent of the issues that matter to you. (Chapter 20 goes into these traditional exits, plus some innovative alternatives to consider, in more detail.)

Pam Marrone of Marrone Bio Innovations says it breaks her heart to see entrepreneurs who lose their companies. "It's just so common!" she laments. Ben Cohen, cofounder of Ben & Jerry's, believes it's critical to finance a business so that it's not dependent on a liquidity event or a sale of the business.

"I think it's a waste of time and energy to build a business that's based on progressive social values and then end up selling it to some valueless entity," he says. "You've built a brand, and you've built a relationship with your customers based on a set of values, and then you toss them out the window if you end up getting owned by an entity that doesn't share those values." Yet he is quick to admit that there are still very few alternatives when a company gets to a certain size and its capital needs grow. So what is a company to do if it wants to raise equity financing in a way that preserves management control as much as possible for as long as possible? The sections toward the end of this chapter present some options, but first, here are some more basics.

—— Anatomy of an Equity Term Sheet ——

Within the formal documentation related to your equity offering will be a list of key terms, or a term sheet. If you're working with more sophisticated individuals or investment firms, you might start by negotiating the term sheet, formalizing the rest of the documentation after you've come to an agreement about the key terms. The following are basic terms that will likely be part of your equity term sheet. Not every term sheet will include all of them, and there is an endless list of additional terms that you might encounter, especially if you're dealing with venture capital or private equity firms. The better you understand these terms, the more likely it is that you'll be able to draft or negotiate a term sheet that will really work for you—or at least the more likely you'll be able to spot terms that might make you think twice about signing a deal.

Common stock. Every corporation has common stock, the most basic class of stock. When you first incorporate your business, all of its stocks will be issued to you and your cofounders, if you have partners. Each share is usually entitled to one vote, although you can choose to alter this ratio for different classes of stock (e.g., you can assign multiple votes to Class A common stock and only one vote per share of Class B common stock). **Preferred stock** is the other most basic class of stock for entities that can offer more than one class (see chapter 3). Your offering will specify the class of stock being sold.

Series A, Series B, Series C (etc.). Once you start raising equity financing by selling stock, it's likely that you will raise several separate rounds, which are traditionally named in alphabetical order for each subsequent series. You might also encounter the terms **seed round** (the first round of funding, which could be equity or debt) and **angel round**. These are names for the first two rounds (if they are named at all), which often include friends and family, followed by angel investors, although both groups may very well participate in subsequent rounds as well.

Stock price. When you incorporated your company, you issued a certain number of stock shares to yourself and any partners. The stock price is equal to the value of the company divided by the total number of shares issued, which is why company valuation is ultimately more important than stock price, except when it comes to the psychological effects of choosing a price that seems high or low relative to similar companies. Your term sheet will include the stock price for the offering, as well as the number of shares that are available in the offering. (See the following section for a more in-depth exploration of company valuation.)

Funding target. This is how much you plan to raise with a particular offering. You will usually specify the offering's objective amount (how much you are hoping to raise), as well as a minimum and maximum amount. The minimum amount is a floor below which you would not be able to achieve the business objectives that prompted the funding round in the first place; the maximum ensures that you do not sell so many shares as to lose your majority ownership, for instance.

Minimum investment amount. The term sheet will specify the minimum number of shares that an investor can purchase, with the associated dollar amount that this represents (based on the stock price). The lower you set the minimum, the more likely it is that less wealthy investors can participate in the case of a public offering. The downside of a lower minimum is that the more people who invest at lower amounts, the more investors you will need to find in order to meet your funding target—and the more investors you will have to manage.

Options. An option is the right to purchase stock in the future, generally at a set price. An option is usually time sensitive; if you do not purchase the stock within a set time frame, you lose the option. If you intend to provide

employee stock options in addition to or instead of giving stock to current employees, you would set aside a certain number of shares in an **option pool**. Savvy investors looking to avoid dilution will take the size of the option pool into account when calculating your company's valuation in order to limit their risk of dilution. **Warrants** are similar to options except that the time frame for exercising them is usually longer. Warrants are often included as "sweeteners" or "kickers" with preferred stock and mezzanine debt offerings.

Antidilution provisions. If the number of shares in a company goes up, the value of the shares that have already been issued goes down, because the value of the company must now be divided by a greater number of shares. This is known as **dilution**, and it can occur when employees exercise their stock options, when convertible debt or preferred stock converts to common stock, when an investor exercises her warrants, or when a company issues additional shares for a new round of equity financing. It can also happen for current shareholders in a **down round** where the company valuation is lower than for previous rounds. Investors are not fans of dilution, for obvious reasons, and they may insist that your term sheet include antidilution provisions. There are a number of ways to do this in a term sheet, most of which involve math too complicated to include here. The important thing to keep in mind when it comes to antidilution provisions is that you can use them to resolve a disagreement about company valuation (as happened in the Native Americans natural foods case in chapter 19 on page 224). But they can also make subsequent equity rounds a bit trickier.

Protective provisions. These exist to serve the investor, not the owner. Similar to antidilution measures, these might specify what percent of which class of shareholders must consent to authorizing the issue of additional shares, but they can also include a minimum number of shareholder votes to approve or veto such events as mergers or dissolution of the company, sales of significant assets, and/or payment of dividends not specified in other stock offerings.

Dividends. You can choose to provide shareholders with a share of your company's profits through a cash payment called a dividend, usually paid quarterly, though you can choose a different payment period. Depending upon how you set it up, the dividend amount can be a fixed value (i.e., a certain percent of the stock's value), or it can vary in proportion to the company's revenues or by the manager's decision; in the latter two cases, in some periods you may not pay any dividends at all. It's much easier to predict how much you will owe in dividends over time if you set a fixed rate, but investors may be more interested in your offering if there is the potential for higher dividends while your company is doing well. If you do not plan on repaying investors through an exit or liquidity event, dividends become a much more important way of giving them a return on their investment.

Callability. There may come a point in the future when you'd rather not have so many shares of a particular class of stock issued. Maybe you have excess cash and want to increase the proportion of common stock, and therefore votes, that remain with the company. In the case of stocks that pay dividends, it may be that you can find less expensive capital from another source and can't justify paying the dividends. Whatever the reason, you might want to **call** the shares, or buy them back from investors at the company's request. Including a clause about callability in your offering makes it clear to investors that you reserve this right.

Redemption. If the investor requests that the company buy back her shares, this is called redemption. The offering's redemption policy describes the circumstances under which this would be allowed. For instance, your term sheet might specify that investors can request redemption within thirty days after the end of any quarter once three years have elapsed after the first close, subject to approval by three-fourths of the board. Your best bet is to include a clause that your company's board must approve all redemption requests, in addition to any policy that gives all outstanding shareholders the right to vote on whether or not to allow redemptions. This will protect the company in the event that it does not have sufficient cash to cover all requested redemptions. However, particularly for direct public offerings, don't underestimate the value of being able to say that you have always been able to redeem shares. If you have a relatively open redemption policy, assume a certain percentage of outstanding shares will be redeemed over the course of the year, and reserve some cash for that likelihood. If you want to get more specific, consider including parameters such as how many shares any one investor can redeem at once, what percent of the total shares issued can be redeemed in any period, and/or how long the company can take to redeem the shares.

ROYALTY FINANCING: DEBT OR EQUITY?

Another way to raise money is to pledge a percentage of future revenues in exchange for a cash advance. In this arrangement, known as royalty financing, you pay your investors their percent of your company's revenues either for a certain period of time or until the sum of their royalty payments hits an agreed-upon figure. But is royalty financing debt or equity? The short answer is neither, unless it's structured as debt. Often used in conjunction with a loan (particularly with mezzanine debt), royalty financing is not always technically debt. Nor is it equity, as investors need not own any portion of your business. (The case of George Weld's restaurant holding company investment deal, covered in chapter 16, is an equity example, since investors own membership units in the LLC and earn a proportionate percentage of the company's profits indefinitely.)

Royalty financing instruments are definitely securities (see chapter 10). Consequently, you need to consult with an attorney to make sure that you properly structure and register any royalty financing agreement before you begin soliciting investors.

Closing date. This refers to the date at which you must complete all of your fundraising for a particular offering. It can specify the date when you have raised all of the funds that the term sheet allows for, if there is a maximum, or you can set an actual date beyond which you will not raise further capital in this round. If you set a minimum funding amount for your offering, you might do a **first close** on the date that you reach that minimum, with subsequent closes until you hit the maximum amount or closing deadline.

—— Company Valuation ——

What is your company worth? This is a totally theoretical concept until it comes time to sell equity, and then it becomes very important. As the company founder, you would find it in your best interest to have a high valuation, because this means you have to give up less equity (fewer shares) for the same amount of money raised than if your company valuation were lower. For the inverse reason, investors usually insist that the company is worth less: they want to own a larger percentage of the company for their investment dollars. Your term sheet will include a pre-money valuation (how much the company is worth before new investment dollars come in) and a post-money valuation (the pre-money valuation plus the anticipated investments).

How do you calculate your company's valuation and the closely related stock price? There are several different ways to do it, and of course it would be too easy if there were hard-and-fast rules that everyone could agree upon. General rules of thumb vary depending on the size of the company and what specific industry it's in. Kevin Murphy is director of Encore Consumer Capital, a private equity firm that has invested in several natural food companies. He notes that tech companies' high valuations have resulted in inappropriately high valuations for consumer products companies. "You see this a lot in friend and family rounds," he says. Many people calculate value as a function of current revenues or, more accurately, current profits; in general, profitable companies are worth more than companies that are operating in the red given the same revenues, and companies with a track record that shows it is reasonable to expect profits to rise will generally be valued higher than those without sufficient data to back up projections of increasing profits. As mentioned in the previous section, the size of the option pool, plus any outstanding warrants, will affect the conversation about stock price. More human factors come into play as well, as Kevin's observation reveals: how experienced are the entrepreneurs and investors who are negotiating? If many investors are interested, valuation can go up as a function of supply and demand. Michael Burgmaier of Silverwood Partners also points out that the valuation that a strategic buyer might offer is not often the same as the value an investor will accept. "Strategics will typically pay more," he explains, "so if you garner a certain price from one, don't necessarily expect that an institutional investor can or will match it."

It's generally a good idea to wait as long as you possibly can to sell equity in your company: the longer you wait, the longer you'll have to get the company to a higher valuation, and the less equity you'll have to give up to raise a comparable amount of money. You'll also have longer to develop a compelling story in terms of the numbers you can bring to the valuation negotiation. "Wait until you can show same-store sales that reveal traction [i.e., the same retail locations are selling more and more of your product], even if you're only selling in one region or even one store," Michael suggests. "You're selling the story, so you want data from which you can extrapolate. Let the numbers do the talking for you, as they are not subjective."

When talking to prospective investors, you do not need to mention valuation right away. Kevin says, "That's like talking about marriage on the first date, or going to a job interview and talking about salary within the first ten minutes." The valuation conversation is more appropriate after your investors have a deeper understanding of your business and after you have a deeper understanding about their values and intentions. If you and your investors cannot agree upon a valuation and yet you still feel confident that you would like to work with them, there are a few ways to proceed. You could hire an outside expert to calculate the valuation for you, letting a third party be the judge. You can agree to include antidilution provisions that appease the investors. You can agree to give up additional board seats, longer time frame on warrants, or better liquidation preferences in exchange for a lower valuation. What you will be willing to offer and what your investors will be willing to accept all comes back to (surprise, surprise) values and priorities.

Convertible Debt

Convertible debt is a form of debt that converts to equity shares, either at the end of its term or when the company sells its first round of equity. Convertible debt is one way to take advantage of many of the benefits of equity financing without having to deal—at least right away—with issues such as agreeing upon a company valuation with your investors or having to give up equity at all. And depending upon how you structure your offering, you won't need to repay the debt until the end of its term (in the case of interest-only debt that does not ultimately convert to equity) or at all (in the case that you do convert the debt to equity—though of course you "pay" by selling equity in this case). Convertible debt offerings are relatively inexpensive to draw up (use an attorney) and usually give investors a discount on the current stock price at the point of conversion. (A 20 percent discount, for instance, would mean that when new investors purchase the stock for $100 per share, the convertible debt would convert at a rate of $80 per share.) In traditional financing, one expects the debt to convert to equity, but this might not be the preferred outcome for a socially responsible business entrepreneur. As the following story illustrates, a fast-growing company that chooses its investors carefully can use convertible debt to its advantage, whether or not it ever converts to equity.

When Tom Stearns started High Mowing Seeds, an all-organic seed company, it was just a hobby. In 2000, four years after its founding, High Mowing Seeds brought in $36,000 in revenues. In the early years, the company's capital needs were simple. Given the seasonal nature of his business, Tom needed lots of cash all at once to buy seeds during the summer and fall, which he took care of with a line of credit from a bank, using the seed inventory as collateral. "We also had two different bank loans, one equipment loan and one working capital line of credit," Tom recalls. "And the only reason I was able to get those at all was because my parents were willing to guarantee them. High Mowing Seeds didn't have anything to put up for collateral other than our inventory, but that was already securing the line of credit."

For the next six years, his company experienced what Tom describes as "crazy, crazy growth," thanks to a number of converging factors that led to ever-increasing demand for his seeds. "People really like our products, and we are one of the only games in town for organic seeds," he explains. "Plus we always have been, and continue to be, deeply engaged in community, social, and political affairs, such as the fight against genetically modified seeds." He also credits High Mowing Seeds' close partnerships with a number of like-minded organizations. "We're lucky that we've been a media darling in terms of our story and activities, and our partners have really helped to tell our story for us."

Though many companies use a line of credit to borrow money to pay for inventory, High Mowing Seeds' experience was a bit different. "A bakery draws down its line of credit once a month. Buy flour, sell bread, pay down the line of credit, repeat," Tom offers as an example. "But we buy all our inventory at once for the whole year, and therefore we needed a pretty big line of credit," he explains. "High Mowing Seeds has the same annual sales as my friend's bakery, but since they draw it down twelve times a year instead of all at once, their line of credit is one-tenth the size of ours. We used the same amount of credit, only differently, and because we carried a higher balance, it cost us a lot more."

By 2006 High Mowing Seeds' annual revenues reached $1 million, after six years of growing 60 percent, 80 percent, even 100 percent annually. In looking at where the company was going to be over the next five years, Tom and the company's new CEO, Meredith Martin Davis, realized that they needed a different kind of financing to take the company through its next phase. "We needed a huge infusion of working capital," Tom recalls. "The company was in the gangly teenager phase. We needed a bigger building than we could afford, a bigger computer system than we could afford, more people than we could afford—all because we were growing so quickly."

Tom and Meredith wanted to invest in the company that High Mowing Seeds was becoming, not the company that it was at the time, but quickly realized that traditional debt wasn't going to help them get there. "Back then banks would have lent us the money we needed, even though we weren't even profitable at the time. But we couldn't have afforded the monthly payments to service that amount of debt," Tom explains. "We needed 'free' money to invest and grow through this stuff."

At the same time, Tom was wary of the hidden costs of selling equity in High Mowing Seeds to raise the capital the company needed to finance its continued growth. He didn't want to sell shares in the company, which would have meant giving up ownership. "I was thirty-one years old in 2006. I was young, and I had a whole career of this seed company ahead of me. I didn't want to start losing ownership and control of the business so early on," Tom says. "But I also had no intention of selling the business any time in the foreseeable future, which was another reason why selling equity didn't feel like the right thing to do."

Tom was confident that his company would outgrow its "gangly teenager" stage and become profitable again, able to pay back their commercial lenders. He needed a way to bring in investors that would make sense for his situation: he needed money. He didn't want to pay it back soon. He had no collateral. He didn't want to give up equity. The company was not profitable, but it was growing quickly. Tom is fortunate enough to live in a state where there are quite a few first-generation sustainable business models, many of which had already pioneered some creative financing models. He spoke to many of those entrepreneurs about their experiences as he structured the terms of his own offering. "The most important thing that I learned was that investors were willing to be patient," he says, noting that many people had invested early on in Seventh Generation, a socially responsible company from Vermont specializing in green cleaning and personal care products, and they waited more than ten years before seeing their return. "And none of the entrepreneurs I talked to planned to sell their companies," he says, "so I knew I didn't have to have an exit plan, either."

Based on everything he learned during these conversations, Tom decided that convertible debt was the right choice. "Developing an offering was totally new territory for me," Tom admits. "I had to learn a whole lot through the process, including what all these terms mean." But he felt it was important to have a very professional, very formal, and totally above-board offering. "In my mind, the crazier the idea, the more formal your paperwork should be. Otherwise you're stretching people's confidence and their ability to think outside the box," he explains. "If someone is already unsure about a creative financing structure, and they're going send the offering to their financial advisers, you don't want to have them send something informal that some yahoo drew up."

Tom and Meredith figured that they wouldn't be able to afford to pay their investors a single penny for the first five years, so they structured the $700,000 convertible debt offering such that investors would receive a balloon payment for all their accrued interest—they decided to compound interest—at the end of five years. "So someone who put in $50,000 would get $16,911 of interest at the five-year mark, to get them caught up," Tom explains. "We could have decided to roll the interest into an equity conversion or a new term loan, but we wanted to give the investors something for waiting for five years," Tom explains. "We want to say, 'Here's a fat check!'" (Meanwhile, Meredith keeps track of the deferred interest payments on the company's profit and loss statement while they use the cash to grow and pay off other debts.)

In the case of High Mowing Seeds, a company with such a popular image in the community, selling the offering was not a big challenge. Tom says that some of the people he approached had actually been waiting for him to call so that they could invest. He told all his prospective investors, "I have an opportunity for you to invest in High Mowing Seeds. You are not going to make a lot of money out of this. It is risky. I want the company to remain independently owned and governed. If none of this scares you off and you want me to keep talking, I'll tell you more." Only then would he continue that High Mowing Seeds had the potential to make a huge social and environmental impact, not only locally but nationally as well, and investors had a chance at making a decent return. "We chose the seventeen people who invested," Tom explains; "they didn't choose us. We turned some people away who wanted to invest because we didn't have as good a feeling about how it would work out." Fortunately, he and Meredith had structured the offering such that they could add a second round, without doing a lot of additional paperwork, after they had raised the initial $700,000. This turned out to be helpful as they raised an additional $400,000 right before the offering's close date.

Another important feature of High Mowing Seeds' convertible debt offering is that at the five-year mark the investors will have the option of what to do with the principal they invested—convert it to equity or extend the loan another term. Tom expects that he and Meredith will have a good sense of what the best option would be for the company at that point. "We're going to do our best to convince all of our investors not to convert to equity, and we are prepared to pay them all back their principal," he explains. "We were pretty conservative in our growth projections, and our 2011–2012 revenues are four times what they were in 2006, more than a year ahead of schedule, so that's helpful." Still, he expects that it will take a few years to pay back all their accrued interest plus the principal. Fortunately, the cost of borrowing money from commercial lenders is now cheaper than the interest rate the company pays its investors, and they can afford the debt service now that they've reached their current size.

One of the great benefits of a convertible debt offering is that it gives you time to figure out what you want to do at the end of the term. "Our model gave me five years to figure that out and keep growing and to consider other possibilities that came up," Tom says. "What if one of our investors was really great, very patient, stayed out of our hair, had lots of money? We might have converted their investment to equity and bought everyone else out. Seventeen people invested in our convertible debt offering, and we knew we didn't want that many equity investors." One of their investors called and expressed regret at taking 6 percent from High Mowing Seeds, given the economy, prompting Tom and Meredith to consider an option such as encouraging everyone to roll their accrued interest and principal into a new term loan at 3 percent in exchange for higher social returns, such as improving employee benefits. The possibilities are endless. "Legally we have to offer the same options to all the investors," Tom says. "We can't offer one-off deals. But we could propose a few scenarios to see what people would respond to."

Of course, your company will need to be in a good position to encourage your investors to consider various alternatives at the end of a convertible debt term, based on the company's finances or the strength of your personal relationships. Otherwise, you will have no choice but to convert the debt to equity at the end of the term. But if you're willing to take this risk in exchange for putting off—perhaps indefinitely—the conversations about valuation and board seats for equity investors, convertible debt is a good option. You'll have to decide on an interest rate; whether or not interest on the debt will be simple or compound; what event(s) might trigger conversion; and what discount to offer on the stock price at the point of conversion.

One caution: if you do expect that you will be seeking equity financing in the future, you need to be careful about how much convertible debt you take on. "Sometimes entrepreneurs get enamored with convertible debt, and over time that debt becomes overly large relative to the size of the next equity financing," Michael Burgmaier explains. For instance, let's say you raise $2 million in convertible debt, and you want to raise a $1 million equity round in the future. The investors who bring in the new $1 million are not going to be excited about $2 million in debt that is going to convert to equity at a discount. "Convertible debt can be an extremely strong and effective tool to use, but entrepreneurs do need to be careful," Michael suggests. "In general, don't let convertible debt become more than 25 percent of what the next round might be. If it becomes much larger than that, you may want to convert it before you raise the next round. With all of these issues, a good lawyer is essential to help with structuring."

—— Preferred Stock ——

If your business is organized as a C corporation, it can issue multiple classes of stock. **Preferred stock** is one of these that gives stockholders preferential treatment compared with common stockholders. A company usually pays dividends on preferred stock before it pays dividends on common stock, and during a liquidity event holders of preferred stock have a higher-priority claim on any of the company's assets than holders of common stock. Preferred stock usually does not come with voting rights for stockholders, which means that it is a handy way to sell equity without giving up management control. However, in the traditional investing world, preferred stock offerings often come with warrants to purchase common stock at a discount or set price at some point in the future, so you need to be careful about how you structure your offering if you want to avoid giving up management control.

You can structure a preferred stock offering so that it behaves a lot more like interest-only debt than equity from the company's perspective: paying regular dividends to preferred shareholders is a lot like paying interest on an interest-only loan. You can also structure your preferred stock offering in such a way that your company buys the stock back from investors, or calls it, at the same value that the investors originally paid, which is a lot like paying back the principal on a loan, except that when it comes to buying back preferred shares, you can build in a lot more control over when you can choose to do it. But the most important difference between selling preferred stock and taking out a loan is where the money sits on the balance sheet. Any type of equity, including preferred stock, is considered an asset, whereas all debts, including convertible debt, are considered liabilities. The more equity you have, the easier it is to access more debt financing. If your company has a loyal following of thousands of fans who may be willing to invest, you may also be able to pay back your preferred stock investors (and common stockholders, for that matter) without ever having to go through a liquidity event.

This is exactly how Organic Valley (or rather, its parent entity, the Cooperative Regions of Organic Producer Pools, or CROPP) structured its Class E Series 1 preferred stock offering. This producer-owned marketing cooperative promotes regional farm diversity and economic stability through the sale of its farmer members' certified organic products. Between 2004 and 2010 Organic Valley raised a total of $43.8 million through a preferred stock offering, including $14 million in 2010 alone. Organic Valley's offering was available only in certain states due to differences in state regulations. People living in Pennsylvania and Florida, for instance, were allowed to approach Organic Valley to learn more about the offering, but Organic Valley couldn't approach them.

"Class E [preferred] stock does a lot for us," says Diane Gloede, Organic Valley's investor relations manager. "As an asset rather than liability, it's good for our balance sheet. It's helped us grow tremendously over the last ten years." The proceeds of the preferred stock offering allowed Organic Valley to invest in internal infrastructure, software, and hardware to support this growth. "We built a new headquarters for the first time in our history," she reports. "That cost $4 million, and we had already outgrown it in four years. We also built a distribution center for over $12 million. We may build a new milk plant near the distribution center. With all this growth, we're always looking ahead, and obviously we'll find ways to use the money we raised."

Organic Valley finally closed this particular offering in September 2010, having raised sufficient funds to meet their current needs, plus those in the foreseeable future. Diane says they won't hesitate to do another preferred stock offering if the company anticipates needing additional funds.

The Organic Valley preferred stock offering model can benefit other socially responsible food companies for several reasons:

- Investors have no voting rights and therefore cannot interfere with management (i.e., farmer-owner) decisions.
- No matter how much the company grows, the redemption value of the shares remains the same, which means that any material benefits of growth remain with the company.
- The investors still take on risk that they will not receive their regular dividend or that the company will not be able to buy back their shares at the time of attempted redemption.
- Because their cash position is strong and they have never had a dearth of interest from new investors, the company need not undergo a liquidity event in order to repay their equity investors.

If you choose to offer only certain classes of preferred stock to trusted partners whose values you know to be closely aligned with your mission, you may want to consider giving them certain voting rights, such as the right to veto the acquisition of your company by another that does not share those values. (Note that preferred stockholders can usually vote on whether or not the company can issue new shares; this is a way to protect the value of their shares from dilution.)

When structuring dividends, you will need to decide whether payments are **cumulative**. This would mean that if you choose not to pay your preferred stock investors at the end of one or more dividend periods, you will still have to make good on those "**passed**" dividends when the company is in a position to do so. (With noncumulative stock, the company does not pay passed dividends.)

There may come a point in the future when you'd rather not have so many shares of preferred stock owned by investors, perhaps because you can find capital at a less expensive rate from another source or you just don't need the cash and therefore cannot justify paying the dividends. In this case, you might want to call the shares, or buy them back from investors. Including a clause about callability in your offering makes it clear to investors that you reserve this right.

18

......

Stepping It Up:
Venture Capital and Other Institutional Investors

IS YOUR COMPANY ON THE VERGE of serious growth, with a consumer-focused brand that is poised for national distribution, has the potential for massive scale, and can achieve it within a decade, if not much sooner? Does the thought of having a seasoned investor with industry expertise sitting on your board excite rather than concern you? Can you recite you company's revenue history from memory, speak confidently about your projections for the years to come, and convince others that you have a winning plan to hit all your milestones? Have you already raised an angel round, or at least been able to bootstrap and borrow your way to a million dollars in annual revenues? Is your company at the break-even point or close to it? Are you willing to dedicate the vast majority of your waking hours to your company, lead it down the road to an exit, and share the financial returns with investors? Have you and your team done this before? Would you run the risk that you might not stay with "your" company forever, if it meant that its products could reach even more people than you ever imagined? If you can answer yes to most of these questions, your company would be a good candidate for institutional equity. Otherwise, you probably shouldn't waste your time exploring this path.

Institutional investors include a wide range of actors, including venture capitalists, private equity firms, family offices, investment funds, investment advisers, and pension funds. The primary distinction between individual investors and institutional investors is that individual investors invest their own money, whereas institutional investors invest money on behalf of others. This distinction influences just about every aspect of working with institutional investors, so it's helpful to understand the implications. Because they are the stewards of other people's money, institutional investors tend to be much more risk averse on the whole than individual investors. They also tend to have much stricter criteria for companies they would consider investing in. The due diligence process for institutional investors can be much more involved than that for individual investors (although some individual investors do come from institutional investment fields and so have developed institutional habits). One factor that can weigh heavier for institutional investors than individuals is the transaction cost per investment, which includes both the cost of conducting due diligence and the cost of engaging with (providing mentorship and advisory services as a formal board member or otherwise) the companies they do invest in over time; this means that most institutional investors prefer to invest relatively large amounts of money in each company they work with compared to individual investors.

Of course, different types of institutional investors work in different ways. Venture capital and private equity firms either set up funds or do one-off deals that they pitch to their investors. A fund typically exists for ten years. "Those fund managers still want a job after those ten years," explains Michael Burgmaier of Silverwood Partners, "and so they have to return the money to their investors with an IRR [internal rate of return; see sidebar on page 212] of 25 to 35 percent." During the first several years of the fund's life, the manager will invest in anywhere from a dozen to two dozen companies, with the expectation that at least a third of them will be a complete loss, a third of them will return approximately what was invested, and a third (or even fewer) will generate the returns necessary to meet the fund's overall target IRR. All of this needs to happen by the end of the fund's ten-year cycle, which means that a company will have between five and seven years (or up to ten years in rare cases) to exit. One-off venture capital deals have a similar time line. "The joke about venture capitalists is true," says Michael. "They enter every room with their eyes on the exit." Some so-called evergreen funds have no time line, and the institution may hold the company for up to twenty years before expecting an exit.

Although the process of structuring a deal with institutional investors is much the same as with individual and angel investors, you will have much less flexibility in negotiating terms with them. They will likely drive the process of drafting the term sheet instead of the other way around, and you should expect to compromise in order to close the deal if you are

INTERNAL RATE OF RETURN

///

As part of the due diligence process, most investors will pay close attention to their internal rate of return, or IRR. The calculation takes into account several factors, including how much the investor expects to receive (the larger the amount, the higher the IRR) and when (the sooner the money is received, the higher the IRR). The calculation also assumes that if the money were not invested in your company, it could earn a certain percent return by being invested in some other way. An investor will have an IRR in mind that will justify their perceived risk of investing in your company.

determined to raise equity from this class of investor. After all, institutional equity professionals are hired expressly to earn money on behalf of their investors and have lots of experience crafting term sheets that work in their favor. They are not likely to consider creative financing arrangements, particularly if they are the first one to sign on to the deal. You will definitely want to hire an attorney or an investment banker (or both) with significant experience working on behalf of companies like yours to make sure that the terms most important to you stay on the table.

——— Finding Institutional Investors ———

Where might you find institutional investors, particularly ones that are interested in socially responsible companies? Despite its name, the field of socially responsible investing, or SRI, is not the best place to look. Interpretations of this concept do vary, but it usually refers to the practice of mutual funds investing in publicly traded companies that have been screened to avoid companies that operate in industries such as weapons or alcohol, companies that engage in animal testing, and/or companies that operate in countries where human rights issues make them unappealing to certain investors. While SRI can also encompass the practice of actively investing in companies with positive environmental or social policies, again, it tends to refer to publicly traded companies, and the people making the investment decisions are usually mutual fund managers rather than other types of institutional investors. The emerging field of impact investing is a better fit for

THE GLOBAL IMPACT
INVESTING RATING SYSTEM

//

Some impact investors use GIIN's Global Impact Investing Rating System, or GIIRS, to evaluate their investment opportunities. Similar to the B Impact Assessment (see sidebar on page 41), the GIIRS assessment itself is free and measures a company's impact in the areas of governance, workers, community, and environment. GIIRS ratings, based on the assessment, are designed to help investors decide whether or not a company meets their investment criteria; initial ratings and annual updates are available for a fee that varies based on the size of the company. If you take the assessment and pay for the rating, your company will be listed in the online GIIRS Company Directory. Investors' Circle, for instance, requires all companies that present at their venture fairs to take the GIIRS assessment and makes the ratings available to all investors who attend these events.

private, socially responsible companies looking for institutional investors. According to the Global Impact Investing Network (GIIN), a nonprofit organization dedicated to increasing the scale and effectiveness of impact investing: "Impact investments are investments made into companies, organizations, and funds with the intention to generate measurable social and environmental impact alongside a financial return. Impact investments can be made in both emerging and developed markets, and target a range of returns from below market to market rate, depending upon the circumstances."[21] The impact investing space is by no means limited to institutional investors. In fact, any type investor may self-identify as an impact investor, including individuals and commercial lenders. However, the institutional investors tend to be the most visible players, which is why it makes sense to start your research here. GIIN, for instance, lists its members on its website, and every one is an institution.

In addition to the Investors' Circle conferences, institutional impact investors and managers of green consumer funds gather at events such as the SRI Conference on Sustainable, Responsible, and Impact Investing and the Social Capital Markets conferences, to name two of the longest-running and best-attended national events. A few institutional investors particularly committed to the sustainable food space attend Slow Money conferences.

Unless you happen to be one of the companies presenting at a formal venture fair, however, expect it to be difficult to garner attention at these events without a personal referral or introduction.

No matter how deep your mission and values, you cannot assume that this alone will be enough to attract institutional impact investors. "Although some impact investors are willing to take a lower rate of return, it is important to show that your business is in a position to provide a level of return aligned with the type of capital you are asking for," warns Taryn Goodman, director of impact investing at RSF Social Finance. "Unless you can grow to fit that investment model, institutional investors don't make sense at all."

What kinds of food businesses might fit this growth profile? According to Taryn, "Most institutional investment dollars are going toward consumer products, although there is also interest in land conservation, as well as in food hub financing, since processing and distribution are two major roadblocks in creating healthy, regional food systems. However, there have been very few investments made to date." Attorney Ken Merrit offers similar advice. "Institutional impact investors may be interested in food companies that meet their criteria," says Ken, "but the only segment historically where there's been interest and activity, and I think it's the only segment that fits their parameters, is a value-added food business that creates brand equity, is scalable, can be grown to the point of a liquidity event."

In addition to impact investors, there are many institutional funds that invest in green consumer products. Food-related tech companies—such as companies developing software to help manage small and medium-sized farms, distribution tracking software, apps to help conscious shoppers find healthy food products, or point-of-sale systems for food retail establishments—have access to the larger world of technology funds, green and otherwise. "There is a lot of interest right now in data management and other companies that are helping create an infrastructure for food businesses to scale," says Danielle Gould, founder and CEO of Food+Tech Connect, a media and research company that curates news and hosts events for innovators transforming the business of food. Still, she cautions that institutional investors are usually looking to triple their investment in three to four years. "A lot of venture capital firms have their areas of expertise," she explains. "They're constantly doing research in those areas so they can make better investments. Food and agriculture isn't something that they've been focusing on, but that is changing."

Each institutional investor will define "impact" in its own way, just as each green consumer products investor will have its own idea of what constitutes "green" and each institutional investor will treat an entrepreneur in its own unique fashion. You can never ask too many questions of institutional investors to get a sense of whether or not they might be the type of partner you are looking for (see the due diligence section in the previous chapter, "Individual and Angel Investors"). The last thing you need is a fund manager who is nearing the ten-year mark and willing to throw your company's values out the window in favor of wrapping up a fund with higher returns.

—— A Homegrown Partnership ——

On the other hand, finding the right institutional equity partner can help you take your company to places you never imagined were possible. This is what John Foraker, CEO of Annie's, Inc., discovered in this company's partnership with Solera Capital. (Since his involvement with Annie's, several different entities have controlled the brands collectively known as Annie's, including Annie's Homegrown and Homegrown Natural Foods; for simplicity's sake I'll refer to them all as "Annie's" in this book.) Best known for its all-natural macaroni and cheese (among its other bunny-themed natural and organic products), the company has another aspect to its mission: to continue growing the business and its profitability—a distinction that made institutional equity attractive.

John has been Annie's leader since 1998, when he and a small group of private investors infused $2 million of growth capital into Annie's. At the time the company's annual revenues were $7 million. "When you've got deep values and you are competing with companies that don't, you have to be able to focus on the long term," John says. There are things the company did that both cost a lot of money and made life more difficult in the short term, such as increasing their commitment to organic ingredients at a time when such a decision was very expensive. "But we were always comfortable doing things like that," John explains. "A core part of consumers' connection to Annie's was that they knew we would stay true to our values, whether or not they were looking." John and his management team felt that if they could build a really strong relationship with their customers based on trust, business growth would be the natural extension, and so far this has been the case.

By 2002 the company had reached $7 million in annual sales. "But we needed some serious growth capital," John says, to fully realize the company's potential. He quickly found several interested institutional investors. Of all his options, he chose to work with Molly Ashby and her private equity firm Solera Capital, a rarity in the world of institutional capital in that it is staffed predominantly by women. John says Solera has been a great partner since the beginning and continues to be. "Finding a financial partner that understood our mission was a really important factor in our decision," he says. "We wanted to work with someone who understood the consumer product goods space *and* would really understand our values, letting us continue to invest in them over time." He warns that all institutional investors will say the right things; "it's just a matter of whether or not you believe them," he says.

But what about an exit? "There had always been a lot of interest in Annie's from big consumer product goods firms," John explains. He assumed that the company would eventually be bought out, but he was concerned after having seen what happened to other natural and organic companies that were purchased and wound up straying from their values. John decided the bigger he could grow Annie's, the more likely it was that they could find a buyer that would respect their values. "I always believed that the longer I could hold that off and grow the business, the better I could build connection between the values and the business and what the brand was doing," he says. "Not just from a marketing standpoint but really deeply within the supply chain and within the relationships with our community and how we built the brand and all of the things we stood for. We wanted to make those so integrated that if Annie's were bought, the buyer would have no choice but to respect those values." With the help of Molly and Solera Capital, which ultimately invested over $81 million in the company (representing a controlling ownership of over 90 percent), Annie's grew its revenues to over $117.6 million, with income from operations reaching $15.1 million. For the rest of Annie's story, see "A Homegrown IPO" in chapter 20.

19

......

Working with Foundations

FOUNDATIONS ARE VERY INTERESTING financial creatures. I hear so many questions about how to find foundation grants, perhaps more than I do about any other type of financing, even though foundation funding is usually the last financing channel that I recommend to food entrepreneurs. There is a lot of money sitting in foundations, yes, but it is very hard to access, which is why I would rather promote other financing methods first, such as those that will also build your future customer base (see chapters 8 and 9). Working with foundations to fund food-based businesses can be very challenging at best. At worst, foundations can take up a lot of your time during the courtship process, only to show you the door months after you've begun discussions with them.

That said, if you have a very strong case that your business is engaging in charitable activities, foundation funding might be a viable option for you. Unlike many other sources of potential funding, foundations have several different pools of money that can (theoretically) all work together to support your socially responsible food venture. It is conceivable, for instance, that a foundation could give you a grant and make an equity investment to support your food venture, plus make connections to additional organizations that might be able to amplify your work. If you can find a foundation that will work with you, you will have a partner in many senses of the word. I hope this chapter will help you understand where to focus your efforts with foundations, if it's appropriate for you to bark up this tree at all.

How Foundations Work

There are several different types of foundations, some of which make grants and some of which do not. Private foundations are grant-making entities that are generally started, funded, and at least partially governed by individuals, families, or corporations. The funds that are granted out are usually generated through an endowment (the money that was initially donated to the foundation) that is invested. Private independent foundations are slightly different in that they are governed independently from the individuals, families, or corporations that initially endowed the foundation.

Community foundations are public charities and behave a bit differently from private foundations or private independent foundations. Think of them as institutions where individuals and families have decided to park philanthropic funds, allowing them to take advantage of the administrative infrastructure of the community foundation rather than starting separate private, family, or corporate foundations. A community foundation usually administers many separate charitable funds, often called donor-advised funds, and grants from these funds are suggested by the donors, who may choose to remain anonymous to the organizations receiving the grants. The important thing to keep in mind when seeking grants is that the staff of the community foundation itself is not likely to accept grant proposals, because they do not have discretion over where the grants go. In some cases community foundations may solicit grant proposals on behalf of donor advisers in their community who are looking to support certain types of projects. As a rule (because this is part of the service they offer), community foundations are very careful about protecting the privacy of their community of donors. While the staff at a community foundation might pass along information about your project to a donor, do not expect to find out which donors are interested in specific issues.

All of the foundation types described above are grant-making foundations. They are distinct from operating foundations, which usually focus their efforts on the programmatic aspects of their mission, meaning that they operate projects themselves; most operating foundations do not make grants at all. Although they may be excellent partners if there is a good fit between their activities and those of your project, they are not likely sources of grant funding. (See chapter 3 for more information about structuring your venture as an operating foundation.)

There are many laws that govern what foundations can do with the various pools of money under their control. If they do not abide by the rules governing what types of activities are charitable, for instance, they risk losing their tax-exempt status. It's helpful to understand this as you assess whether or not it would be worth pursuing foundation grants. If your social enterprise is organized as a nonprofit, it is without question eligible for foundation grants. L3C entities are also theoretically eligible, although a foundation will have to file additional paperwork with the IRS to confirm that everything is in order. Even if your business is organized as a for-profit social enterprise of any other form, it is possible though less likely that you could attract grant funding from foundations. It will be easier to do so if you have a specific project that is clearly charitable in nature (see sidebar on page 33).

More interesting than their grant making (to me, at least) is what foundations can do with the money in their endowments. This money is invested in order to generate the funds foundations give away, and there is far more money sitting in foundations' endowments than they give away as grants—usually in a ratio of 95 percent of assets in endowments to less than 5 percent distributed annually as grants. A foundation generally invests in stocks, bonds, mutual funds, and the other usual suspects of the stock market, as well as institutional funds. These investments needn't be mission aligned at all, and in most cases none of a foundation's investments are. In recent years the movement to align foundations' endowments with their philanthropic goals has been growing slowly but surely. The argument is that it doesn't make sense for foundations to pursue a maximum return on investment for their endowment if those investments end up contributing to the same environmental or social problems the foundation is trying to help solve. This means that more foundations are putting endowment money into funds that solve social and environmental problems, such as green consumer products funds. Foundations are also increasingly investing in mission-aligned financial institutions like CDFIs.

In between grant making and the mission-related investing (MRI) just described is a very specific type of investing known as program-related investing. Not everybody understands the legal definition of PRI, and the term is often misused. By law, PRI (debt or equity) counts as part of a foundation's grant making, which means that the investment must be aligned with the foundation's charitable goals, and the foundation cannot make the investment with the intention of making a financial return. Do not take this to mean that foundations doing PRI do not expect to have their PRI loans returned or to make a return on any equity investments: they absolutely do expect to get their money back. Tax-exempt nonprofits are automatically eligible for PRI just as they are for grants; for-profit social enterprises can be, but it is more challenging for them to make the case.

Although more foundations are showing an interest in making loans and other types of investments from their grant-making funds, even to the point of setting up PRI funds, very few foundations are actively engaged in PRI, and even fewer are engaged in MRI. Only a small number of pioneering foundations are making investments directly to individual nonprofits or for-profit social enterprises, including some that are specifically focusing on sustainable food businesses that address issues of food access, food security, health, and economic development (among others). So unless you already have an existing relationship with a foundation and they ask if you are interested in a PRI investment, don't bother asking them. Chances are you would have to do a lot of education to help the foundation understand what PRI is in the first place, much less convince them that they should do it at all, much less to you. The exception would be if you discover a foundation PRI program that is actively seeking financing proposals, in which case, go for it.

—— Finding Foundations ——

There are many ways for mission-minded food entrepreneurs to go about finding foundations that might be interested in their work:

- **Look for grant makers near you.** Leslie Schaller of the Appalachian Center for Economic Networks in Ohio suggests that entrepreneurs develop relationships with local and regional foundations. "More and more foundations have established separate funds for local food and healthy community initiatives," she observes. Although foundations are the obvious players, don't forget to contact grocery stores in your area. "Many corporations have foundations for small grant programs, including Kroger and Lowe's. Most grocery chains and big-box retailers have foundations and a policy that allows each store to make small, local grants under $5,000," says Leslie. She adds that many big-box retailers and grocery warehouses can be great partners for donating such things as forklifts, pallet jacks, pallet racks, walk-in coolers, and other capital-intensive equipment. "It helps to be prepared with a list of equipment, renovation and expansion needs."
- **Look for grant makers that focus on your issue area.** In addition to local funders, there may be national funders committed to supporting projects like yours. The Sustainable Agriculture and Food Systems

Funders website includes a list of their members, and you can also search by geography: http://www.safsf.org/who/members. The Council on Foundations has a complete list of grant-maker affinity groups on their website: http://www.cof.org/about/affinitygroups.cfm.

- See who is funding similar projects or events. Many nonprofit websites list the names of foundations (and possibly also individuals) that support them, so you can do some research into which funders have supported projects similar to yours. The same goes for events centered around kindred issues, such as those that gather organic farming practitioners, promote local businesses, or advocate for green business practices.

—— Funders and the Element of Chance: —— Native American Natural Foods

Karlene Hunter, a member of the Oglala Sioux Tribe, has over twenty-five years of experience working on educational and economic development on the Pine Ridge Reservation in South Dakota. She has received numerous awards, including the 2011 Social Venture Network Innovation Award, and she is also CEO and cofounder of Native American Natural Foods. "We are focused on creating a family of nationally branded food products that are delicious and that promote a Native American way of wellness that feeds mind, body, and spirit," she explains. "Our vision is not to go back to a traditional way of life but to bring the heritage of wisdom from our traditional healthy lifestyle into the twenty-first century. We imagine a world filled with healthy foods that add to the restoration and preservation of our lands and ecosystem—a world without the pain of starvation or obesity."

Their Tanka products, named for the Lakota word for "outstanding" or "great," exemplify Native American Natural Foods' vision. "When we started working on the recipe for Tanka Bar, we were trying to meld authentic Native ingredients and flavors into a bar that would honor our past yet fit how we live today," Karlene recalls. "We started with the traditional recipe for *wasna*, the original Native trail mix made from dried buffalo meat and berries. We tried all sorts of ideas to improve on *wasna* but discovered it could not be improved. We're convinced our ancestors knew what they were doing. Tanka products honor their wisdom." First released in 2007, Tanka Bars were an instant success, and orders poured in from around the country after a feature on the front page of the *New York Times*'s "Dining In" section. Despite some significant challenges during the economic downturn of 2008 ("People just stopped buying products that weren't staples," Karlene observed), the company has experienced remarkable growth.

Meanwhile, Karlene and Native American Natural Foods cofounder and president Mark Tilsen have experienced firsthand the challenges associated with raising capital to keep up with this growth, primarily as it relates to purchasing raw materials to fulfill the orders that keep coming in. "When we first launched, we both mortgaged everything we had to finance the business," Karlene says. But after Tanka Bar sales starting taking off in the beginning of 2008, they needed still more capital to purchase the buffalo and cranberries to fulfill those orders. "We were able to get a loan from the First National Bank of Gordon, Nebraska, because we qualified for a 90 percent guarantee through the Bureau of Indian Affairs," Karlene explains. "But when orders slowed way down at the end of 2008, and our operating losses began to grow, we still needed cash to cover our operating expenses. That's when we started looking to foundations that might be able to help us."

It wasn't hard for Karlene and Mark to make the case that their company helps meet charitable goals. "Pine Ridge Reservation is one of the poorest communities in the United States, with an unemployment rate of more than 70 percent," says Karlene. "Our company is committed to creating jobs for young people from the Pine Ridge Reservation, and 95 percent of our staff are tribal members who live on the reservation." Ultimately, they discovered two foundations willing to consider making equity investments in Native American Natural Foods. An equity investment from Northwest Area Foundation through Lakota Funds, a local CDFI, allowed Native American Natural Foods to get through their cash crunch in 2008. The company continued to grow, reaching over $1.4 million in gross sales in 2011. "We had a proven product, and the market was exploding, but we still didn't know how we were going to be able to fulfill our orders on an ongoing basis," Karlene explains. "With traditional banking, if you don't have collateral, you're not going to get a loan. Native American Natural Foods has a six-thousand-square-foot building—we built it from scratch and it's entirely paid off—but we can't use it as collateral because it's on leased tribally owned land, which means the bank can't repossess it. If the majority of your assets are in land and structures, but you can't use those as collateral, what the heck are you going to use?" Karlene asks, reflecting a struggle faced by many Native American entrepreneurs. "You need to find people and institutions with creative alternatives."

Sometimes those people find you. One day in 2011, Sonja Swift came by the Native American Natural Foods offices at the suggestion of a mutual friend. "We always stop what we're doing to talk with people who want to come in and learn more about what we're doing," Karlene says. "We have a lot of interesting conversations that way." She figured this would be just another one of those interesting conversations. "I didn't know who Sonja was, what her background was. All I knew was that she was a very nice person who obviously really cared about what was going on at Pine Ridge Reservation and the issues we face," Karlene recalls. "We talked about everything: what the company was doing, the importance of the land and of using the land. We were deep into our financing conundrum at the time, and I joked that I could also tell her all about the difficulties of financing our inventory. She actually wanted me to go into those details. It was pretty shocking when she called a few weeks later and said, 'I think we can help you.' We said, 'We who?' Then she started giving us her background, and told us about the Swift Foundation."

Sonja explained that she served on the board of her family's Swift Foundation, which supports local stewards and their allies who are dedicated to protecting biological and cultural diversity, building resilience amidst climate change, and restoring the health and dignity of communities globally.[22] Like many foundations, the Swift Foundation does not accept unsolicited proposals, so it was quite fortunate for them that Sonja discovered Native American Natural Foods. "This company is having such an amazing impact," Sonja says. "Their employees are receiving training so they can own part of the company. And they are providing a way for people to make a living off of the land again by purchasing the prairie-raised buffalo that goes into the Tanka products." Despite her own enthusiasm, Sonja still needed to gain the support of the rest of her family foundation's board. "The timing of my meeting with Karlene and Mark was serendipitous, because the Swift Foundation board meeting happened soon afterward," she reports. "We were able to approve an investment, and this transaction turned out to be one of the more unique transactions the foundation has ever made."

Morgan Roberts of Manchester Capital Management is the investment adviser who worked with the Swift Foundation as it tried to decide how best to help Native American Natural Foods in a way that aligned with their values. He coordinated the due diligence effort, poring over the company's operating agreement, capital structure, balance sheet, income statements, and other documentation. "In this particular case, we decided it was a little too risky to make a straight loan," he explains. "There was a community development bank that was willing to do a large loan if Native American Natural Foods could find an equity investor to place $150,000, so the real opportunity was for us to buy a little equity in the company." But first they had to agree on a valuation for the company, which proved to be a challenge. "Mark thought the company was worth $5 million, but I said, 'No, it's not, but here's what we can do,'" Morgan recalls. "We knew that they would need additional financing later on, so we drafted an antidilution clause [into the term sheet] that would ensure that when other investors came in, nobody would be able to buy stock at a lower price than we paid. Or if they do get a lower price, Native American Natural Foods will have to credit us with additional shares so that effectively we would be paying the lower price." Now the Swift Foundation owns 3 percent of the company, and Morgan connects with them several times a year to make sure they're following their business plan and optimizing use of their resources.

This was not the first food-related investment for the Swift Foundation. Among its other investments, they had both made a loan and bought equity in Guayakí, another high-impact food company. Morgan notes that although the Native American Natural Foods deal is a high-risk investment for the foundation, it's a relatively small one, and it's very much mission aligned. "We have a certain amount of money dedicated to mission-related investments," he explains. "We don't do program-related investments per se; we treat all investments as investments. PRI is really just an accounting device for a foundation's tax return. We vet everything as an investment."

Karlene has nothing but praise for Sonja and her family, who "are doing it right. They are really getting in there and doing the research, getting involved with organizations and companies that are impacting change." Almost more important than that, though, according to Karlene, is that she and Sonja "clicked." "I really love her. She's a sweetheart," Karlene says of Sonja. "It all goes to show, you just never know who you're talking to," Karlene warns other entrepreneurs. "We could have said, when she first wanted to come in and talk to us, 'No, we don't have time to talk. We're busy; we're tired.' We might never have had the support of the Swift Foundation."

This is quite a remarkable story for several reasons. First, it is very rare that a foundation has such innovative policies that allow this type of investment directly into a project. That the deal worked out so quickly—thanks to an imminent board meeting and a team that could make snap decisions —is also nothing short of miraculous. And I probably don't need to point out that counting on a foundation representative's approaching you is a rather irresponsible fundraising plan. But these aspects help highlight the double-edged nature of pursuing foundation funding. Unless your venture is a nonprofit, it takes an unusual confluence of factors to make it a realistic option. On the other hand, if you do have that rare combination of ingredients, foundation funding can be really creative and high impact.

20

......

Selling without Selling Out

"I'LL NEVER FORGET THE DAY that Coke bought Odwalla." Will Rosen-zweig sat on stage in front of a roomful of institutional investors in the fall of 2011, just days away from the ten-year anniversary of Odwalla's sale to the Coca-Cola Company. He told a rapt audience about his UC Berkeley students' reaction to the news a decade earlier. "You could hear half the class groan, 'There goes the neighborhood!' The other half was like, 'Ooh! Now just think of how many people will have access to that fresh, healthy juice!'"

In recent years many socially responsible food companies have been purchased by larger companies, particularly in processing, distribution, and retail.[23] In one sense this has been a good thing for fundraising entrepreneurs, because an active acquisition market can help attract equity investors, who can look forward to an acquisition as their exit. But so often when a values-based food company becomes the domain of a larger, bottom-line-focused company, any number of things can happen. Longtime employees have been let go. The company headquarters and other facilities have been moved out of the communities that nurtured them. Founders have been fired. Company commitments, whether related to sourcing sustainable ingredients, packaging and other inputs, community giving programs, or employee benefits, have been weakened or gone away altogether.

If you're reading this book, chances are you believe in the power of social entrepreneurship to solve many of the problems we face today, both in our communities and on our living planet. It's harder to guess how you feel about socially responsible companies selling to multinational corporations or going public on an international stock market. Many committed sustainable food system advocates believe that any sale or public offering means that a founder has sold out, regardless of circumstances; others believe that you can have real impact only if you achieve the kind of scale possible solely through a multinational, publicly traded company.

There is no one right answer, but one thing is certain: no founder can run a company forever. Not only are you mortal, but sometimes you just know it's time to turn your attention to something other than your business. Sooner or later you might also be ready to realize the financial gains from your investment of time and money over the course of your business's evolution. (If you have sold stock in your company, your investors might be ready to cash out themselves.) There is an endless list of reasons a founder might want to move on or cash out. The trick is coming up with a succession plan that is aligned with your values, and it's never too soon to start thinking about how to finance your transition out of the company.

If you do decide to sell your company—to another person, to a group of people, to another company, or to the public market—there are some things you can do to minimize diluting the values that you built into it. This chapter won't tell you everything you need to know about succession plans. That could be a book in itself, and many of the lessons are still being lived and learned by some of the first-generation sustainable food entrepreneurs. Even if there are no easy answers, I hope the following stories will inspire you to think about which questions to start asking about how your business might carry on under new ownership, with or without you in charge.

Classic Acquisitions

There are a few well-known instances of organic food company acquisitions that I won't describe in great detail because so much has been said about them already. But I will mention them briefly here, just in case you want to research them further.

Ben & Jerry's, whose DPO story I described in chapter 10 was ultimately purchased by Unilever in 2000 for $326 million, very much against the founders' intentions. This now legendary cautionary tale for social entrepreneurs occurred after a long series of very well-intentioned decisions, including taking the company public on NASDAQ to give the DPO shareholders a way to realize the value of their stocks and hiring a new CEO to take the company to the next level who, according to Ben, turned out not to share quite the same values as the founders. For years, the general understanding has been that Ben & Jerry's had no choice but to sell the company when

Unilever made an offer that was so much greater than the company's values, given the legal responsibility of the board to maximize shareholder value.[24]

In April of the same year Ben & Jerry's sold to Unilever, Gary Erickson turned down a $120 million offer to sell the natural energy bar company he founded and co-owned, Clif Bar, to Quaker Oats. Gary had spent the previous ten years growing the company to a $40 million business with sustainability at its core, permeating everything from its organic ingredients to its innovative program for keeping employees happy and healthy to its active role as a community player. Rather than run the risk that these values might disappear after he sold the company, Gary literally left his company's suitor at the altar or, rather, the boardroom table, on the day he was supposed to have finalized the sale. In his book *Raising the Bar: Integrity and Passion in Life and Business* (2004), Gary writes thoughtfully about the fears that so often lead people to sell their companies, his decision not to sell Clif Bar, and the consequences of making his choice—for one, he had to quickly come up with the money to buy out his business partner at Clif Bar, who had wanted to go through with the Quaker Oats deal. A year later, Quaker Oats, an American multinational food and beverage company, merged with Pepsico; two years after turning down the $120 million offer, Clif Bar committed to making all its products organic. Who knows if this would have been possible as a Pepsico company? Gary Erickson is still glad he decided not to sell and is proud of what Clif Bar continues to accomplish.

Gary Hirshberg took an entirely different route with the organic yogurt company he cofounded in 1983 and is equally pleased with the results. When he was ready to give Stonyfield Farm's early investors, many of whom were friends and family, a way to get their money out of the company, Gary spent a couple of years exploring his options. Eventually he worked out a unique arrangement with Groupe Danone, a $600 million French multinational food company, to purchase 40 percent of the company's shares from existing shareholders in 2001. Groupe Danone would also serve as a strategic partner, giving Stonyfield access to the expertise of its worldwide team. Groupe Danone was interested in Stonyfield because it would enable them to benefit from the rapid growth in the organic and natural dairy segment. This first deal was a test of sorts, as Gary wanted to be sure that he would still be able to manage the company in accordance with his ambitious organic, environmental, and social missions with such an enormous partner, relative to the size of Stonyfield. Indeed, Groupe Danone continued to let Gary keep control over the vast majority of Stonyfield's management, even after the two parties agreed in 2003 that Groupe Danone would become a majority shareholder by purchasing all of the remaining shares that weren't owned by employees. Groupe Danone even made Gary managing director for a new initiative that would bring a joint venture overseas, and it adopted some of Stonyfield's other environmentally friendly practices. (Stonyfield did not receive any capital from Groupe Danone in either transaction, which merely bought out the other shareholders.) "This has been a win-win-win-win for Stonyfield's customers, shareholders, employees, and for Groupe Danone," Gary said in a Stonyfield statement from 2003. Gary, who is still chair of the board of Stonyfield as of this writing but stepped down as the company's "CE-Yo" in 2012, believes that we need to work with larger companies in order to combat the larger climate issues that we face nowadays. If you feel the same way, you might want to consider his not-quite-a-traditional-sale model.

A Homegrown IPO

John Foraker of Annie's and Molly Ashby of Solera Capital (we met them in chapter 18) had a hunch that Annie's could do better than be swallowed up by another company. John knew he wanted to stay with the company, continuing to grow it and further its mission, and he wasn't sure if that would be possible if they sold the company. He and Molly pondered the company's future in many of their collaborative conversations over the years. "We always knew Annie's was a unique company with great growth potential and wondered if it could stand alone as a public company," he recalls, adding that selling the company would certainly be the easier route, although it was unclear what financial return the shareholders would realize if that happened. "We always had a sense of pragmatic reality about an IPO," he says, even as they began to talk to a few big investment bankers about the possibility in early 2011, "because few food companies had gone public in the preceding decade." In fact, no organic food company had gone public for thirteen or fourteen years at that point, he reports. But John and Molly were pleasantly surprised that the investment bankers thought there would be real institutional interest in a company like theirs. They decided to forge ahead with an IPO, choosing Credit Suisse and J. P. Morgan to serve as the underwriters.

In 2012 the company's shares were originally offered at $19 apiece, primarily to a group of interested investors John calls "the bluest of blue-chip institutional investors and the best firms in the U.S. and the world," whom they courted during an eight-day investor road show. (Prior to that, all shares of preferred stock were converted to common stock in anticipation of the IPO.) He says that without exception they all understood how integral Annie's mission is to its customers and the financial value of the company. "We really led with that, because we believe that's a really important factor that differentiates us from other companies. At the time I wondered if we should be so out there about our values," John recalls, "but it wasn't a hard decision; that's how we've always been." By all accounts, the market agreed. On March 28, 2012, Annie's stock opened to public trading on the New York Stock Exchange under the symbol BNNY. Share value soared above $35, giving Solera Capital a hefty return on their investment and the company a market value of close to $600 million.

John says that the IPO has brought Annie's many more benefits than the capital necessary to continue growing the business. Though he cannot calculate just how much the company benefited, he knows the IPO helped create awareness about Annie's among the public. "To put it in perspective, in a regular year, we were getting about 400 million media impressions across all of our advertising channels," he reports. "The quarter we went public, we received 1.3 billion impressions and generated amazing media stories about Annie's."

As of this writing, John is still CEO of Annie's, and he expects to stay in this role for years to come. Solera Capital still owns 28 percent of the company, and John reports that he is grateful that Molly and Solera Capital continue to be such close strategic partners.

—— Employee Stock Ownership Plans ——

Are you committed to building wealth for your employees? Do you want to reward them for helping grow your company into the success that it has become? Is your company a C corporation rather than an LLC, sole proprietorship, or partnership? If so, an employee stock ownership plan (ESOP) might be a transition strategy that can help you meet your goals.

Jim Cochran was an early organic farming pioneer, becoming the first California strawberry farmer to move to organic methods starting in 1983.

His farm, Swanton Berry Farm, now grows several types of berries, plus broccoli, cauliflower, artichokes, and other vegetables, all certified organic, on five different leased locations on the Northern California coast. In 2004, recognizing the challenges that young people have today in starting to farm, particularly if they do not have money of their own to invest, he implemented a version of an employee stock ownership plan for Swanton Berry Farm. Jim awards all employees on the farm, which is under a union contract, with stock bonuses through the plan, making them part owners of the operation. Over time the employees will come to own a substantial portion of the business, building more equity in the farm during years when the business does well and less during bad years. Stockholders have full access to the farm's financials and other records, and they participate in much of the decision making at Swanton Berry Farm, making this arrangement less like working as someone else's employee than working on their own family's farm—but without many of the disadvantages. "They are guaranteed a modest income and benefits package, without the serious downside risk faced by independent farmers who regularly work all year long and still lose money," Jim explains. "Further, they have colleagues who can spell them so that they can spend more time with their families. Both of these factors will reduce the amount of stress they face and will hopefully make farming a psychologically sustainable option for them."

Jim says it took him ten years to save the $50,000 required to handle the accounting and legal paperwork to implement Swanton Berry Farm's ESOP, and it can get more expensive than this, depending on how complicated your situation is. All things considered, however, ESOP paperwork can cost you much less than, say, selling to another company, assuming there is one interested in the sale. Swanton Berry Farm has annual revenues just above $2 million, making it a relatively small company. But if you think that ESOPs are only for small-scale businesses, think again.

On February 15, 2010, Bob Moore of Bob's Red Mill Natural Foods Company celebrated his eighty-first birthday. He also surprised the employees with an ESOP that made them 100 percent owners of this multimillion-dollar Milwaukie, Oregon, company, which produces over four hundred whole grain products, many of them organic. An announcement to customers on the company's website explains, "This means . . . that Bob's Red Mill has secured its own destiny, committing to the long term that the values and high standards we all cherish will last into the future."[25] Roger Farnen, quality assurance manager, adds, "By creating the ESOP, Bob and [his business] partners have fulfilled their ultimate quest for sharing success among all employees. And it provides tangible incentives for optimal achievement no matter what their position in the company. Bob is basically passing the entrepreneurial torch on to his employees and is instilling in us that hard work provides rewards."

According to operations vice president Dennis Vaughn, "The partners could have sold this company many times for a lot more money, but to them this company is about so much more than the money." At the time he implemented the ESOP, the value of the company amounted to hundreds of thousands of dollars for each of the two hundred nine employees. As in all ESOPs, however, the individual employees do not own the stock directly. Instead, the stock is held in a trust, and when an employee retires or leaves, the trust will buy back the stock attributed to that employee based on its particular vesting arrangement. A year later Bob was still running the company, along with a group of stakeholders who, according to the company's blog, "help steer decisions that affect the company." The company also points out that Bob's Red Mill is genuinely a team effort, involving every employee.[26]

Of course, you need not be as generous as Bob and give your company away all in one fell swoop in order to do an ESOP successfully. You can make the transition slowly, as Jim is doing with Swanton Berry Farm. Many commercial banks make special loans to companies who are in that process, and depending on your situation, there can be tax advantages to both the owners and the employees involved in an ESOP. They aren't appropriate for all entity types, however, and you need to be careful when you add new employees to the plan, as this dilutes the value of existing shares. But the ESOP is an exciting model for certain entrepreneurs, particularly if there are employees in your company who are poised to take over leadership. If you're interested in learning more, the National Center for Employee Ownership offers a wealth of information on their website: https://www.nceo.org. You can also check out the 142-page book, *Understanding ESOPs*, by Corey Rosen and Scott Rodrick (2008).

—— Keeping the Brand Close ——

In 1983 Judy Wicks founded the White Dog Café in Philadelphia as a takeout coffee and muffin shop. Always deeply passionate about supporting her fellow local entrepreneurs (she cofounded the Business Alliance of Local Living Economies, after all), Judy continued to deepen her commitment to sustainable food systems as the business grew. When she learned about the plight of pigs in industrial factory farms, she took meat off the menu until she could figure out a way to source locally from farms where animals were raised on pasture and treated humanely. Eventually, the White Dog Café came to purchase all of its meat, poultry, and eggs, as well as vegetables and fruits when in season, from local family farms. Many other products, such as office supplies and cleaning products, come from local, independently owned, green purveyors, too. Sustainable fishing is also important to Judy, so she made the commitment that 75 percent or more of the restaurant's fish must be from the "best choices" list specified by the Monterey Bay Aquarium's Seafood Watch program, and they won't serve any fish from the program's "avoid" list. On hearing about the social and financial challenges faced by the workers and growers of coffee, tea, chocolate, table sugar, and even spices like cinnamon and vanilla, Judy instituted a policy that the café source only certified Fair Trade forms, many of which are also certified organic. All electricity is purchased from 100% renewable sources, and the restaurant recycles and composts as much as it can. Also dedicated to her employees, Judy ensured that the highest-paid person in the restaurant would make no more than a certain ratio higher than the lowest-paid worker, and she developed a generous employee benefits plan, including an employee charitable giving program and interest-free loans for employees who wanted to buy their first computers.

By 2008 the White Dog Café had grown to a two-hundred-seat restaurant, and for twenty years a sister retail store (now closed), named the Black Cat, offered locally made and fair trade gifts in the next-door brownstone building. Between these two businesses, revenues had reached $5 million annually. And Judy knew that the time had come for her to transition away from her roles there, so she could turn her attention full time to other humanitarian and social efforts. "I had spent a couple of years looking into employee stock ownership plans, going to ESOP conferences, and even hiring a lawyer who specialized in them," Judy explains. "But I finally realized: although an ESOP would have addressed the ownership issue, it wouldn't address the leadership issue. Unfortunately, I hadn't groomed any of my employees for that role, and no one was showing an interest in the responsibility of running the company, so I needed to find another entrepreneur to take over the leadership of the White Dog Café." Through her social network, she managed to identify a local restaurateur who was very interested in the White Dog Café because it is a beloved Philadelphia institution. But how would she ensure that the values of her business would remain intact with another person at the helm?

While Judy had been researching ESOPs, the trademarks for both the name and logo of the White Dog came up for renewal. Rather than renew these under the ownership of the corporation, she had the foresight to renew them under her own name, figuring that this might one day come in handy during the succession of the business to new owners. And in fact when she sold the company, "the most important aspect of the sale was that I owned the name and the logo," Judy says. With the help of a savvy friend she knew from the Social Venture Network, she concocted an innovative arrangement that would allow her to sell the restaurant while maintaining control of its values.

Judy put the name and logo into a new LLC, which in turn licenses these two assets back to the new owner—along with a social contract. "This contract identifies the business practices that the new owner must adhere to in order to do business under the name White Dog," Judy explains. The social contract outlines the basic philosophy of the restaurant, including all of the local, organic, humane, and fair trade procurement policies that Judy developed and a stipulation about maintaining at least 51 percent local ownership for any new location should the new owner want to open additional restaurants under the White Dog name. The agreement calls for quarterly meetings for Judy and the new owner to go over any concerns, and if any aspect of the social contract is broken, Judy reserves the right to take back the name and logo.

The finances of the deal were tricky to work out. The sale of the business in 2009 included the corporation itself and all of the other assets of the business, but the really valuable part was the brand—the name and the logo—which were not part of the sale. So Judy took home a lot less money than she could have if she had sold everything all together, but with the help of her friend and a licensing lawyer, she worked out an arrangement that would allow her to recoup the full value of the business over the next fifteen years (65 percent in the first five years) through the licensing fees for the name and logo, plus royalty payments on a percentage of all sales from the restaurant or from merchandise that displays the White Dog name or logo. If Judy finds the new owner in violation and they cannot agree to a recourse prior to the fifteen-year mark, she would forfeit whatever licensing fees and royalties have yet to be paid. "We tried to work it out so that if they violated the social contract, they would have to pay the licensing fees anyway, but their lawyer wouldn't go for that," she says. "But what is more important to me than the money is the social contract, the values. If White Dog is not going to have the same values behind it, I don't want anyone else to use the name, and that is worth a lot of money to me." (Judy also still owns the building and receives lease payments from the new owner.)

So far, the agreement, which has been in effect for three years, has worked well, and there is now a second White Dog Café in a town near Philadelphia and near the residence of the primary owner. "It is doing very well, which gives twice the business to local farmers and fair trade suppliers," Judy says, adding, "Older customers who live closer to the new location appreciate not having to make the trip into the city to eat food they can trust."

One weakness that Judy has identified is that the only tool she has if the values start to erode is to take away the White Dog name. As she explains, "The problem is that this would hurt me as much as it would hurt the new owners. This is my life work, and my name is behind the White Dog Café. I would suggest that other people build in an intermediary penalty, such as a fine, before taking back the name." She would also prefer that the social contract had more policies that could actually be measured quantitatively; she thinks there's far too much gray area as it currently stands. Ultimately, though, Judy is excited about this model and looks forward to getting more ideas from others about how to make it even better to help the next entrepreneurs who want to use such a scheme. You can read more about Judy's experience with the White Dog Café in her new book, *Good Morning, Beautiful Business: The Unexpected Journey of an Activist Entrepreneur and Local-Economy Pioneer* (Chelsea Green, 2013).

EPILOGUE

......

Putting the Layers Together

As YOU HAVE NO DOUBT NOTICED by now, from both your own experience and the case studies in this book, no single form of financing will satisfy your business's capital needs from the time you first launch it to the time when you're ready to move on. Rather, you will likely need to use several types of capital from a variety of different sources as your business grows and evolves over time.

Sadly, the process of fundraising can often end up feeling like trying to put together a jigsaw puzzle when not all the pieces even exist yet: the capital markets are not quite there when it comes to efficiently matching the people and institutions that want to invest in socially responsible food businesses with those entrepreneurs who want to put that money to work. I was once at a conference where the topic at hand was sales channels for farmers. One of the speakers—I wish I could remember who it was—quipped, "There is a market for every farmer, but not every market is for every farmer." In the world of raising capital, the saying would go something like this: "There is not financing for every entrepreneur, and not every type of financing is for every socially responsible food business."

Fortunately, as I have mentioned before, the field of food finance is shifting in a positive direction, more rapidly now than at any other time since I've been paying close attention. Financing options have multiplied, even if they can still be somewhat difficult to find, particularly for those who have historically had less access to resources. Thanks to the work of many of the organizations and financial institutions mentioned in this book and the pioneering foundations and people who support them, more and more money is becoming available, and under more appropriate terms, for socially responsible food businesses.

I hope this book has helped make some sense of all the different options currently available, both in terms of understanding when each might be appropriate and understanding where to go and what to do to maximize your chances of accessing this capital in a way that aligns with your values. Whatever new forms or sources of financing might arrive in the near term are unlikely to deviate significantly from what I covered here, so the advice for accessing the main categories of financing should still hold true. The major players currently involved in this movement, all of whom I tried to cover in this book, will probably continue to stay at its cutting edge, so if you want to make sure you're the first to know about any new capital opportunities that arise, sign up for their updates; I will also continue to post relevant news and resources on my website, http://www.financeforfood.com.

If your own experiences working with the different categories of financiers has been completely different from what you have read here, for better or for worse, I do hope that you will take the time to tell your story. Of course, I'd love to hear from you so I can share your story through Finance for Food's work. In addition, there are many other ways to relate your experience in a forum where other socially responsible food entrepreneurs can benefit from your insights, including through the networks mentioned in chapter 1. I cannot close without offering my gratitude: I would never have been inspired to write this book in the first place had it not been for the generosity of the food entrepreneurs who shared their stories with me, including those featured in this book and many more that I did not have the space to mention explicitly. Every one of them understood the importance of sharing their lessons with a wider audience. We are going to need to work together if we want to continue building momentum in the sustainable food movement. Thank you, reader, for your role in this ever-growing puzzle.

ACKNOWLEDGMENTS

FIRST AND FOREMOST, I am grateful to Sarah Bell and the entire board and staff of the 11th Hour Project. Their generous financial support of Finance for Food made this book possible. Thank you to the Trust for Conservation Innovation for serving as the nonprofit home of Finance for Food, the project that resulted in this book and several workshops organized around its content; Finance for Food will receive all author royalties generated from this book's sales. Additional financial support for this project came from the Food and Community Fellowship program of the Institute for Agriculture and Trade Policy, funded by the Woodcock and W. K. Kellogg Foundations, and from the GRACE Communications Foundation.

I thank my parents, Michele and Kwei Ü, for being the first to show me food's role in cultivating all that is valuable in life. I am also grateful to the following people and organizations that provided physical space, moral support, and nourishing food at critical times: Elizabeth Grace; Adam Ü; Mahea Campbell and Alea Malay; Peter Barnes and the Mesa Refuge writing retreat program; Katy Mamen, the Sowers Circle, and the Occidental Arts and Ecology Center; John Bloom, Gary Schick, and the entire staff of RSF Social Finance; Charlie Callahan; and Geoffrey Fleming.

Thanks to Elliott Hoffman for making a critical introduction at exactly the right time, and to Sarah Bird and John Foraker, Greg Steltenpohl and Jon Ramer, Mari Mielcarski and Woody Tasch, and Don Shaffer (in his case, three times over). Their confidence in me resulted in a decade's worth of professional experience at the intersection of sustainable agriculture and social finance, which ultimately culminated in this book. I have always appreciated—even if I have not always heeded—Don's advice to stay out of the weeds.

I am honored to have such a talented and supportive kitchen cabinet of advisers. Virginia Clarke, Brian Snyder, and Mike Roberts have provided endless inspiration and hours of laughter, and I am eternally grateful for our ongoing collaborations and adventures. Warren Langley and John Katovich have watched this project evolve from its first incarnation as an assignment for the capital markets class they designed for the Pioneer Cohort of the Presidio Graduate School's MBA in sustainable management; thank you for helping cultivate that little seed. Simran Sethi and Brahm Ahmadi were right there beside me in the pioneer cohort of that program, and I've learned as much about both dedication and public speaking from them as I have from anyone. Kathleen Fluegel and Martin Ping have both humbled me in their commitment to and reminders of what is truly important. Michelle Long has shown me time and time again that hosting what she calls "a better party" is an incredibly effective way to foster positive change in the world, and I'm delighted to be able to attend so many of hers. I send much gratitude to Eric Becker, Jim Cochran, Jeff Rosen, Ricardo Salvador, Josh Viertel, Mas Masumoto, and Leslie Schaller, who have each mentored and supported me in unique and wonderful ways.

Thanks to Brianne Goodspeed and all the good folks at Chelsea Green (an employee-owned publishing company) who have helped get this book out of my head and into your hands. I have Jenny Kassan and the Sustainable Economies Law Center to thank for vetting (and, often, drafting) the legal portions of this book, although I take full responsibility for any errors. Thanks to the many food entrepreneurs and finance experts who took the time to help me understand various pieces of the puzzle, including those whose stories did not make it into the final cut. I am very grateful for the organizational skills of Kate Poole, who helped me keep track of the many quotes in this book, and to Gary Sprague for his excellent editing skills. Finally, thanks to Sylvia Sukop, fellow Mesa "refugette," for revealing to me the wonders of Scrivener.

NOTES

1. "The Slow Money Principles," Slow Money, accessed November 29, 2012, http://slowmoney.org/principles.
2. Internal Revenue Code Section 501(c)(3), accessed November 11, 2011, http://www.irs.gov/Charities-&-Non-Profits/Charitable-Organizations/Exemption-Requirements-Section-501%28c%29%283%29-Organizations.
3. "S Corporations," accessed November 27, 2012, http://www.irs.gov/Businesses/Small-Businesses-&-Self-Employed/S-Corporations.
4. The states that have enacted benefit corporation legislation are California, Hawaii, Illinois, Louisiana, Maryland, Massachusetts, New Jersey, New York, Pennsylvania, South Carolina, Vermont, and Virginia. "State by State Legislative Status," accessed January 15, 2013, http://www.benefitcorp.net/state-by-state-legislative-status, accessed January 15, 2013.
5. Regulation §20.2031-1, accessed April 13, 2012, http://www.irs.gov/businesses/small/article/0,,id=108139,00.html
6. Regulation §20.2031-1, accessed April 13, 2012, http://www.irs.gov/businesses/small/article/0,,id=108139,00.html.
7. IRS Publication 950, accessed November 29, 2012, http://www.irs.gov/publications/p950/ar02.html.
8. "Gift Cards and Gift Certificate Statutes," accessed November 29, 2012, http://www.ncsl.org/issues-research/banking/gift-cards-and-certificates-statutes-and-legis.aspx.
9. "Kickstarter Stats," accessed April 10, 2013, http://www.kickstarter.com/help/stats.
10. SEC Securities Act of 1933, accessed November 29, 2012, http://www.sec.gov/about/laws/sa33.pdf; Jenny Kassan, personal communication, October 24, 2012.
11. "Small Business and the SEC," accessed November 15, 2011, http://www.sec.gov/info/smallbus/qasbsec.htm#eod1.
12. Jenny Kassan, personal communication, October 24, 2012.
13. Rule 501 of Regulation D, accessed September 28, 2012, http://www.sec.gov/answers/accred.htm.

14. "SCOR Overview," accessed November 29, 2012, http://www.nasaa
    .org/industry-resources/corporation-finance/scor-overview/.

15. "US Securities and Exchange Commission, "Guide to Broker-Dealer
    Registration," accessed March 4, 2013, http://www.sec.gov/divisions
    /marketreg/bdguide.htm.

16. IRS Publication 535 Chapter 4, accessed November 20, 2012, http://
    www.irs.gov/publications/p535/ch04.html.

17. http://www.opportunityfinance.net/about/, accessed 3/1/13.

18. "Halo Report: 2011 Angel Group Year in Review," accessed March 1,
    2013, http://www.angelresourceinstitute.org/en/Research/~/media
    /ARI/Images/Site%20Images/Halo-Report-Infographic3c.jpg.

19. Ibid.

20. Kawasaki, Guy. "The 10/20/30 Rule of PowerPoint," accessed March 1,
    2013, http://blog.guykawasaki.com/2005/12/the_102030_rule.html.

21. GIIN homepage, accessed November 26, 2012, http://www.thegiin.org.

22. "Swift Foundation Mission," accessed March 4, 2013, http://swift
    foundation.org.

23. If you want to visualize what consolidation within the organic and
    natural food world looks like, Philip H. Howard, associate professor
    at Michigan State University, has created some fascinating graphics
    to illustrate the ownership structure within these industries: see
    his website, accessed December 29, 2012, https://www.msu.edu
    /~howardp/infographics.html.

24. As of this writing, on the website for the article "The Truth About Ben
    and Jerry's," *Stanford Social Innovation Review* (Fall 2012), various at-
    torneys and other socially responsible business specialists were debat-
    ing whether or not this interpretation of the corporate law is actually
    true. The article, which discusses among other things the need for new
    entity structures to address the demands of socially responsible busi-
    nesses, plus the comments that follow, make for fascinating reading:
    "The Truth About Ben and Jerry's," accessed October 29, 2012, http://
    www.ssireview.org/articles/entry/the_truth_about_ben_and_jerrys.

25. "Letter to Bob's Redmill Customers," accessed November 9, 2012,
    http://docs.bobsredmill.com/index2.php?option=com_docman
    &task=doc_view&gid=5225&Itemid=29.

26. "ESOP, a year later," accessed November 9, 2012, http://www.bobsredmill
    .com/blog/featured-articles/esop-a-year-later.

RESOURCES

I MENTION MANY OF THESE RESOURCES in the preceding chapters, and I have done my best here to explain what I think are the most useful aspects of each. All of the links were accurate as of this writing, but the web is an ever-changing universe; if a link no longer works, you can often still find the resource mentioned by typing its title or key words into your favorite search engine.

Networks and Organizations

The Slow Money website provides information about upcoming conferences and events, local chapters, and videos from past entrepreneur showcases. It also features a list of investment funds that operate in accordance with the Slow Money Principles (see sidebar on page 13), which you will find under the resources for investors; take a look to see if there is one that invests in companies like yours: http://slowmoney.org/other-resources.

The Social Venture Network (SVN) website includes information about membership, a directory of sustainable products and services from current members, and upcoming events and workshops: http://svn.org.

The Business Alliance for Local Living Economy (BALLE) website includes links to local networks, information about upcoming events and workshops (including the Accelerating Community Capital webinar series), and a sign-up form for the BALLE Buzz e-newsletter: http://www.bealocalist.org.

Business Planning and Mentorship

Marjorie Kelley's book, *Owning Our Future: The Emerging Ownership Revolution* (Berrett-Koehler, 2012), explores key design elements of businesses with deep values at their core. It includes some very interesting observations about generative (as opposed to extractive) ownership structures.

The Corporation for Enterprise Development website offers information about individual development accounts (IDAs), including a directory of programs: http://cfed.org/programs/idas/ida_basics/. California FarmLink pioneered an IDA program designed to help beginning and underserved farmers finance their agricultural endeavors, and there is a federal project under way that could, if all goes well, introduce similar IDA programs in another fifteen states, so keep an eye out for an announcement of such a program in your state.

Most local Small Business Development Center (SBDC) offices have their own websites describing the services they provide. Find the office nearest you using the directory at America's Small Business Development Center Network's website: http://www.asbdc-us.org/. You can also search using their map-based interface: http://www.asbdc-us.org/About_Us/SBDCs.html.

The U.S. Small Business Administration offers a wealth of information on starting and managing a business, including templates and outlines for business plans and financials: http://www.sba.gov/.

Learn more about SBA's Service Corps of Retired Executives (SCORE) services, find a local office, or find an online mentor at their website: http://www.score.org/.

SCORE's website also offers information about putting together financial statements, including links to several financial statement templates: http://www.score.org/resources/business-plans-financial-statements-template-gallery.

The National Business Incubator Association can provide you with a referral to nearby business incubators that work with food-based businesses: http://www.nbia.org/contact. You can also browse their website's state-by-state list of general business incubators: http://www.nbia.org/links_to_member_incubators/index.php.

The Midwest Organic and Sustainable Education Service has published a useful guide entitled *Fearless Farm Finances: Farm Financial Management Demystified*, which you can order from the organization's website: http://www.mosesorganic.org/farmfinances.html.

The Field Guide to the New American Foodshed project seeks to educate and promote opportunity for young, beginning, and small farmers in foodshed-related businesses. Their website includes templates for a one-page business plan and one-page financial plan, primarily for food producers, plus an hour-long webinar on these topics: http://foodshedguide.org/planning.

The William James Foundation's website lists many useful resources for social entrepreneurs, including lists of business plan competitions, conferences, business accelerators, and other organizations that may be of assistance: http://williamjamesfoundation.org.

Online Crowdfunding

The two largest and most popular online crowdfunding platforms are IndieGoGo and Kickstarter: http://www.IndieGoGo.com and http://www.Kickstarter.com.

Credibles and Three Revolutions are both designed specifically for food companies:

  https://credibles.org and http://threerevolutions.com.

  StartSomeGood is a crowdfunding platform for social enterprises only: www.StartSomeGood.com.

Kickstarter School and the Insights section of IndieGoGo's blog offer advice and tips for successful crowdfunding: http://www.kickstarter.com/help/school and http://www.indiegogo.com/blog.

Crowdsourcing.org offers general advice for tapping the wisdom of crowds, including crowdfunding resources: http://www.Crowdsourcing.org.

Raising Money from Your Community

Economist, attorney, author, and entrepreneur Michael Shuman wrote his book *Local Dollars, Local Sense: How to Shift Your Money from Wall Street to Main Street and Achieve Real Prosperity* (Chelsea Green, 2012) primarily for people who are looking to invest in their local businesses, but this fascinating and well-researched book is also an excellent read for entrepreneurs looking to raise capital from nonaccredited investors.

Amy Cortese's book *Locavesting: The Revolution in Local Investing and How to Profit from It* (Wiley and Sons, 2011) is another well-researched book that includes specific examples in which entrepreneurs have raised capital from local community members.

Securities Law

If you really want to get into the nitty-gritty details of securities law as it relates to capital-raising entrepreneurs, check out Jenny Kassan's chapter 6 of Janelle Orsi's book *Practicing Law in the Sharing Economy: Helping People Build Cooperatives, Social Enterprise, and Local Sustainable Economies* (American Bar Association, 2012). Because the book was designed for practicing attorneys, you might consider sharing a copy with your lawyer if she seems a little unclear on the possibilities.

The Securities and Exchange Commission (SEC) maintains a list of answers to frequently asked questions about the JOBS Act of 2012. This law should make it easier to engage in the type of crowdfunding in which you can offer investors a financial return: http://www.sec.gov/divisions/corpfin/guidance /cfjjobsactfaq-title-i-general.htm.

Personal Credit Options

The Federal Reserve Board website offers a helpful guide to shopping around, comparing, and negotiating the best possible mortgage, including a mortgage shopping worksheet: http://www.federalreserve.gov/pubs /mortgage/worksheet.pdf. They also offer helpful advice for understanding credit card offers, plus tips for paying off credit card debt: http://www .federalreserve.gov/creditcard.

The two major peer-to-peer (P2P) lending sites are Lending Club and Prosper. Their websites include more details about how to use their services and the specific terms they offer: http://www.lendingclub.com and http:// www.prosper.com.

The Lend Academy blog covers a variety of topics related to P2P lending, including valuable insights for borrowers: http://www.lendacademy.com.

If you're interested in analyzing some raw data related to P2P lending, check out these no-frills (and investor-oriented) websites: http://www.LendStats .com and http://www.nickelsteamroller.com.

Drafting Loan Terms

Nolo Press has published a very helpful book called *Business Loans from Family and Friends* by Asheesh Advani (2009). It includes several forms on an included CD-ROM, such as simple promissory notes and a loan request letter.

Current Applicable Federal Rates are available at the IRS website: http://www.irs.gov/app/picklist/list/federalRates.html.

Microfinance

The SBA publishes lists of the specialized intermediary lenders they work with to provide credit through their microloan program, or you can call your local office for referrals: http://www.sba.gov/content/microloan-program.

The Association for Enterprise Opportunity supports the development of strong and effective U.S. microbusiness initiatives to assist underserved entrepreneurs in starting, stabilizing, and expanding businesses. It maintains an online, searchable list of their members, many of which provide microloans and other financial services: http://www.aeoworks.org/index.php/site/page/category/find.

Kiva is a popular nonprofit microlending website where people can search for borrowers around the world to support with microloans. Unlike crowdfunding or peer-to-peer lending websites, you cannot request a loan directly via the website. If you want to apply for a microloan from one of Kiva's "field partners" (the term they use for the lending institutions that actually process the loans in their system), search their field partner list for organizations in North America, and look for the U.S. partners: http://www.kiva.org/partners.

Community Development Financial Institutions

The CDFI Fund website includes a searchable database for finding CDFIs: http://www.cdfifund.gov/what_we_do/need_a_loan.asp. (A note of caution while you're at the CDFI Fund website: don't get confused by the invitations to apply for grants and awards. These awards are not designed for specific businesses but for CDFIs themselves. This is why the database refers to CDFIs as "awards"; they are the financing institutions that have been awarded funds through the national CDFI program.)

The Opportunity Finance Network also maintains a searchable online list of their members. Since they include organizations that are not certified by the CDFI Fund, their list is larger than the one above: http://www.opportunityfinance.net/industry/industry_locator.asp.

The CDFI Coalition is a national organization promoting the work of CDFIs. Through its member organizations, the coalition represents CDFIs working in all fifty states and the District of Columbia. Their website has links to a variety of listings of CDFIs, including by state and city, type, and organization name: http://cdfi.org/index.php?page=info-4

If you are looking for data to help you make the social case for your food-based business to CDFIs or other impact investors, the Food Environment Atlas, released by the USDA in 2010 as part of HFFI, provides county-by-county data on the food environment, local food choices, health and well-being, and other community characteristics, such as the prevalence of poverty: www.ers.usda.gov/FoodAtlas.

Credit Unions

The National Credit Union Association's website has a locator that you can use to identify credit unions in your area. You can also link through to local credit unions' websites to see if you qualify for membership and whether or not they offer business lending services: see http://www.ncua.gov.

The following lenders are covered in more detail in chapter 14, and you can learn more about them at their websites:

http://www.farmcreditnetwork.com

RSF Social Finance: http://www.rsfsocialfinance.org

New Resource Bank: http://www.newresourcebank.com

Whole Foods Market's Local Product Loan Program: http://www.wholefoodsmarket.com/mission-values/commitment-society/loan-program-details

The following U.S. Small Business Administration and the U.S. Department of Agriculture resources are covered in more detail in chapter 15, and you can learn more about them at their websites:

The SBA's loan programs: http://www.sba.gov/loanprograms

USDA's Know Your Farmer Know Your Food Compass: www.usda.gov
/kyfcompass

USDA's service center locator: http://offices.sc.egov.usda.gov/locator/app

USDA's Food Hub site, where you can access the Regional Food Hub
resource guide: www.ams.usda.gov/foodhubs

NSAC's *Guide to Federal Funding for Local and Regional Food
Systems*: http://sustainableagriculture.net/blog/new-nsac-guide-to
-usda-funding-for-food-systems/

SARE's book *Building Sustainable Farms, Ranches, and Communities: Federal Programs for Sustainable Agriculture, Forestry, Entrepreneurship, Conservation and Community Development* (2009):
http://www.sare.org/Learning-Center/Books/Building-Sustainable
-Farms-Ranches-and-Communities

USDA's SARE program: http://www.sare.org

Equity Investors

Gust (formerly Angelsoft) is an online platform that streamlines the process
of connecting start-up companies with angel investors; most angel investor
networks use Gust to manage their submissions and assess opportunities.
As an entrepreneur, you create a company profile that contains all the
information that investors will want to see. Parts of your profile are public,
and you can also choose to share more private company information with
individual investors or angel groups, which the platform lets you search.
You can also view information such as how many investors—and which
ones—have viewed which parts of your company profile. Gust's video gal-
lery includes hundreds of tips from investors: http://gust.com.

The Angel Resource Institute publishes a list of angel groups: http://www
.angelresourceinstitute.org/angels/angelgroups/findagroup.aspx.

Presentation Zen: Simple Ideas on Presentation Design and Delivery
by Garr Reynolds (New Riders, 2008) is popular book among fundraising
entrepreneurs that can help you hone your investor pitches.

OwnYourVenture.com's equity simulator is an excellent online tool for
visualizing what will happen given various equity investment scenarios:
http://ownyourventure.com/equitySim.html.

In *Venture Deals: Be Smarter Than Your Lawyer and Venture Capitalist* (Wiley, 2013) Brad Feld and Jason Mendelson, two managing directors of the Foundry Group venture capital firm, break down everything you need to know about equity term sheets. Though the authors work in the information technology field and this book is therefore written from that angle, there are so many excellent insights in this book that it's definitely worth a read.

Organic Valley's entire stock offering is available on their website if you want to see exactly how they structured it: http://www.organicvalley.coop /about-us/invest/stock-prospectus.

TheFunded.com is a members-only community website (membership is free for company CEOs) where thousands of entrepreneurs are attempting to level the playing field between institutional investors and companies seeking capital. Members can view very detailed profiles of venture capital firms, including ratings from companies that have received—or failed to receive—funding from each. Most of the funds are in the tech industry, but you still might find the shared term sheets, advice, and other resources on the site valuable: http://www.thefunded.com.

I highly recommend Food+Tech's e-newsletter for keeping tabs on the latest in food technology and information trends; it also includes the occasional interview from an institutional food investor. You can sign up for the e-newsletter on their website: http://www.foodtechconnect.com.

The website for the Global Impact Investing Network (GIIN) contains resources related to the field of impact investing. It also lists its investor members and can link you to the Global Impact Investing Rating System (GIIRS): http://www.thegiin.org.

The Mission Investors Exchange is a membership organization for foundations and other philanthropic organizations that want to increase the impact of their capital. Its website includes a searchable list of members and quite a bit of information about how PRI and MRI work. It is geared toward funders, so you'll have to pick and choose which information will be most relevant to you as a fundraiser: http://www.missioninvestors.org.

Foundations

The Foundation Center provides data, training, and connections to resources related to philanthropy, including a searchable database on grant makers and their grants. It also operates an associated organization, GrantSpace, which offers information and resources that are specifically designed to meet the needs of grant seekers. Most of the Foundation Center's tools and resources are available for nominal fees, but it operates five regional library/learning centers where you can access many of their services and publications for free. There is also a Foundation Center partner network of more than four hundred information centers, which are located in public libraries, community foundations, and educational institutions. http://www.foundationcenter.org and http://grantspace.org.

The Chronicle of Philanthropy is a print and online publication for nonprofit leaders, fundraisers, grant makers, and other people involved in the philanthropic enterprise. Their website has an entire section dedicated to fundraising. Though many of the articles (especially the most recent) are premium content and therefore only available to paying subscribers, there is plenty of free, general information that people seeking philanthropic grants will find useful: http://philanthropy.com.

INDEX

ABOUT THE AUTHOR

Elizabeth Ü is executive director of Finance for Food, a nonprofit that educates food-system entrepreneurs in the United States about the full range of financing options available to support them. Elizabeth has extensive experience at the intersection of sustainable food systems and social finance—helping food-based business owners identify appropriate–and mission-aligned–financing opportunities based on their unique situations and values.

GIOVANNI AGNOLI

Elizabeth previously served as manager of strategic development at RSF Social Finance, helping launch a loan fund to support high-impact, sustainable food ventures. She has served on staff at the Business Alliance for Local Living Economies (BALLE), and spent two years as program officer of Slow Money, then a project of Investors' Circle. Elizabeth regularly speaks and gives workshops on the topics of impact investing, social finance, and sustainable food systems at conferences geared toward foundations, financiers, investors, philanthropists, nonprofits, and social entrepreneurs.

A Food and Community Fellow of the Institute for Agriculture and Trade Policy, Elizabeth holds a BS in geography from McGill University and an MBA in sustainable management from Presidio Graduate School. She lives in San Francisco, California.

—— About the Foreword Author ——

Michael Shuman is an attorney, economist, and author of eight books, including most recently *Local Dollars, Local Sense: How to Shift Your Money from Wall Street to Main Street and Achieve Real Prosperity* (Chelsea Green, 2012).

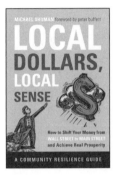
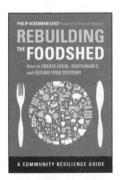

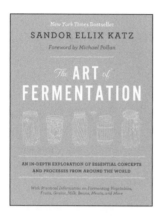
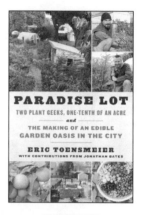
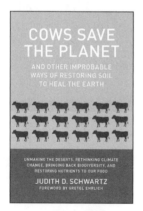
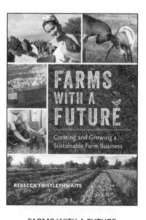